Digital Progress and Trends Report 2025

Scan to see all titles in this collection.

Digital Progress and Trends Report 2025

Strengthening AI Foundations

WORLD BANK GROUP

Contents

Figures

Map

Table

Foreword

Artificial intelligence (AI) is advancing at an extraordinary speed, reshaping how people learn, work, and live. Its ability to unlock access to knowledge, boost productivity, and open new markets holds immense potential to accelerate development—creating jobs, new industries, and economic transformation.

Expanding digital access will be one of the greatest drivers of future employment: 10 of the 15 fastest growing jobs globally are now in technology or technology-enabled roles. In addition, AI-related job postings are now rising faster in middle-income economies—up 16 percent in upper-middle-income and 11 percent in lower-middle-income countries—compared to just 2 percent in high-income countries.

This report, *Strengthening AI Foundations,* is the second in the *Digital Progress and Trends Report* series, providing a comprehensive, data-driven snapshot of the global AI landscape. It highlights a stark divide: Most innovations remain concentrated in high-income countries. Yet, a promising trend is emerging, as low- and middle-income countries are actively adopting "small AI" solutions. While these immediate, localized impacts are crucial, continued investment in strengthening the broader AI foundations is needed to embrace AI at scale over time.

To seize this opportunity and facilitate the growth of small AI, governments need to prioritize investment in what we call the foundational "4Cs":

- *Connectivity,* encompassing reliable digital infrastructure, energy, and device access, is the indispensable baseline.
- *Compute,* covering AI chips, servers, data centers, and cloud services, is increasingly becoming the "new electricity" of the AI era.
- *Context,* or locally relevant data and content, is essential to build trusted, inclusive, and effective AI systems.
- *Competency* is the set of robust digital skills that are indispensable for adopting, adapting, and innovating with AI.

Governments have a pivotal role to play in building and strengthening these critical foundations so that AI can take root and flourish in developing countries. The World Bank Group is committed to helping countries harness AI for inclusive and sustainable development, including supporting the 4Cs, strengthening data governance, championing regulatory and institutional reforms, and investing in the human capital essential to thrive in today's digital era.

Our new World Bank Group digital strategy includes AI readiness as a core pillar. It also emphasizes the importance of having dynamic local innovation ecosystems and ensuring that AI tools are aligned with local realities and priorities. Policies that promote competition and equitable distribution of AI gains will be critical for mitigating risks and ensuring broad-based benefits.

As the AI era accelerates, developing countries need to be prepared to leap forward. Small AI offers a unique opportunity to bypass traditional development barriers and spark homegrown innovation and inclusive growth.

This report is a call for collective and strategic action. To ensure that AI becomes a force for shared prosperity—rather than a new source of inequality—we must work together to expand access, close skill gaps, manage risks, and shape a future where the transformative power of AI truly benefits everyone.

Axel van Trotsenburg
Senior Managing Director
World Bank

Acknowledgments

The *Digital Progress and Trends Report 2025* was prepared by a World Bank team led by Yan Liu, under the guidance of Christine Zhenwei Qiang, Global Director for Digital Foundations. The core team consisted of Yan Liu, Antonio Martins Neto, Sharada Srinivasan, Saloni Khurana, He Wang, and Juan Porras. Key inputs were received from Hans Christian Boy, Nnamdi Itefchi-Fred, Ozzeir Nisar Khan, Roman Kovalenko, and Oleg V. Petrov.

- The overview was authored by Christine Zhenwei Qiang and Yan Liu (refer to https://hdl.handle .net/10986/43822).

- Chapter 1 was authored by Yan Liu and Sharada Srinivasan, with input from Oleg V. Petrov, Ozzeir Nisar Khan, and Roman Kovalenko.

- Chapter 2 was authored by Saloni Khurana, with input from Antonio Martins Neto and Nnamdi Itefchi-Fred.

- Chapter 3 was authored by Yan Liu, with input from Hans Christian Boy.

- Chapter 4 was authored by He Wang, with input from Yan Liu.

- Chapter 5 was authored by Saloni Khurana, Yan Liu, and Juan Porras.

- Chapter 6 was authored by Yan Liu.

- Appendix A was authored by Antonio Martins Neto.

- Case Study 1, "Exploring AI's Disruptive Promise for Education Systems in Low- and Middle-Income Countries," was authored by Sharada Srinivasan and Alex Twinomugisha (refer to https:// hdl.handle.net/10986/43822).

- Case Study 2, "Harnessing AI for Efficiency: Transforming Agriculture and Energy Sectors," was authored by Antonio Martins Neto (refer to https://hdl.handle.net/10986/43822).

- Case Study 3, "Co-worker, Coach, or Competitor? How AI Is Transforming Digitally Deliverable Services," was authored by Johan Bjurman Bergman and He Wang (refer to https://hdl.handle .net/10986/43822).

The team is grateful to the many reviewers who provided thoughtful insights and guidance at various stages of the report's preparation. Anton Korinek, Professor in the Department of Economics and Darden School of Business, University of Virginia, served as the external peer reviewer. Internal peer reviewers included Gabriel Demombynes, Tim Kelly, Auguste Tano Kouame, Aart Kraay, Gaurav Nayyar, Michel Rogy, Stephane Straub, Davide Strusani, and Marie-Chantal Uwanyiligira. Additional written comments were received from Doerte Doemeland, Amy Jean Doherty, Elisabeth Huybens, Martin Raiser, David Satola, and Renaud Seligmann, as well as from the People Vice Presidency.

The team particularly appreciates the guidance and support of Axel van Trotsenburg, Indermit Gill, Sangbu Kim, Christine Zhenwei Qiang, Stephane Straub, and Ozan Sevimili.

Special thanks are due to Kelly Suzanne Alderson, Sharmista Appaya, Andrea Barone, Johan Bjurman Bergman, Breen Byrnes, Peter Kusek, Monica Yanez Pagans, Camila Saad, Ghislain de Salins, Clara Stinshoff, Casey Torgusson, and Christopher Tullis for their helpful comments and suggestions. The team also appreciates contributions from colleagues across Verticals and the International Finance Corporation (IFC) during workshops with IFC and the Agriculture, Education, Energy, and Finance, Competitiveness, and Innovation Global Departments on the sectoral case studies.

The team thanks the following organizations for participating in various stakeholder consultations and providing valuable inputs: Meta, Microsoft, and Peking University.

The report was funded by the World Bank and the Digital Development Partnership 2.0 Trust Fund, a World Bank initiative supported by development partners aiming to advance digital transformation in low- and middle-income countries by building strong digital foundations and enablers while facilitating use cases for digital economies to thrive.

Jewel McFadden was the acquisitions editor, Christina Davis was the production editor, Kathie Porta Baker was the copy editor, Ann O'Malley was the proofreader, and Veronica Elena Gadea, World Bank Group, and William Pragluski designed the cover and interior.

Main Messages
The AI Imperative:
A Race against the Widening Divide

AI brings new opportunities and responsibilities

Artificial intelligence (AI) offers unprecedented potential to expand access to services, enhance workers' and businesses' capabilities, boost productivity, and open new economic pathways. However, to fully realize its benefits, countries need to address the rising risks of inequality, concentration of innovation, and ethical and accountability concerns.

Small AI brings immediate and tangible impact

For low-income countries (LICs) and middle-income countries (MICs), "small AI"—affordable, accessible, and designed for everyday devices—provides a vital avenue to achieve an immediate and tangible impact with limited resources. This ground-up innovation already is transforming development-relevant sectors like agriculture, education, and health, demonstrating AI's power at the community level. While potentially limited in scale, small AI enables developing countries to leapfrog traditional barriers and harness AI's benefits today.

AI evolution is uneven: Innovation, adaptation, and adoption

AI innovation remains concentrated largely in high-income countries (HICs), although some LICs and MICs are beginning to catch up. The rapid pace and concentration of innovations pose adaptation challenges, but open-source technologies are democratizing AI participation, allowing developing countries to tailor AI to local contexts without reinventing foundational technologies. While individual adoption of AI, particularly in MICs, has surged, its uptake by businesses and governments remains in its nascent stages.

- HICs account for 87 percent of notable AI models, 86 percent of AI start-ups, and 91 percent of cumulative venture capital funding in AI start-ups as of July 2025. They also are the source of 54 percent of AI research papers and 32 percent of generative AI (GenAI) patent applications (2014–23), compared to 17 percent of the global population and 64 percent of the global gross domestic product (GDP).

- Excluding China and India, LICs and MICs account for 4 percent of AI start-ups; less than 1 percent of AI start-up funding, GenAI patents, and notable AI models; and 23 percent of global AI papers, compared to 48 percent of the global population and 15 percent of the global GDP.

- Over 40 percent of ChatGPT's global traffic came from MICs in mid-2025, with Brazil, India, Indonesia, and Viet Nam among the top users. LICs lag behind, making up less than 1 percent of global traffic, highlighting a stark gap.

- In HICs, 24 percent of internet users used ChatGPT in April 2025, compared to 5.8 percent in upper-middle-income countries (UMICs), 4.7 percent in lower-middle-income countries (LMICs), and just 0.7 percent in LICs.

Realizing AI's potential hinges on four foundational investments: The "4Cs"

The four foundational investments for AI include connectivity, compute, context, and competency.

Connectivity: The gateway to AI participation

Internet access continues to expand, and satellites are opening new possibilities for closing the remaining gaps. Despite this progress, huge disparities in affordability, speed, and data usage remain between richer and poorer countries. Cohesive policy is critical to expand affordable connectivity, including reliable electricity, and lay the groundwork for AI-ready economies.

- From 2022 to 2024, the share of population using the internet increased by only 2 percentage points (p.p.) in HICs (reaching 93 percent) but increased by 4 p.p. in UMICs (reaching 81 percent), 5 p.p. in LMICs (reaching 54 percent), and 3 p.p. in LICs (reaching 27 percent in 2024).

- The data consumption gap is widening, with HICs increasingly leaving others behind. In 2023, total data traffic per capita reached 1,400 gigabytes (GB) in HICs, 400 GB in UMICs, 100 GB in LMICs, and 5 GB in LICs.

- By 2024, 84 percent of the population in HICs was covered by the 5G mobile network, compared to 65 percent in UMICs, 35 percent in LMICs, and 4 percent in LICs.

- The number of communication satellites in orbit deployed for commercial purposes is 14 times greater than it was a decade ago, growing to 5,300 between 2015 and 2023.

Compute: The "new electricity" of the AI era

The transformative power of AI is fundamentally reliant on compute, but its supply is concentrated. While many countries access compute through importing cloud services, this trade remains imbalanced. Developing countries face strategic decisions about building domestic compute capacity (for example, data centers) versus securing affordable international cloud access.

- In 2024, 50 percent of global secure internet servers were in the United States, 41 percent were in other HICs, and just 9 percent were in the rest of the world. On a per capita basis, the United States has 200 times more servers than typical MICs and 20,000 times more than LICs.

- HICs accounted for 77 percent of global co-location data center capacity as of June 2025. LICs and MICs accounted for only 23 percent, with UMICs at 18 percent, LMICs at 5 percent, and LICs representing less than 0.1 percent.

- In 2023, 87 percent of global cloud computing exports are from the United States, predominantly destined for HICs (approximately 84 percent in 2023), where demand is concentrated, with the other 16 percent going to MICs (a negligible percentage, close to 0, goes to LICs).

Context determines AI capabilities

AI model capabilities depend on the quantity, quality, and diversity of training data. While English still dominates, emerging formats like video offers new opportunities for LICs and MICs to participate. Developing countries are navigating AI adoption of open-source and proprietary models. Adapting global models to local economic, cultural, and institutional contexts can turn global data resources into locally relevant AI solutions.

- As of 2024, 85 percent of AI training data start-ups are based in HICs—leaving LICs and MICs behind in localized data.

- Venture capital investment in AI training data is led by the United States at 56 percent, followed by China at 17 percent, the European Union at 15 percent, India at 3 percent, and the United Kingdom at 2 percent, with the rest of the world accounting for the remaining 6 percent.

- More than 50% of open-source AI training data sets are in English, limiting accessibility for non-English speakers. Emerging formats like video and audio offer new ways for LICs and MICs to participate. For example, 8 percent of YouTube videos are in Hindi, and 3 percent are in Arabic.

Competency is a prerequisite for AI participation and jobs

Digital skills are now a baseline across many occupations, with AI reshaping labor markets globally. Skills gaps are uneven, but AI-related jobs are growing faster in MICs than in HICs. Many LICs and MICs face significant talent challenges from supply shortages—due to the lack of quality, industry-aligned education and training programs—to brain drain, hindering full participation in the AI economy.

- Basic digital skills were held by 66 percent of people in HICs, 38 percent in UMICs, 21 percent in LMICs, and less than 5 percent in LICs in 2023. For intermediate skills, the figures drop to 57 percent in HICs, 26 percent in UMICs, 13 percent in LMICs, and only 3 percent in LICs. Advanced digital skills are limited globally, with less than 10 percent of the populations in HICs having them versus 3.5 percent in UMICs, 1.6 percent in LMICs, and less than 1 percent in LICs.

- Job vacancies requiring AI skills are rising faster in developing countries than in HICs, growing by 16% in UMICs, 11% in LMICs, and just 2% in HICs from 2021 to 2024. Vacancies doubled in the Arab Republic of Egypt, Pakistan, and the Philippines, and grew fourfold in Kenya, albeit from a very low base. Job vacancies requiring GenAI skills surged ninefold globally from 2022 to 2024.

- Brain drain further challenges AI development and adaptation, with talent outflows 3–4 times higher than inflows in countries like Bangladesh, Lebanon, Nigeria, and Ukraine.

Strategic AI investment: The time to act is now

AI presents a defining moment for global development, especially for LICs and MICs. Investment in AI, tailored to each country's readiness, is a strategic imperative. AI is reshaping global comparative advantages and is poised to unlock new opportunities for export-led growth, job creation, and long-term transformative benefits. By localizing and customizing AI models, developing countries can strategically solve pressing development challenges; connect their citizens to new opportunities; and, ultimately, profoundly transform lives. The time for strategic action is now.

Abbreviations

ABDI	Brazilian Agency for Industrial Development
AGI	artificial general intelligence
AI	artificial intelligence
ASEAN	Association of Southeast Asian Nations
AVs	autonomous vehicles
AWS	Amazon Web Services
BMGF	Bill and Melinda Gates Foundation
BPM	business process management
BPO	business process outsourcing
BTOS	Business Trends and Outlook Survey
CBRN	chemical, biological, radiological, and nuclear
CSPs	cloud service providers
CV	coefficient of variation; computer vision
DDS	digitally delivered services
DPTR	*Digital Progress and Trends Report*
DRAM	dynamic random-access memory
DT	digital transformation
EAP	East Asia and Pacific
ECA	Europe and Central Asia
edtech	educational technology
EMDE	emerging and developing economy
EU	European Union
FAO	Food and Agriculture Organization of the United Nations
FCDO	Foreign, Commonwealth, and Development Office
FDI	foreign direct investment
fintech	financial technology
4Cs	connectivity, compute, context, competency
GB	gigabytes
GDP	gross domestic product
GenAI	generative AI
GHG	greenhouse gas

GPTs	general-purpose technologies
GPUs	graphics processing units
GSO	geosynchronous orbit
HICs	high-income countries
HPC	high-performance computing
HR	human resources
HVAC	heating, ventilation, and air conditioning
IBPAP	IT and Business Process Association of the Philippines
ICT	information and communication technology
IDEs	integrated development environments
IoT	Internet of Things
IP	intellectual property
IPM	integrated pest management
IT	information technology
LAC	Latin America and the Caribbean
LEO	low Earth orbit
LICs	low-income countries
LLMs	large language models
LMICs	lower-middle-income countries
LRLs	low-resource languages
mbps	megabits per second
MENA	Middle East and North Africa
MEO	medium Earth orbit
MICs	middle-income countries
ML	machine learning
NGOs	nongovernmental organizations
NGSO	nongeosynchronous orbit
NITDA	National Information Technology Development Agency
NLP	natural language processing
NTNs	nonterrestrial networks
OECD	Organisation for Economic Co-operation and Development
PPP	public-private partnership
PV	photovoltaic
QA	quality assurance
R&D	research and development
RN	registered nurse
ROI	return on investment
SAR	South Asia; semiautonomous region
SMEs	small and medium enterprises

SMS	short message service
SSA	Sub-Saharan Africa
TAP	Technology Access Program; The Apprentice Project
UMICs	upper-middle-income countries
UNCTAD	United Nations Trade and Development
UNESCO	United Nations Educational, Scientific and Cultural Organization
UNICEF	United Nations Children's Fund
USAID	US Agency for International Development
VC	venture capital
VoIP	voice-over-internet protocol
WTO	World Trade Organization
XAI	explainable artificial intelligence

Harnessing AI for Development: Can It Work? | 1

KEY MESSAGES

- The future trajectories and impacts of artificial intelligence (AI) are highly uncertain, bringing new opportunities and new risks:

  - AI's future capabilities and impacts are highly uncertain. In the short term, modest benefits may come with uneven distributional effects. Long-term gains hinge on both technological advancements and societal factors, including infrastructure and skills, organizational and process changes, development of complementary innovations, evolving regulations, and social norms.

  - AI further lowers barriers to accessing information, opportunities, services, and expertise; unlocks productivity gains; expands market access; and spurs trade. Over time, it may enable the creation of new products, jobs, and industries, offering a pathway to higher living standards and economic transformation.

  - AI can potentially intensify competition among workers and firms, devalue human capital, and exacerbate inequality between and within countries. Developing economies that lag in AI adoption risk premature de-professionalization, with shrinking space to create high-skilled, high-income jobs.

- Although AI innovation is dominated by high-income countries, AI adaptation and localization are key to relevant and effective adoption.

  - The United States has led innovation with 62 percent of notable AI models ever created and more than 73 percent of funding in AI start-ups globally.

  - China now leads the world in AI research paper publication and patent applications. Argentina (0.1 percent), China (13 percent), and India (0.2 percent) are the only three middle-income countries (MICs) creating notable AI models. Low-income countries (LICs) and most other MICs play a marginal role in AI innovation.

  - Many AI applications require deep localization to be relevant and effective. Most developing countries may not need to develop foundational AI models, and they can benefit from localized innovation and practical adaptation of existing open-source platforms.

- Generative artificial intelligence (GenAI) is spreading at record speed, but a stark usage divide exists between LICs and the rest of the world.

- ○ GenAI tools have been used by more than half a billion people (13 percent of the global workforce) in more than 200 countries within 2 years of ChatGPT's launch.
- ○ Over 40 percent of ChatGPT's global traffic came from MICs in April 2025, with Brazil, India, Indonesia, and Viet Nam among top users. Yet LICs lag—making up less than 1 percent of global traffic—highlighting a stark gap.
- ○ Intentional AI adoption by firms remains limited (8 percent) even in advanced economies, and it is lower in developing countries.
- Promising use cases are emerging across developing countries and across sectors. Realizing the potential of AI hinges on the foundational 4Cs: connectivity, compute, context (training data, models, and applications), and competency (digital skills).
  - ○ In Brazil, the Arab Republic of Egypt, India, Nigeria, the Philippines, and Uzbekistan, teachers use AI for lesson planning, nurses for patient tracking, contact center agents for coaching, and farmers for agronomic advice. In these roles, AI acts more as a co-worker or coach—enhancing human capacity—than a replacement.
  - ○ However, the scale, equity, and sustainability of benefits hinge on the 4Cs.

AI definitions, ecosystem, and significant trends

Artificial intelligence (AI) is a branch of computer science dedicated to creating systems capable of performing tasks that typically require human intelligence. Although the concept dates to the 1950s, in recent years, AI capabilities have improved significantly due to the availability of massive data, better training data, and more powerful computer hardware.

AI is an umbrella term used for a set of loosely related technologies. No consensus exists on what is and is not AI (Narayanan and Kapoor 2024). As technological capabilities grow, tasks once exclusive to humans are now within the purview of machines. As a result, experts in the field often joke that AI is everything that computers cannot currently do. AI also has become a marketing buzzword, with companies rushing to label products as being AI based to ride the hype. Hence, it is challenging to provide a precise definition of AI or even of its types or subfields.

This publication defines AI broadly, encompassing subfields such as predictive AI based on machine learning (ML), natural language processing (NLP) and speech recognition, computer vision (CV), transformer model-based generative AI (GenAI), autonomous driving, and robotics. Each type has distinct characteristics and applications. Although the report's primary focus is GenAI—the latest frontier in AI development—it also explores other AI types, reflecting that the ongoing advancements in AI are a continuum and are reshaping the economy and society in diverse ways.

GenAI

GenAI marks a leap forward in AI innovation. Traditional AI approaches are typically task focused, primarily used for data analysis and predictive modeling. GenAI takes this a step further by not only performing tasks but also creating new content. Leveraging advancements in large language models (LLMs), GenAI can interpret natural language prompts and generate content in a wide variety of outputs, including text, images, audio, video, code, 3D models, and even synthetic data. This has directly translated to GenAI models outperforming the average human benchmark in common tasks, such as reading comprehension, language understanding, and image recognition. Such capabilities have enabled new applications across industries and domains, notably in office productivity, creative industries, design, and marketing.

GenAI also complements and enriches traditional AI approaches across various subfields. Together, GenAI and traditional AI approaches expand the tool kit of AI practitioners and researchers, working in tandem to push the boundaries of AI capabilities.

AI ecosystem

The modern AI ecosystem is a vast, intricate, and rapidly evolving landscape (refer to figure 1.1). The ecosystem relies on a foundational energy and telecommunications infrastructure. Capitalizing on this basic infrastructure is the compute layer, where specialized AI chips, servers, storage solutions, and data centers form the physical backbone to store and process data for AI workloads. Cloud computing platforms offer scalable access to compute and integrate AI services.

FIGURE 1.1 Key layers and segments of the AI ecosystem

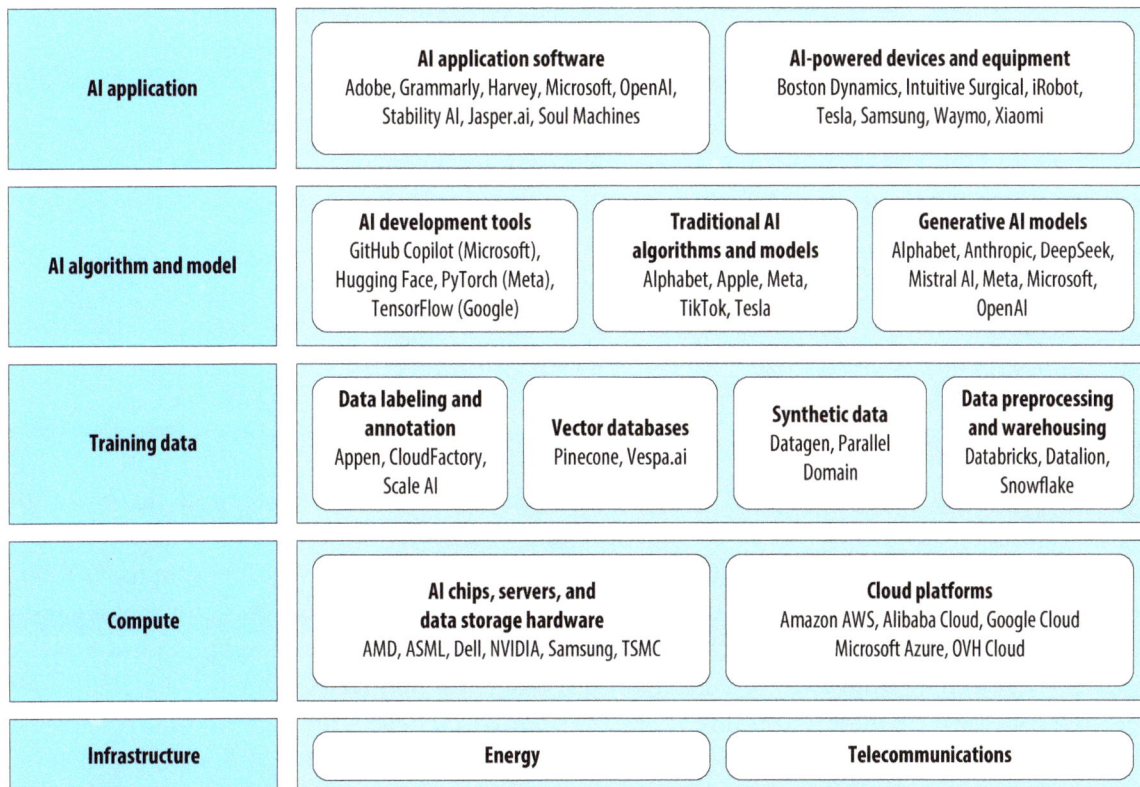

AI application	**AI application software** Adobe, Grammarly, Harvey, Microsoft, OpenAI, Stability AI, Jasper.ai, Soul Machines	**AI-powered devices and equipment** Boston Dynamics, Intuitive Surgical, iRobot, Tesla, Samsung, Waymo, Xiaomi	
AI algorithm and model	**AI development tools** GitHub Copilot (Microsoft), Hugging Face, PyTorch (Meta), TensorFlow (Google)	**Traditional AI algorithms and models** Alphabet, Apple, Meta, TikTok, Tesla	**Generative AI models** Alphabet, Anthropic, DeepSeek, Mistral AI, Meta, Microsoft, OpenAI
Training data	**Data labeling and annotation** Appen, CloudFactory, Scale AI	**Vector databases** Pinecone, Vespa.ai	**Synthetic data** Datagen, Parallel Domain	**Data preprocessing and warehousing** Databricks, Datalion, Snowflake
Compute	**AI chips, servers, and data storage hardware** AMD, ASML, Dell, NVIDIA, Samsung, TSMC	**Cloud platforms** Amazon AWS, Alibaba Cloud, Google Cloud Microsoft Azure, OVH Cloud	
Infrastructure	**Energy**	**Telecommunications**	

Source: Original figure for this publication.
Note: AI = artificial intelligence.

Training data are yet another critical part of this ecosystem, which can be gathered from various sources such as digital devices, sensors, digital platforms, business transactions, and public data sets. These data are then aggregated into central repositories, labeled, and annotated. Data preprocessing is key to ensuring accuracy and relevance, and it precedes data use for algorithmic training. Data feed into the training data and model layer, where AI development tools are used to build and train AI models.

Traditional AI training data such as ML are already deeply integrated into everyday technologies, powering digital devices, search engines, social media, and e-commerce platforms. Foundational models are large, pretrained models that serve as a general-purpose starting point for a variety of tasks across domains. At the application layer, AI applications leverage and fine-tune foundational models for specific tasks and use cases, and AI-powered devices and equipment embed AI capabilities for localized operation. The boundaries between these layers and segments are often fluid, with many companies operating across multiple segments within the ecosystem.

Significant trends

Although GenAI is still in the early stages of development and adoption, researchers are already exploring new frontiers. Two significant near-term trends are the move toward multimodality and the pursuit of advanced reasoning.

Multimodal AI refers to systems that can process and synthesize information from multiple data types simultaneously. Instead of only "understanding" text or images, a multimodal model can watch a video, listen to the audio, read the subtitles, and generate a comprehensive summary of what occurred. This allows for a much richer, more contextual understanding of the world and enables more fluid and intuitive interactions with technology, moving it closer to how humans perceive reality.

Beyond better perception, the field is intensely focused on *advanced AI reasoning*. Although current models are excellent at pattern recognition, they can struggle with multistep problems that require logical deduction, strategic planning, or creative problem-solving. The next frontier is to develop AI that can not only retrieve information but can also reason with it to analyze a complex problem, break it into smaller steps, form a coherent plan, and execute it. This capability is essential for tackling grand challenges in science, medicine, and engineering.

Agentic AI allows computers to go beyond chat and content generation and carry out all sorts of tasks by delegating them to other software and even people. Traditional AI requires human input to navigate complex scenarios or shifting priorities. Agentic AI autonomously sets subgoals, resolves conflicts, and adjusts its strategies using real-time feedback—often anticipating needs before they arise. Agentic AI can handle complex, multistep reasoning, orchestrate entire workflows, negotiate trade-offs, and integrate cross-domain knowledge to achieve higher-order objectives. Instead of static retraining cycles, agentic AI models evolve continuously, learning from new environments and outcomes, leading to sustained adaptability in fluid and uncertain contexts. Despite agentic AI's great potential, meaningful deployment and adoption remain rare. Agentic AI also creates several critical challenges, including reliability, accountability, trust, and bias amplification risks.

Beyond virtual agents, another promising trajectory involves *physical AI*—notably, autonomous vehicles (AVs) and robotics. Physical AI captures data directly from its environment, for example, through sensors or Internet of Things devices. These capabilities present immense potential for AI to create economic and societal value, with applications ranging from industrial process automation to AVs and personal assistive robots in health care.

The global adoption of AVs is rapidly accelerating, particularly in the ride-hailing sector, with key players demonstrating significant growth. Waymo, Alphabet's self-driving division, recorded more than 700,000 monthly paid trips in California as of March 2025, a remarkable 55-fold increase since August 2023. In April 2025, Waymo was reportedly serving 250,000 paid trips per week in the United States, a fivefold increase year over year (Kolodny and Elias 2025). Similarly, Baidu's Apollo Go robotaxi service has seen substantial deployment in China, with Wuhan alone boasting a fleet of more than 500 vehicles and becoming a major operational area for autonomous driving services. Baidu reported more than 7 million cumulative robotaxi rides across 11 Chinese cities as of July 2024, with 899,000 rides in second-quarter 2024, representing a 26 percent year-over-year increase ("In Leaked Reports" 2024). Although the broader market for fully autonomous private vehicles is still in its nascent stages, the growth in robotaxi services underscores a significant shift in urban mobility.

Scope of this report

This report focuses on recent trends in AI development and the foundational building blocks required to support AI adoption and innovation in developing countries. To provide context and motivation, this chapter briefly discusses the potential economic and social implications of AI, emphasizing the urgency of global coordination and investment to strengthen the foundational 4Cs of AI readiness: connectivity, compute, context (training data, model, and applications), and competency (digital skills). The report acknowledges the wide range of expert views and the uncertainty surrounding AI's long-term development impacts. A more in-depth exploration of these implications will be provided in the *World Development Report 2026*.

This report draws on a range of data sources to track trends in AI innovation and adoption. It benchmarks country performance on the 4Cs, identifies key market failures and externalities that underpin public intervention, and reviews emerging policy approaches—highlighting their benefits, risks, and trade-offs. More detailed and context-specific policy recommendations will be developed in forthcoming reports.

Potential impacts of AI on the global economy and society

Expert perspectives on the pace of future advances in AI and their impacts vary significantly. Some AI researchers and technology entrepreneurs anticipate the arrival of *artificial general intelligence* (AGI), when AI surpasses human intelligence and can solve any intellectual task that a human being can, within 5–20 years (Hinton 2023; Kurzweil 2024). Although AGI could boost output growth substantially, it will necessitate an inexorable decline in the role of human labor in the economy. This shift will require a fundamental reevaluation of economic structures, income distribution mechanisms, social systems, the economic value of education, and the meaning of work (Korinek 2024).

On the one hand, figures such as Sam Altman, Geoffrey Hinton, Elon Musk, and Mustafa Suleyman have talked up AI's superhuman potential and warned about its existential threats to humanity. On the other hand, skeptical market analysts such as Jim Covello from Goldman Sachs have argued that the technology is not designed to solve the kind of complex problems that would justify its enormous cost (Mickle 2024). Scientist and writer Gary Marcus has criticized that the LLMs powering GenAI have too many flaws to be transformative (Zinn 2025). AI experts such as Yann LeCun have argued that today's AI models are far from rivaling the intelligence of people's pets (Mims 2024). Sayash Kapoor and Arvind Narayanan have contended that current AI benchmarks do not measure real-world utility—that much of the world's knowledge is tacit and uncodified and, thus, can hardly be passively learned by machines. They believe AI's economic impacts are likely to be gradual, unfolding over decades as complementary innovations emerge and organizational practices and institutional frameworks adapt.

AI differs from previous general-purpose technologies such as electricity, internal combustion engines, and computers in two key aspects:

1. *Learning and adaptability, which allow it to complement or substitute for human decision-making and judgment.* Unlike traditional technologies, which are rule based and static, AI systems can learn from data, adapt to new information, and improve over time. This makes AI more dynamic and capable of handling complex problems. Hence, AI systems can operate with a degree of autonomy, making decisions based on the data they have learned from and tackling more complex cognitive problems. This autonomy in optimization and decision-making allows AI to either substitute for or complement human decision-making and judgment.

2. *Data dependency.* AI relies heavily on large data sets for training and operation. This contrasts with technologies such as the steam engine, electricity, internal combustion engine, telecommunications, computers, and the internet, which require infrastructure but not vast data inputs. Computers, the internet, social media, and digital platforms all use and generate data, but they can operate without much data. They also primarily process or transmit data according to predefined rules. They do not learn and adapt in the same way AI does.

GenAI further differs from previous AI in the following aspects:

- Prediction with unstructured data, enabling content generation;
- Simplified human-machine interaction through natural language, enhancing user accessibility;
- Enhanced capabilities in cognitive and creative tasks that primarily affect high-skilled, nonroutine white-collar jobs;
- Flexibility and versatility, allowing more general applications than previous AI approaches;
- Stronger scaling laws, requiring even bigger data sets and more compute power; GenAI applications are also more computer intensive than predictive AI; and
- *Hallucination,* generating plausible but incorrect or entirely fictitious content, making reliability a challenge.

Economic implications and the potential magnitude of impacts

Given the significant uncertainties surrounding AI's future capabilities, adoption patterns, and potential regulatory and societal responses, predicting its precise longer-term impact is almost impossible.

Furthermore, the diverse nature of AI technologies, their varied applications, and the complex channels through which they exert influence add to this complexity. This section does not attempt a comprehensive analysis of various possible scenarios. Instead, it selectively focuses on four interconnected key aspects—(1) labor markets and human capital; (2) industrial organizations; (3) economic geography and international trade; and (4) aggregate productivity, living standards, and income distribution—discussing some of the likely scenarios and their potential consequences to guide policy actions.

Labor markets and human capital

AI can help democratize access to education and health care, particularly in underserved countries and regions. In education, the integration of GenAI into schools, colleges, and universities can enable skill-adaptive and personalized learning, instantaneous feedback, and on-demand student guidance and support. In health care, AI can support clinicians and doctors with diagnosis, screening, prognosis, and triaging, alleviating the burden on health care practitioners. These uses could be meaningful in developing countries and regions where access to quality education and health care remains limited. Yet challenges like unequal access, data fragmentation, privacy laws, and distrust can delay widespread adoption.

GenAI could potentially reduce the incentives for people to invest in higher education and skills acquisition. Traditionally, high-skilled, well-paid jobs have demanded specialized expertise, with the promise of higher income and more fulfilling careers motivating individuals to invest in college degrees and advanced training. GenAI tools could commodify expertise by allowing average workers to emulate their top-performing peers. This will reduce the returns on skills (Bloom et al. 2024), making individuals less incentivized to acquire advanced expertise because of the diminished prospects of securing rewarding employment, leading to further downsides to productivity and wages (Capraro et al. 2024). However, the future impact of AI on the demand for expertise is highly uncertain, and how AI will affect people's incentives to acquire various expertise remains to be seen.

The impact of AI on labor demand is complex and uneven. AI can automate certain tasks, reducing the demand for workers primarily engaged in such tasks and occupations. AI can also augment some tasks by making workers more productive. Augmentation has an ambiguous effect on labor demand, hinging on the balance between AI-driven productivity growth and growth in final product demand. Product demand is influenced by multiple factors and general equilibrium effects, including own-price effects, cross-price dynamics with substitutes and complements, the emergence of new products, and changes in consumer income and preferences.

AI may also shift demand toward less-experienced or lower-cost workers by transferring tacit knowledge from experts, enhancing productivity, and narrowing performance gaps (Brynjolfsson, Li, and Raymond 2025; Dell'Acqua et al. 2023; Noy and Zhang 2023). This could spur services outsourcing and offshoring, benefiting workers from developing countries. However, the opposite can occur: Experienced workers may use AI to automate entry-level tasks, displacing novices and reducing jobs outsourced to low-cost countries (Hui, Reshef, and Zhou 2024; Yilmaz, Naumovska, and Aggarwal 2023). Studies show that AI can also widen performance disparities in some tasks, amplifying the output of top performers while reducing the productivity of others (Otis et al. 2023)—potentially increasing demand for elite talent while squeezing out the rest.

The ultimate impact also depends on AI's ability to spur new products, industries, and occupations. If AI catalyzes such breakthroughs, it could generate demand for entirely new jobs and raise incomes.

AI has generated some new occupations and jobs, although these jobs tend to be highly polarized, and the high-income roles are limited in scope and number. High-skilled, high-income roles such as AI scientists, AI developers, robotics specialists, and data scientists are concentrated in a small number of AI firms, cities, and countries. The number of workers needed to meet global demand is negligible to overall employment. The new occupations created specifically by GenAI, such as prompt engineers, have so far been underwhelming in scale, as have peripheral roles such as AI governance and ethics specialists. Conversely, AI has created hundreds of thousands of low-skilled, low-income gig jobs, such as data labeling, further contributing to labor market polarization.

AI is likely to shift bargaining power away from workers to firms, potentially exerting downward pressure on wages and labor income share. As GenAI lowers the barrier to entry in previously elite occupations and potentially devalues some forms of cognitive and analytical expertise, it could suppress wages for a wider range of workers, excluding those at the very top.

AI could further constrain the potential for creating quality jobs in high-skilled services, particularly in developing countries. If the productivity growth in high-skilled services jobs outpaces growth in labor demand, the employment share of high-skilled services will likely stagnate or even decline because of AI. Similar to how computer-driven automation has led to premature deindustrialization, AI may lead to premature de-professionalization, where employment share in high-skilled services peaks earlier, lower, and at lower income levels (Liu 2024).

Industrial organizations

Data have become a critical resource and production factor in the AI age, creating new markets for data collection, storage, and processing. However, the unique characteristics of data complicate data exchange and AI usage. AI and recent GenAI have ignited a surge in investments in AI chips and data centers. In addition, organizations and governments are increasingly recognizing data as a critical asset, prompting a significant ramp-up in training data investment.

Because data are nonrival and can be reused limitlessly, their economic value varies significantly depending on size, quality, timeliness, specific application, context, and user. The challenge to determine the economic value of data, coupled with privacy and security concerns, has impeded the development of data exchange markets. Ambiguities surrounding data property rights and intellectual property (IP) of AI-generated content could also slow AI adoption.

Data exhibit strong economies of scale and scope, leading to a concentration of economic, social, and political power in the hands of those with privileged access to vast data sets. Data-driven businesses can leverage these data sets to solidify their market power and potentially stifle innovation. Furthermore, the increasing reliance on data in decision-making can introduce bias, discrimination, and systemic risks if the data are not representative or the algorithms are flawed.

AI solution providers with large data sets, abundant computational resources, top talent, and superior AI capabilities can benefit from significant economies of scale and scope, entrenching their competitive advantages and potentially leading to higher market concentration. However, GenAI tools tend to require much more computing power than traditional software, particularly during the inference phase. The nonnegligible marginal cost per additional user or service, coupled with the fact that LLMs do not necessarily exhibit network effects, may weaken economies of scale and scope for GenAI providers. This could limit the monopoly-like power often enjoyed by digital platforms. The increased demand for computing power—called *compute*—strengthens the position of compute suppliers such as NVIDIA and benefits cloud service providers who distribute LLMs. This dynamic could squeeze LLM providers such as OpenAI from both sides ("OpenAI's Latest Model" 2025).

The returns on digital and AI adoption tend to increase disproportionately with firm size and data intensity, potentially leading to higher market concentration across various sectors. Conversely, the cost of GenAI adoption tends to be lower than that of predictive AI because of GenAI's versatility and flexibility. This lower adoption barrier could mitigate the increasing returns to scale associated with traditional information technology (IT) investments, potentially acting as a counterforce to rising market concentration.

Economic geography and international trade

If AVs and robots eventually match or exceed human flexibility and dexterity, their widespread adoption could expand suburban areas and create more efficient urban environments. AVs would enable longer commutes, allowing people to live farther from city centers while continuing to work during travel, potentially leading to the expansion of suburban areas. By reducing the need for proximity to workplaces, AVs and remote work technologies could encourage the growth of larger, more dispersed cities. In addition, robots could take over many physical and manual tasks, which would allow workers to control or monitor these tasks remotely. This shift could reduce the need for workers to be physically present at traditional job sites, further decentralizing cities. Moreover, AVs and robots could optimize road usage, reduce traffic congestion, and decrease the need for parking, thereby creating more efficient urban environments (Legêne et al. 2020).

AI could shift global value chains, reshaping global trade patterns and labor demand in the outsourcing and offshoring of digitally deliverable services. The effects, however, remain uncertain. On the one hand, if AI significantly boosts the productivity of workers in advanced economies, there may be less demand to outsource jobs to workers in developing countries. Tasks that were once cost-effectively outsourced might be automated or performed more efficiently by domestic workers in rich countries using AI tools. On the other hand, if AI enables workers in developing countries to emulate the performance of their counterparts in more advanced economies, the demand for outsourcing and offshoring of white-collar jobs could increase. In this scenario, AI could help equalize global high-skilled labor markets, creating new opportunities for developing countries to attract higher-value jobs in sectors such as professional services and IT. GenAI could also bridge language barriers and facilitate international trade.

Aggregate productivity, living standards, and income distribution

AI has the potential to boost efficiency and accelerate innovation across various industries. Its ability to create and scale solutions without explicit programming, combined with the shift toward general-purpose AI applications, promises broader productivity gains. AI can optimize resource allocation, reduce inefficiencies, increase personalization, and accelerate scientific discovery and innovation. Automation of routine tasks frees human workers to focus on higher-value activities. Improved accessibility of GenAI tools can further enhance productivity, especially for smaller firms and a wider range of employees. GenAI could even take on some managerial functions, enabling more efficient organizational structures. A few experimental studies have documented substantial productivity gains for white-collar workers using GenAI, especially for less productive or lower-performing workers (Brynjolfsson, Li, and Raymond 2025; Dell'Acqua et al. 2023; Noy and Zhang 2023).

However, current AI's inherent flaws may limit its broader economic significance. First, the hallucinations that GenAI tools produce are rooted in the mathematical and logical structure of LLMs (Banerjee, Agarwal, and Singla 2024), making them unreliable in business environments where mistakes can be costly. Second, current AI tools remain pattern recognition engines without true understanding, common sense, or logical reasoning (Mirzadeh et al. 2024). Third, much economically valuable knowledge is tacit, context specific, and difficult to codify in a form that AI can learn from (Narayanan and Kapoor 2025).

AI will become more useful when it can "understand" and interact with the physical world. At present, AI models are used mainly to optimize software and generate information, text, and images, affecting a narrow range of activities that are mostly confined to virtual spaces. For AI to have a broader impact, it needs to be able to perceive, comprehend, and respond to physical environments reliably even in novel and unique situations. By bridging the gap between digital intelligence and physical action, AI could revolutionize more industries and solve practical challenges in ways that go far beyond current applications.

However, it is unlikely that robots and AVs will soon match the dexterity, emotional intelligence, and judgment that human workers bring to physical and manual jobs such as driving, child care, and nursing. Beyond the physical realm, emotional intelligence is crucial in jobs such as child care and health care, where reading nonverbal cues, offering empathy, and adjusting on the basis of emotional states are essential for building trust and providing support.

In addition, human judgment, shaped by experience and a deep understanding of context, ethics, and split-second decision-making, plays a vital role in navigating unpredictable situations. Although AI excels at data-driven tasks, replicating the intricate combination of physical dexterity, emotional intelligence, and ethical judgment required for these roles remains a monumental technical and ethical challenge.

Furthermore, low risk tolerance in the physical world, as well as legal and regulatory hurdles, complicates the widespread adoption of robots and AVs. Despite years of development and testing, no clear timeline exists on when AVs will be adopted widely and replace human drivers. However, within months of the release of ChatGPT, companies and people were using it widely in producing and editing communication materials and generating digital content. A crucial difference between the two is that people are much more risk averse when algorithms are brought into the physical world and, in particular, public spaces (Frey and Osborne 2023).

Therefore, AI's overall effect on aggregate productivity and living standards is likely to be modest in the short term, and even more limited in lower-income countries. AI primarily boosts labor productivity in high-skilled, white-collar services. Acemoglu (2024) estimates that fewer than 5 percent of all tasks in the United States can be profitably automated in the next decade. Therefore, AI will raise gross domestic product (GDP) by only 1 percent over the next decade, with even more limited positive effect on wages. The lack of infrastructure and digital skills further diminishes AI's impact in low-income countries (LICs) (Gmyrek, Winkler, and Garganta 2024).

AI is also likely to exacerbate inequality between capital owners and labor (Acemoglu 2025). Its distributional effect among workers is complex, potentially exerting downward pressure on wages for many workers. Autor (2024) argued that, unlike previous digital technologies, GenAI offers an opportunity to expand the middle class by enabling middle-skilled workers to perform higher-stakes decision-making tasks currently reserved for elite experts. In contrast, Frey and Osborne (2023) suggested that, by lowering barriers to entry in cognitive occupations, GenAI will increase competition, eventually driving down wages across the income ladder.

In the medium to long term (>10 years), AI's potential to drive more substantial positive impacts is greater but depends on several critical factors: advancements in AI capabilities, co-inventions and the creation of transformative new products, breakthroughs in energy supply, the development of complementary infrastructure and skills, organizational and process changes, and concomitant shifts in institutions and regulations.

AI presents both opportunities and threats for LICs and middle-income countries (MICs). AI has the potential to enhance human capital and generate new employment, particularly in digitally deliverable services. However, uneven access and adoption could exacerbate existing inequalities in education, skills, and health outcomes. Furthermore, AI may lead to premature de-professionalization, shifting employment toward low-skilled service jobs and potentially worsening unemployment and underemployment. The prospect of declining returns to higher education could disincentivize investments in human capital development.

AI can greatly benefit small businesses in developing countries by making knowledge and expertise more accessible, improving decision-making, expanding market access, and boosting productivity. However, increased economies of scale in AI-driven industries may also make it more challenging for LICs and MICs to develop competitive domestic firms and participate effectively in global markets. Although AI could stimulate a new wave of services outsourcing and boost services exports, it could also have the opposite effect, making export-led growth more difficult to achieve. Finally, although AI may elevate productivity and living standards, the income gap between rich and poor economies may widen further.

Uneven progress in AI innovation, adaptation, and adoption

This report defines AI innovation, adaptation, and adoption as follows:

- *AI innovation: The creation of new AI technologies, models, training data, or methodologies that advance the state of the art.* This includes publishing fundamental research (for example, in scientific publications), developing and launching notable AI models, patenting novel AI techniques, commercializing original AI products, and forming AI-focused start-ups.

- *AI adaptation: The modification or customization of existing AI technologies for specific contexts, sectors, or applications.* Examples include building industry- or domain-specific

AI tools on top of general-purpose models (for example, services built using the ChatGPT application programming interface), fine-tuning open-source AI models for local languages or government service delivery, or integrating AI components into specialized products.

- *AI adoption: The use of AI technologies without in-house modification by public organizations, private enterprises, or individuals.* This can include deploying AI-powered software, using off-the-shelf AI tools such as Gemini, or integrating ready-made AI features into workflows.

Although analytically distinct, these categories are interconnected. Adaptation often builds on innovation, and adoption may involve minor adjustments that edge into adaptation. In practice, many AI activities sit along a continuum rather than in discrete boxes. Investment is a measure for AI innovation and adaptation.

AI innovation and adaptation

Advancements in AI research have been driven primarily by high-income countries (HICs) notably the United States, and increasingly by industry over academia. Researchers in all LICs and MICs combined produced only 46 percent of the global AI scientific publications during 2000–24 and received only 31 percent of global citations (refer to figure 1.2). Articles from upper-middle-income countries (UMICs) and lower-middle-income countries (LMICs) are driven by China and India, respectively.

Although the United States accounts for only 26 percent of HICs' academic articles and 35 percent of the overall citations, China and India account for 70 percent and 68 percent of UMIC and LMIC publications, respectively. Among the more than 900 notable AI models[1] published since the 1950s, 62 percent of lead contributors come from the United States; 25 percent from other HICs; 13 percent from China; 0.2 percent, or only 2 models, from India and 0.1 percent, or only 1 model, from Argentina.

FIGURE 1.2 AI innovation and adaptation activities, by country income group

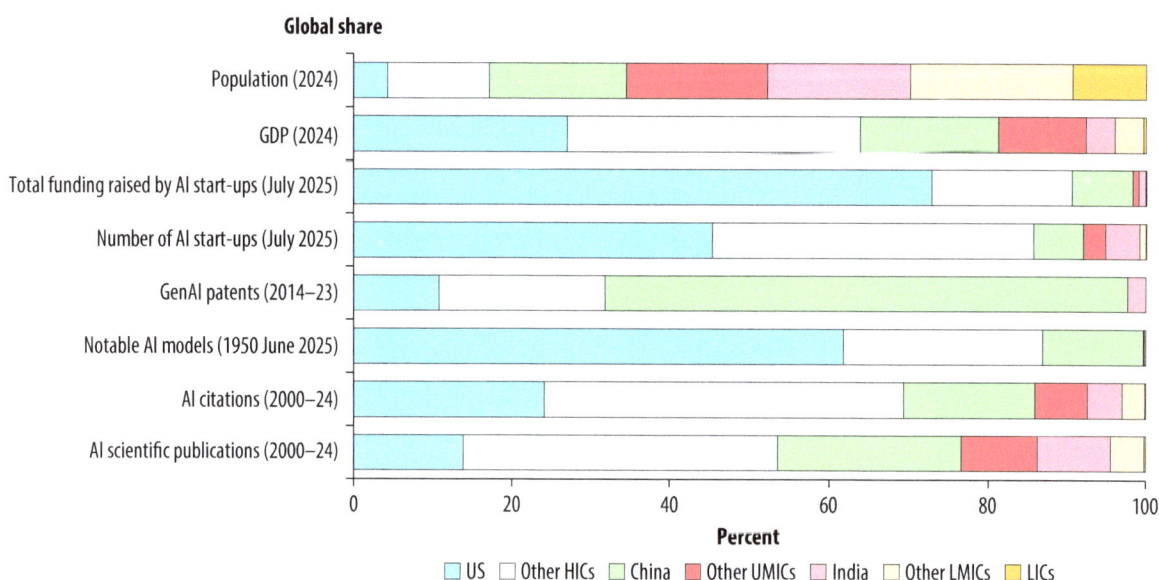

Sources: Original figure for this publication based on analysis of various indicators from Epoch (https://epoch.ai/), OECD.AI (https://oecd.ai/en/), and WIPO (https://www.wipo.int/en/web/ip-statistics).
Note: For models with multiple contributors, only the nationality of the first or leading contributor is counted. AI = artificial intelligence; GDP = gross domestic product; GenAI = generative artificial intelligence; HICs = high-income countries; LICs = low-income countries; LMICs = lower-middle-income countries; UMICs = upper-middle-income countries; US = United States.

The creation of notable AI models is dominated increasingly by industry over academia. Before 2022, 51 percent of the models' lead contributors were from academia, compared with 47 percent from industry; however, since 2022, nearly 80 percent of notable AI models' lead contributors are from industry, whereas only 20 percent are from academia.

Patent filings in AI, particularly GenAI, have experienced ninefold growth since 2017, primarily driven by China. The geographic landscape of GenAI patenting is highly concentrated, with five countries emerging as dominant players: China, India, Japan, the Republic of Korea, and the United States. Over the past decade, Chinese companies and research institutions have led the world in patenting AI applications, with a meteoric rise in filings since 2019. China accounts for 66 percent of global total GenAI patent filings during 2014–23 (WIPO 2024). Although initial concerns were raised about the quality of these Chinese patents, recent research suggests that patent quality has improved, and the approval rate is now aligned with other major patent systems (Thomas and Murdick 2020).

China dominates the overall GenAI patenting landscape, but India has the highest growth rate at 56 percent per year. In GenAI specifically, European countries, notably Germany and the United Kingdom, lag significantly behind, together accounting for less than 3 percent of GenAI patent families (Shoaib 2024). These findings suggests a potential innovation gap for these countries, with potential long-term implications for their technological competitiveness.

No LICs filed patent applications pertaining to AI in the past decade. Importantly, data on patenting trends across LICs and MICs remain sparse. This paucity of data underscores the need for improved monitoring and reporting of AI innovation activities in the developing world. The underrepresentation of diverse groups in AI research and patenting can impede the creation of more inclusive AI models.

The world's leading tech companies—all headquartered in the United States—are leading investments in AI infrastructure and development, reflecting the tech industry's strategic pivot toward AI capabilities across their product portfolios. In 2024, Microsoft allocated US$19 billion in capital expenditures, with half dedicated to data center expansion and the remainder to processing units. Meta has reportedly spent US$37–US$40 billion in 2024 on capital expenditures, including the acquisition of 350,000 NVIDIA graphics processing units. Google has invested US$3 billion in data centers and reportedly spent US$60 million on training AI models using Reddit data. Amazon has committed to a US$230 million investment in GenAI start-ups and plans to invest US$150 billion in data centers over 15 years, while also developing its own AI chips to reduce dependency on NVIDIA.

Although most big technology investments are focused on the United States, some are diversifying to developing countries, too. For example, between January and July 2024, Amazon, Google, and Microsoft announced 21 investments across 15 countries for a total of US$130 billion (Schoeberl and Corrigan 2024), including in Indonesia and Malaysia in Southeast Asia. This US$130 billion in announced investments represents approximately 23.2 percent of their combined first-half 2024 revenues.

Although big technology firms are leading the charge in large-scale AI investment, venture capital (VC) and private equity firms are pouring funds into AI start-ups. However, just as with academic and technical innovations, LICs and MICs represent only a fraction of venture-backed AI start-ups and an even smaller share of funding. Start-ups and the flow of VC investments measure the commercialization of innovation in AI across countries. Start-ups often serve as agile innovators, quickly adapting to new technologies and market needs, and VC investments can provide a quantitative measure of the confidence in a country's start-up ecosystem.

However, data on AI start-ups in LICs and MICs remain limited. One collection of AI global start-ups compiled by CB Insights, consisting of around 21,000 start-ups as of July 2025, counts 45 percent of them as from the United States. Other HICs house another 40 percent of AI start-ups, with the United Kingdom ranking second with 6.8 percent (1,456 start-ups). China ranks third with 6 percent (1,352 start-ups), and India ranks fourth with 4 percent (27 start-ups). Most LICs and MICs have few AI start-ups.

The cumulative funding received by these AI start-ups is much more uneven. AI start-ups in the United States received more than $500 billion in VC funding as of July 2025, 73 percent of the global total. Other HICs received another 18 percent. China accounts for 8 percent of global VC funding of AI start-ups. Other MICs and LICs combined make up less than 2 percent of global VC funding of AI start-ups, indicating limited local AI innovation, adaptation, and commercialization.

The analysis of AI innovation and adaptation globally suggests that few developing countries are engaged and dominant in AI innovation and significant adaptation. China's and India's exceptional positions in AI development leverages three critical foundations: a vast science, technology, engineering, and mathematics talent pool; government support for AI research and development; and mature technology industry ecosystems. Both countries have large-scale technical workforces and established digital infrastructure to provide the necessary foundation for AI innovation.

However, both countries have leveraged these advantages differently. China's AI innovation has benefited from coordinated state support and integrated digital ecosystems, whereas India capitalizes on its global IT services leadership and entrepreneurial culture. Both countries' large domestic markets and strong digital adoption rates create natural testing grounds for AI applications. These structural advantages create self-reinforcing cycles: Success attracts more talent and investment, which further strengthens AI capabilities. This cycle helps explain why they have pulled ahead of other developing nations in AI development and commercialization. Other low- and middle-income economies will also benefit from investments in these fundamentals to develop a domestic entrepreneurial and research ecosystem that leverages the power of AI for their own economic ends.

AI adoption

The adoption and global diffusion of GenAI by individuals has been much faster than that of previous technologies.[2] It took 75 years for the telephone to reach 100 million users, 33 years for cars, 7 years for the internet, 3.3 years for WhatsApp, and only 2 months for ChatGPT (Ebert and Louridas 2023). By June 2025, at least hundreds of AI tools were available, with the top 60 most-visited tools attracting nearly 6 billion monthly visits. Chatbots, because of their versatility and wide range of applications, dominate this space, accounting for 95 percent of traffic among these top tools.

Notably, ChatGPT alone commands nearly 80 percent of the total traffic, with 500 million monthly users—equivalent to 13 percent of the global workforce. By March 2024, ChatGPT had reached 209 of 218 economies worldwide (refer to map 1.1, panel a). The top five economies for ChatGPT traffic in March 2024 were Brazil, India, Indonesia, the Philippines, and the United States. Colombia, Mexico, and Viet Nam have also seen impressive total traffic.

However, LICs and MICs lag far behind HICs in GenAI tool penetration. By April 2025, 24 percent of internet users in HICs used ChatGPT, compared with 5.8 percent in UMICs, 4.7 percent in LMICs, and 0.7 percent in LICs (Liu, Huang, and Wang, 2025). When adjusted for internet users, a clear divide exists between advanced economies and the rest of the world (refer to map 1.1, panel b). Although each internet user in Singapore visits ChatGPT 2.7 times on average each month, most developing countries record less than 0.4 visit per internet user.

MAP 1.1 ChatGPT traffic, by country, 2024

a. Total traffic, March 2024

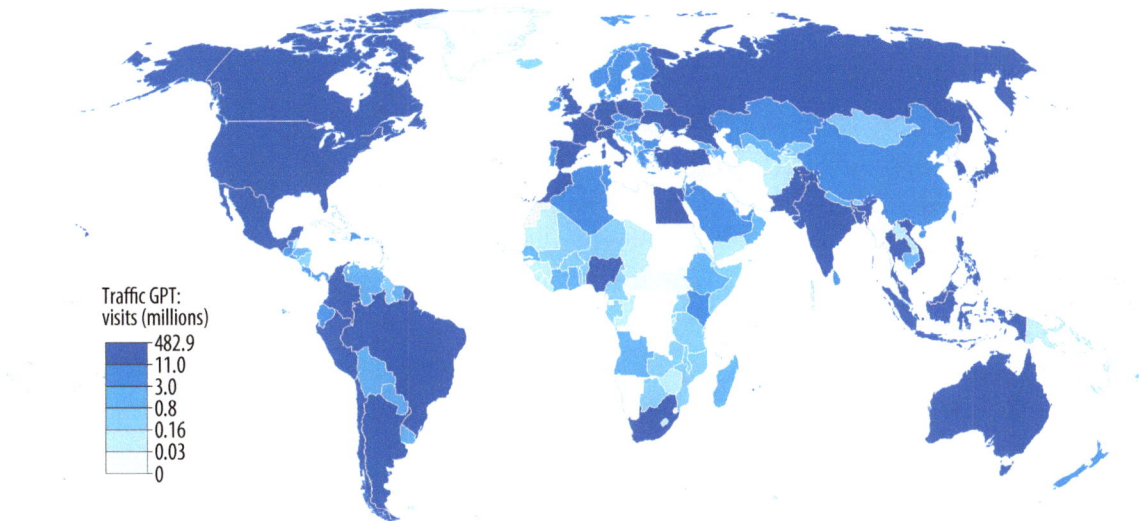

IBRD 48264 | July 2024

b. Traffic per internet user, March 2024

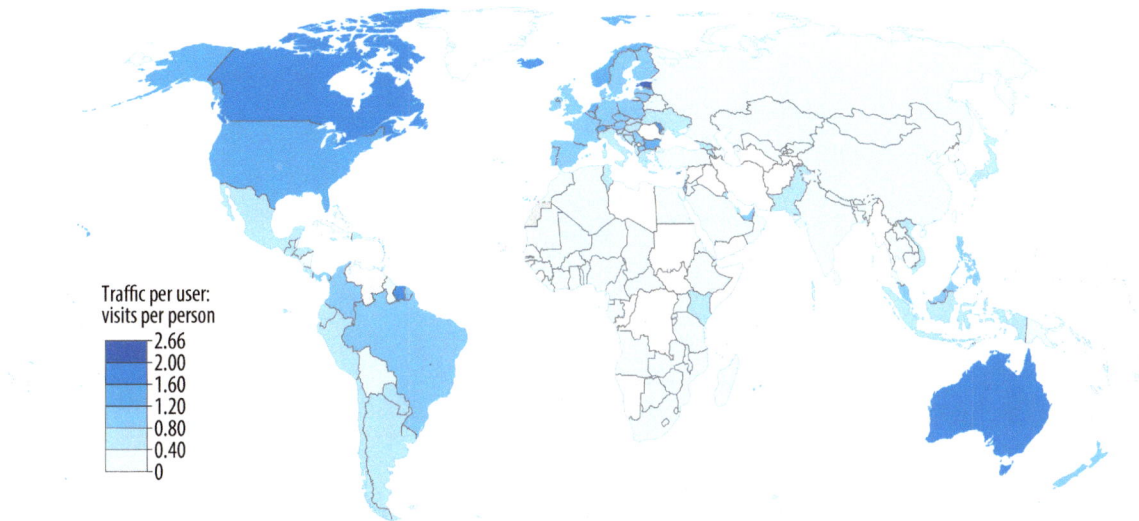

IBRD 48263 | July 2024

Source: Liu and Wang 2024.
Note: GPT = general-purpose technology.

Still, MICs show disproportionately high GenAI adoption relative to their economic size. The share of US traffic to ChatGPT plummeted from 70 percent to 25 percent within 1 month after its debut, but middle-income economies contributed more than 50 percent of global traffic only 6 months later (refer to figure 1.3). MICs have a disproportionately high adoption rate of GenAI relative to their GDP, electricity consumption, and search engine traffic, although low-income economies remain underrepresented, accounting for less than 1 percent of global ChatGPT traffic.

Robust digital infrastructure, specialization in digital services, higher human capital, and a large youth population are key factors driving higher GenAI adoption at the country level. Specifically, higher fixed broadband penetration, faster internet speed, a large share of white-collar workers, comparative advantage in digitally deliverable services, widespread English fluency and digital skills, and a higher share of youth population predict higher GenAI adoption when GDP per capita, population, and internet penetration are controlled for.

The demographics of GenAI users as captured by Semrush[3] reveal a clear skew toward young, highly educated men. Women account for only one-third of ChatGPT users, a stark contrast to the more balanced gender splits seen on platforms such as Google (48 percent female) and Wikipedia (52 percent female). The most-active GenAI user group is those ages 18–24, particularly for video-based GenAI tools. Nearly half of chatbot users hold a college degree, exceeding the educational attainment of Google's user base.

This gender gap in GenAI usage is significantly more pronounced than the global gender divide in internet use overall. According to International Telecommunication Union data, 70 percent of men are internet users worldwide, compared with 65 percent of women. In HICs and UMICs, this gap has nearly closed, with 94 percent of men and 93 percent of women online in HICs and 81 percent of men and 80 percent of women online in UMICs. Around 32 percent of US men use

FIGURE 1.3 ChatGPT and GenAI traffic over time, by income level and country

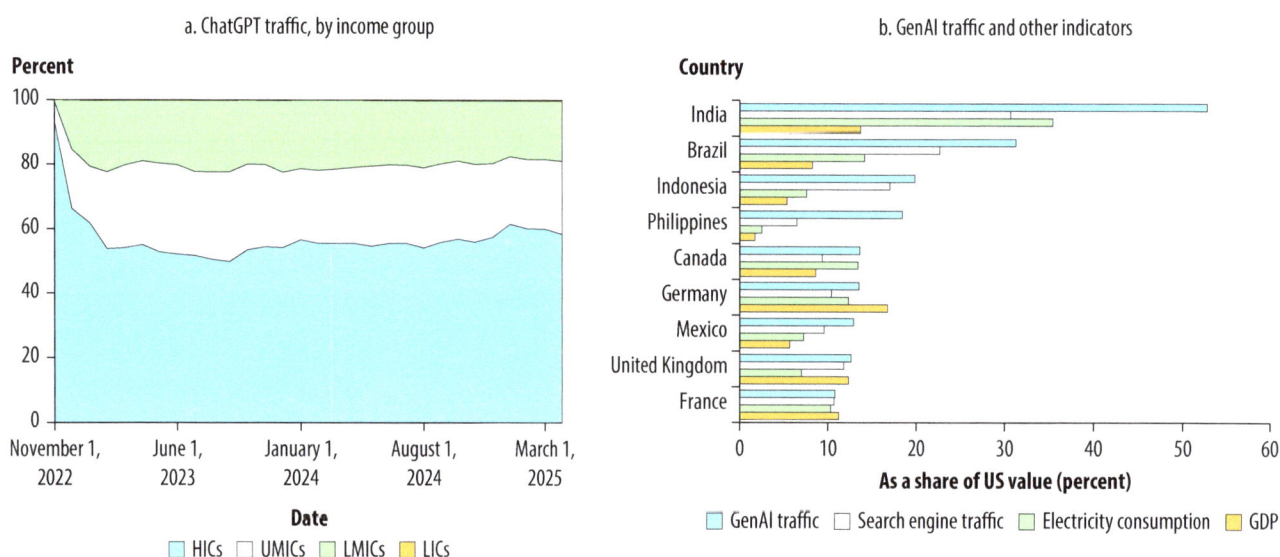

a. ChatGPT traffic, by income group

b. GenAI traffic and other indicators

Sources: Liu, Huang, and Wang 2025; Liu and Wang 2024.
Note: GDP = gross domestic product; GenAI = generative artificial intelligence; GPT = general-purpose technology; HIC = high-income countries; LICs = low-income countries; LMICs = lower-middle-income countries; US = United States.

GenAI at work, compared with just 23 percent of women (Bick, Blandin, and Deming 2024). In Denmark, women are 18 percentage points less likely to use ChatGPT than comparable men in the same occupation, of the same age and experience, and at the same earnings level (Humlum and Vestergaard 2024). The gender usage gap is likely much greater in developing countries.

GenAI tools are primarily accessed via desktop computers during weekdays, reflecting their role in professional and academic environments. Although Netflix sees binge-watching spikes over the weekend, ChatGPT usage peaks during the work week. Weekend traffic drops to about two-thirds to one-half of its weekday highs, indicating that people primarily turn to GenAI for work-related tasks.

People primarily use GenAI for writing communications both at work and for personal use. In the United States, nearly 40 percent of people list writing as the top one or two tasks for which GenAI is most useful, and 27 percent use GenAI for writing outside of work (Bick, Blandin, and Deming 2024). Other common tasks for which people most often use GenAI include administrative tasks, interpretation, translation, and information summarization.

Employees are moving faster than companies to integrate GenAI into the workplace. A global survey of 31,000 workers across 31 countries by LinkedIn and Microsoft in 2024 (Microsoft Source 2024) indicated that 75 percent of global knowledge workers are already using GenAI. Without guidance or clearance from the top, 78 percent of employees are bringing their own AI to work. This is even more common at small- and medium-size companies, where 4 of 5 workers bring their own AI. GenAI adoption is high in administrative support, real estate, and retail industries, with countries such as China, India, Indonesia, and Thailand reporting usage rates above 90 percent.

GenAI adoption at work is highest for IT, management, business, and finance occupations and industries. In the United States, nearly half of workers in these occupations and industries use GenAI frequently (Bick, Blandin, and Deming 2024). Software developers report the highest GenAI adoption. A survey conducted in May 2024 of 65,000 developers on Stack Overflow suggested that 76 percent are using or plan to use GenAI tools in their development process in 2024—a 6 percentage point increase from 2023 (Stack Overflow 2024). In the next year, surveyed developers believed that AI tools will be more integrated into documenting code (81 percent), testing code (80 percent), and writing code (76 percent). Of all the available AI tools, ChatGPT is used most— and 74 percent want to keep using it next year.

However, GenAI usage is not limited to white-collar workers. Interestingly, 22 percent of workers in blue-collar jobs—construction and extraction, installation and repair, skilled production, and transportation and moving occupations—use GenAI at work in the United States.

In Denmark, IT-prone and high-skilled occupations similarly report the highest GenAI adoption at both the extensive and the intensive margins. Around 80 percent of software developers, marketing professionals, and journalists used ChatGPT in 2024, and 20 percent of them have a ChatGPT Plus subscription (Humlum and Vestergaard 2024).

In contrast, AI adoption by firms—for use in firms' business processes, for instance—remains limited even in advanced economies, with large firms leading the way. Firm surveys in OECD countries show that, on average, only 8 percent of firms used AI in 2023 (refer to figure 1.4). In contrast, allied technologies such as cloud computing were used by nearly half of the firms in OECD countries (OECD 2024). Korea leads OECD economies in firm AI adoption, with 28 percent of all firms reporting AI adoption. At the other end of the spectrum, only 2 percent of firms in Romania use AI.

FIGURE 1.4   **Firm AI adoption rate across OECD countries, 2024**

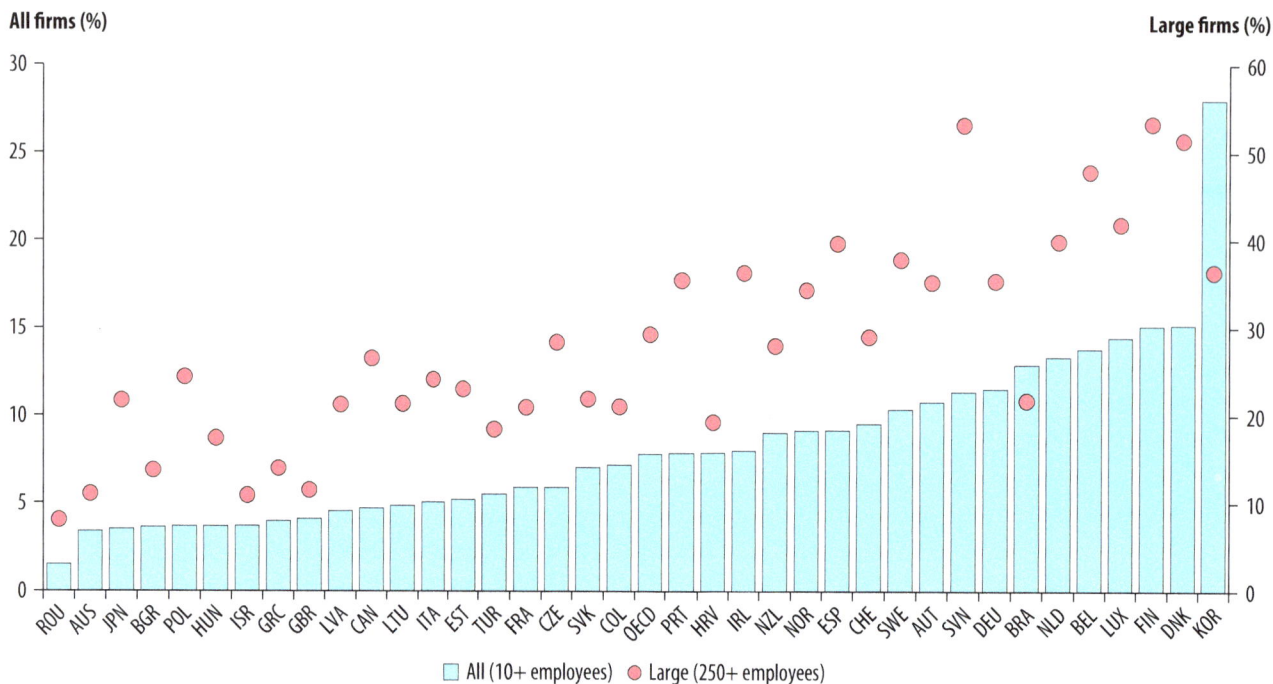

Source: Original figure for this publication using data from OECD 2024 (https://www.oecd.org/content/dam/oecd/en/publications/reports/2024/05/oecd-digital-economy-outlook-2024-volume-1_d30a04c9/a1689dc5-en.pdf).
Note: For a list of country codes, refer to https://www.iso.org/obp/ui/#search. AI = artificial intelligence; OECD = Organisation for Economic Co-operation and Development.

Large firms with at least 250 employees tend to have much higher AI adoption rates. In Belgium, Denmark, Finland, and Slovenia, around half of large firms are using AI. In the United States, fewer than 6 percent of firms are currently using AI-related technologies.

Adoption is concentrated among very large firms; those in "superstar" cities; and businesses owned by younger, more educated individuals. Recent data from the Business Trends and Outlook Survey (BTOS) indicate a modest increase in AI adoption, from 3.7 percent in September 2023 to an expected 6.6 percent by fall 2024 (Bonney et al. 2024). Among developing countries, 13 percent of firms in Brazil use AI, nearly twice the 6 percent and 7 percent in Türkiye and Colombia, respectively. AI adoption is higher for firms with more than 1,000 employees. Nearly 60 percent of firms in India, 50 percent of those in China, and 47 percent of those in Latin America report actively deploying AI, based on the IBM Global AI Adoption Survey 2023 (IBM 2024).

Firms in IT, professional services, and financial services are most likely to adopt AI. The US BTOS shows that more than 20 percent of firms in IT services use AI, followed by about 17 percent in professional services and 9 percent in finance and insurance (Bonney et al. 2024). The IBM Global AI Adoption Survey 2023 and McKinsey's GenAI adoption survey show similar results (McKinsey 2025). These three industries tend to top all other industries in the share of workers with advanced degrees, average earnings, and dependence on digital inputs, and they show high trade intensity. Thus, they are at the forefront of AI adoption.

When surveyed, firms report inaccuracy as the top risk in their GenAI use, and nearly one-quarter have already experienced negative consequences. As businesses begin to see the benefits of GenAI, they are also recognizing associated diverse risks. These can range from data management risks such as data privacy, bias, or IP infringement to model management risks, which tend to focus on inaccurate output or lack of explainability.

A third big risk category is security and incorrect use. GenAI hallucinations and inaccurate output are the top concern for firms, with 63 percent of firms reporting it as a relevant risk in 2024, up from 56 percent in 2023. Inaccuracy—which can affect use cases across the GenAI value chain, ranging from customer journeys and summarization to coding and creative content—is the only risk that firms are significantly more likely to mitigate in 2024 than in 2023. Nearly one-quarter of firms also reported negative consequences from GenAI's inaccuracy. However, given the inherent nature of hallucinations in GenAI, this will likely limit its use cases and effectiveness for firms.

Firms most often see meaningful cost reductions from AI in human resources (HR), risk, legal, and compliance functions. The McKinsey Global Survey on AI in 2024 (McKinsey 2025) indicates that 31 percent of firms report cost reductions of at least 10 percent in HR because of GenAI adoption, by far the area in which firms see the largest cost reduction among all business functions. Of firms, 15 percent also see cost reductions of at least 20 percent in risk, legal, and compliance because of GenAI adoption. Similarly, analytical AI adoption reduces costs in HR and compliance by at least 20 percent in more than 8 percent of firms.

Developing countries face significant challenges in fostering AI innovation and adaptation because of a complex interplay of economic, educational, and infrastructural factors. The lack of substantial research funding from both government and private sectors hampers long-term AI projects—including basic and applied research relevant to developing use cases within countries. Limited access to VC and angel investors creates a fundamental funding gap. High interest rates and stringent collateral requirements from traditional banks make debt financing challenging for AI start-ups, which typically have few tangible assets.

The innovation ecosystem is further strained by limited access to advanced computing resources, with insufficient high-performance computing infrastructure and prohibitively expensive cloud computing services. Moreover, market constraints, such as smaller domestic markets and limited ability to monetize AI solutions, affect revenue potential. Many local firms may lack the digital maturity to adopt AI solutions, resulting in a narrower customer base. This creates a chicken-and-egg problem in which limited market demand inhibits investment in development of applied AI solutions.

In addition, the inadequacy of specialized AI education and training programs in universities creates a skills gap at the entry level, hindering the growth of a robust AI workforce. Weak IP protection in many developing countries can also discourage innovation and commercialization, because researchers and companies may fear that their AI innovations may be stolen or copied without legal recourse.

The exodus of AI talent from developing to developed nations represents a severe impediment to building local AI applications. The salary disparity driving this migration is substantial—for example, in Latin America, the average AI engineer earns approximately US$30,000 annually, compared with US$150,000 in the United States. Career growth limitations further accelerate this drain. These barriers collectively create a challenging environment for AI innovation, limiting the ability of developing countries to contribute to and benefit from advancements in AI technology.

The adoption of AI technologies in developing countries is similarly hindered by a range of structural, economic, and social challenges. Limited digital infrastructure, characterized by unreliable internet connectivity and insufficient access to smart devices, forms a fundamental barrier to widespread AI adoption. A significant skills gap in the workforce can make it difficult for organizations to effectively implement and manage AI systems. Cultural and language barriers also play a crucial role, because many AI systems are not adapted to local languages or cultural nuances, leading to reduced effectiveness and acceptance.

Financial constraints pose another significant hurdle, with the high initial costs of AI implementation often out of reach for local businesses and government agencies. Moreover, a general lack of AI awareness and trust among decision-makers and the public can result in skepticism about AI's potential benefits and concerns about its impact on employment. These multifaceted barriers create a complex landscape that significantly slows the adoption and integration of AI technologies in developing countries, potentially widening the global digital divide.

4C pillars of AI foundations

This report highlights the importance of strengthening the foundational 4Cs that underpin a country's capacity to adopt, adapt, and innovate with AI: connectivity, compute, context, and competency (refer to figure 1.5). These four pillars represent the critical enablers of an inclusive and effective AI ecosystem.

- *Connectivity*—including reliable energy and digital infrastructure and access to and ownership of digital devices—is essential to ensuring that individuals, firms, and institutions can access and use AI technologies.

FIGURE 1.5 **The 4Cs of AI foundations**

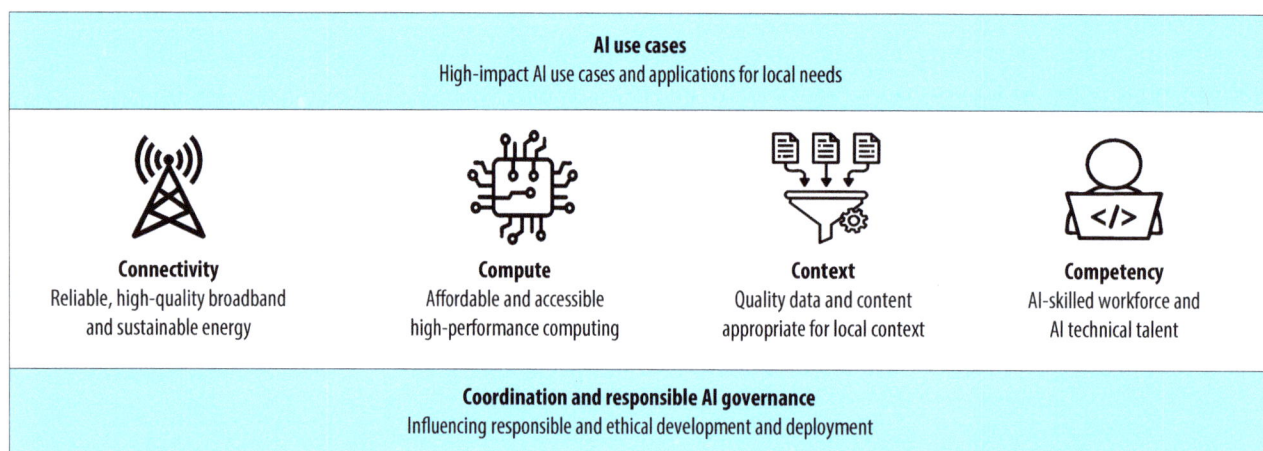

AI use cases
High-impact AI use cases and applications for local needs

| **Connectivity** | **Compute** | **Context** | **Competency** |
| Reliable, high-quality broadband and sustainable energy | Affordable and accessible high-performance computing | Quality data and content appropriate for local context | AI-skilled workforce and AI technical talent |

Coordination and responsible AI governance
Influencing responsible and ethical development and deployment

Source: Original illustration for this publication.
Note: The "coordination and responsible AI governance" topic is covered in a companion publication (World Bank 2024, https://hdl.handle.net/10986/42500). AI = artificial intelligence.

- *Compute* refers to the availability and affordability of processing power, such as AI chips, data centers, and cloud computing, which are necessary to train and deploy models at scale.
- *Context* encompasses the training data, models, and applications tailored to local languages, cultures, needs, and governance frameworks, without which AI tools may remain irrelevant or untrusted.
- *Competency* captures the digital skills and broader capabilities required to integrate AI into workflows and build new solutions.

Although all four components are necessary across the board, their relative importance and required sophistication differ depending on whether a country is focused on adoption, adaptation, or innovation. For basic adoption of off-the-shelf AI tools, countries must prioritize widespread connectivity and foundational digital skills. Adaptation—modifying AI tools to local contexts—demands more advanced data governance, locally relevant content, and specialized talent. Innovation, such as developing frontier models or novel applications, requires high-end computer infrastructure, robust venture and research ecosystems, and globally competitive expertise.

Thus, the 4Cs offer a practical policy framework for diagnosing readiness, identifying binding constraints, and tailoring interventions. They can help governments set priorities based on their AI ambitions and capabilities while also fostering coherence across infrastructure, innovation, education, labor, and data strategies. A balanced and coordinated investment in the 4Cs is essential not just for enabling AI but also for ensuring it delivers broad-based economic and social impact.

About this publication

After this introduction, this publication proceeds as follows: chapters 2–5 delve into the four foundational pillars crucial for AI success. For each of the 4Cs, these chapters examine supply and demand dynamics, benchmark country performance, pinpoint market failures and other obstacles, and offer policy insights. Chapter 6 synthesizes these findings and proposes high-level policy considerations for how developing countries can leverage the 4Cs to unlock the potential benefits of AI. Finally, Appendix A summarizes key findings from three thematic case studies; the full cases are available online at https://hdl.handle.net/10986/43822.

Notes

1. Creation of notable AI models measures both AI innovation and adaptation.
2. Due to the fast pace of innovation, a consistent definition and measurement of AI adoption is difficult. AI is often an invisible component of existing products and services, leading to "unintentional adoption" and significant underreporting in surveys. The challenges are amplified by the lack of consistent, cross-country, and longitudinal surveys, particularly in developing nations with limited resources. Given these issues, this section focuses on the intentional adoption of GenAI, which is more easily tracked.
3. Semrush (https://www.semrush.com/) calculates user demographics through data gathered via hundreds of partnerships with clickstream data providers, bringing in over 2 million events every minute. All the data collected is anonymized to protect individual identities but provides insights on socioeconomic characteristics of users (such as age, gender, and location) that are made available for analytics. With this anonymized clickstream data, Semrush uses a neural network algorithm to create realistic estimates of various subgroups and conducts error testing to validate these estimates.

References

Acemoglu, D. 2025. "The Simple Macroeconomics of AI." *Economic Policy* 40 (121): 13–58.

Autor, D. 2024. "Applying AI to Rebuild Middle Class Jobs." Working Paper w32140, National Bureau of Economic Research, Cambridge, MA.

Banerjee, S., A. Agarwal, and S. Singla. 2024. "LLMs Will Always Hallucinate, and We Need to Live With This." Preprint, submitted September 9, 2024. https://arxiv.org/abs/2409.05746.

Bick, A., A. Blandin, and D. J. Deming. 2024. "The Rapid Adoption of Generative AI." Working Paper 32966, National Bureau of Economic Research, Cambridge, MA.

Bloom, D. E., K. Prettner, J. Saadaoui, and M. Veruete. 2024. "Artificial Intelligence and the Skill Premium." Working Paper 32430, National Bureau of Economic Research, Cambridge, MA.

Bonney, K., C. Breaux, C. Buffington, E. Dinlersoz, L. S. Foster, N. Goldschlag, J. C. Haltiwanger, Z. Kroff, and K. Savage. 2024. "Tracking Firm Use of AI in Real Time: A Snapshot from the Business Trends and Outlook Survey." Working Paper 32319, National Bureau of Economic Research, Cambridge, MA.

Brynjolfsson, E., D. Li, and L. Raymond. 2025. "Generative AI at Work." *Quarterly Journal of Economics* 140 (2): 889–942.

Capraro, V., A. Lentsch, D. Acemoglu, S. Akgun, A. Akhmedova, E. Bilancini, J. F. Bonnefon, P. Brañas-Garza, L. Butera, K. M. Douglas, and J. A. Everett. 2024. "The Impact of Generative Artificial Intelligence on Socioeconomic Inequalities and Policy Making." *PNAS Nexus* 3 (6): 191.

Dell'Acqua, F., E. McFowland, III, E. R. Mollick, H. Lifshitz-Assaf, K. Kellogg, S. Rajendran, L. Krayer, F. Candelon, and K. R. Lakhani. 2023. "Navigating the Jagged Technological Frontier: Field Experimental Evidence of the Effects of AI on Knowledge Worker Productivity and Quality." Unit Working Paper 24-013, Harvard Business School, Technology and Operations Management, Boston.

Ebert, C., and P. Louridas. 2023. "Fig. 1: Time to Reach 100 Mio Users." https://www.researchgate.net/figure/Time-to-reach-100-million-users-for-different-technologies-in-months-after-initial_fig1_372212988.

Frey, C. B., and M. Osborne. 2023. "Generative AI and the Future of Work: A Reappraisal." *Brown Journal of World Affairs* 30: 161.

Gmyrek, P., H. Winkler, and S. Garganta. 2024. "Buffer or Bottleneck? Employment Exposure to Generative AI and the Digital Divide in Latin America." Working Paper 121, International Labour Organization, Geneva.

Hinton, G. 2023. "I Now Predict 5 to 20 Years but without Much Confidence." X, May 3, 2023, 5:08 a.m. https://x.com/geoffreyhinton/status/1653687894534504451.

Hui, X., O. Reshef, and L. Zhou. 2024. "The Short-Term Effects of Generative Artificial Intelligence on Employment: Evidence from an Online Labor Market." *Organization Science* 35 (6): 1977–89.

Humlum, A., and E. Vestergaard. 2024. "The Adoption of ChatGPT." Becker Friedman Institute for Economics Working Paper 2024–50, University of Chicago, Chicago.

IBM. 2024. "Data Suggest Growth in Enterprise Adoption of AI Is Due to Widespread Deployment by Early Adopters, but Barriers Keep 40% in the Exploration and Experimental Phases." News, January 10, 2024. https://newsroom.ibm.com/2024-01-10-Data-Suggests-Growth-in-Enterprise-Adoption-of-AI-is-Due-to-Widespread-Deployment-by-Early-Adopters.

"In Leaked Reports, Baidu Shows It's in the Global Robotaxi Race." 2024. *Bamboo Works,* October 14, 2024. https://thebambooworks.com/in-leaked-reports-baidu-shows-its-in-the-global-robotaxi-race/.

Kolodny, L., and J. Elias. 2025. "Waymo Reports 250,000 Paid Robotaxi Rides per Week in U.S." https://www.cnbc.com/2025/04/24/waymo-reports-250000-paid-robotaxi-rides-per-week-in-us.html.

Korinek, A. 2024. "Economic Policy Challenges for the Age of AI." Working Paper w32980, National Bureau of Economic Research, Cambridge, MA.

Kurzweil, R. 2024. *The Singularity Is Nearer: When We Merge with AI.* New York: Penguin.

Legêne, M. F., W. L. Auping, G. Homem de Almeida Correia, and B. van Arem. 2020. "Spatial Impact of Automated Driving in Urban Areas." *Journal of Simulation* 14 (4): 295–303.

Liu, Y. 2024. "Generative AI: Catalyst for Growth or Harbinger of Premature De-Professionalization?" Policy Research Working Paper 10915, World Bank, Washington, DC. http://documents.worldbank.org/curated/en/099520009172451039/.

Liu, Y., and H. Wang. 2024. *Who on Earth Is Using Generative AI?* Washington, DC: World Bank.

Liu, Y., J. Y. Huang, and H. Wang. 2025. *Who on Earth Is Using Generative AI? Global Trends and Shifts in 2025.* Washington, DC: World Bank.

McKinsey. 2025. "The State of AI: How Organizations Are Rewiring to Capture Value." *QuantumBlack: AI by McKinsey,* March 12, 2025. https://www.mckinsey.com/capabilities/quantumblack/our-insights/the-state-of-ai.

Mickle, T. 2024. "Will AI Be a Bust? A Wall Street Skeptic Rings the Alarm." *Seattle Times,* September 23, 2024. https://www.seattletimes.com/business/will-ai-go-bust-a-wall-street-skeptic-rings-the-alarm/.

Microsoft Source. 2024. "Microsoft and LinkedIn Release the 2024 Work Trend Index on the State of AI at Work." *Microsoft Company News,* May 8, 2024. https://news.microsoft.com/source/2024/05/08/microsoft-and-linkedin-release-the-2024-work-trend-index-on-the-state-of-ai-at-work/.

Mims, C. 2024. "This AI Pioneer Thinks AI Is Dumber Than a Cat." *Wall Street Journal,* October 11, 2024. https://www.wsj.com/tech/ai/yann-lecun-ai-meta-aa59e2f5.

Mirzadeh, I., K. Alizadeh, H. Shahrokhi, O. Tuzel, S. Bengio, and M. Farajtabar. 2024. "GSM-Symbolic: Understanding the Limitations of Mathematical Reasoning in Large Language Models." Preprint, last revised August 27, 2025. https://arxiv.org/abs/2410.05229.

Narayanan, A., and S. Kapoor. 2024. *AI Snake Oil: What Artificial Intelligence Can Do, What It Can't, and How to Tell the Difference.* Princeton, NJ: Princeton University Press.

Narayanan, A., and S. Kapoor. 2025. *AI as Normal Technology.* New York: Knight First Amendment Institute, Columbia University, New York. https://knightcolumbia.org/content/ai-as-normal-technology.

Noy, S., and W. Zhang. 2023. "Experimental Evidence on the Productivity Effects of Generative Artificial Intelligence." *Science* 381 (6654): 187–92.

OECD (Organisation for Economic Co-operation and Development). 2024. *The Digital Economy Outlook (Volume 1).* Paris: OECD. https://doi.org/10.1787/a1689dc5-en.

"OpenAI's Latest Model Will Change the Economics of Software." 2025. *The Economist,* January 20, 2025.

Otis, N., R. P. Clarke, S. Delecourt, D. Holtz, and R. Koning. 2023. "The Uneven Impact of Generative AI on Entrepreneurial Performance." SSRN. Unpublished manuscript, February 27, 2024. http://dx.doi.org/10.2139/ssrn.4671369.

Schoeberl, C., and J. Corrigan. 2024. "Funding the AI Cloud—Amazon, Alphabet, and Microsoft's Cloud Computing Investments, Part 1: If You Build Cloud, They Will Come." Center for Security and Emerging Technology, Georgetown University, Washington, DC. https://cset.georgetown.edu/publication/funding-the-ai-cloud-computing-investments-part-1/.

Shoaib, Z. 2024. "Big Tech Moves More AI Spending Abroad." *Wall Street Journal,* May 23, 2024. https://www.wsj.com/tech/ai/big-tech-moves-more-ai-spending-abroad-088988de.

Stack Overflow. 2024. "2024 Developer Survey." https://survey.stackoverflow.co/2024/.

Thomas, P., and D. Murdick. 2020. *Patents and Artificial Intelligence: A Primer.* CSET Data Brief. Washington, DC: Center for Security and Emerging Technology, Georgetown University. https://cset .georgetown.edu/wp-content/uploads/CSET-Patents-and-Artificial-Intelligence-1.pdf.

WIPO (World Intellectual Property Organization). 2024. *Generative Artificial Intelligence.* Patent Landscape Report. Geneva: WIPO. https://www.wipo.int/web-publications/patent-landscape-report -generative-artificial-intelligence-genai/assets/62504/Generative%20AI%20-%20PLR%20EN _WEB2.pdf.

Yilmaz, E. D., I. Naumovska, and V. A. Aggarwal. 2023. "AI-Driven Labor Substitution: Evidence from Google Translate and ChatGPT." Working Paper 2023/24/EFE, INSEAD, Fontainebleau, France. http://dx.doi.org/10.2139/ssrn.4400516.

Zinn, A. 2025. "Generative AI's Most Prominent Skeptic Doubles Down." Techxplore, May 29, 2025. https://techxplore.com/news/2025-05-generative-ai-prominent-skeptic.html.

Connectivity | 2

KEY MESSAGES

- Internet access gaps have narrowed, but affordability and quality gaps between richer and poorer countries have widened.

  ◦ *Internet users.* Lower-middle-income countries (LMICs) drove global internet penetration (68 percent in 2024, up from 64 percent in 2022), but one-third of the global population remains offline. Urban-rural gaps widened across income groups, despite narrowing gender-age gaps.

  ◦ *Affordability.* Broadband costs dropped significantly in low-income countries (LICs) between 2022 and 2023 (18 percent for fixed broadband; 8 percent for mobile broadband) but still remain prohibitive given the low income level in LICs.

  ◦ *Speed inequality.* High-income countries (HICs) and upper-middle-income countries (UMICs) saw a 50-percent increase in internet speed between 2023 and 2024, reaching 143 megabits per second (mbps) and 74 mbps, respectively; the median speed in LICs and LMICs stagnated below 25 mbps.

  ◦ *Data consumption.* The data consumption gap has widened, with HICs increasingly leaving others behind. In 2023, median data traffic per capita reached 1,400 gigabytes (GB) in HICs (up from 1,200 GB in 2022), 400 GB in UMICs, and 100 GB in LMICs, and it stalled at 5–6 GB in LICs.

- Information and communication technology (ICT) goods trade has slumped, whereas digital services trade continues to record strong growth.

  ◦ ICT goods trade plunged by 13 percent in 2023 (US$2.5 trillion) compared with 2022 because of slowing demand and trade frictions. China, the Republic of Korea, and Mexico experienced the sharpest declines. As firms diversified sourcing locations to enhance resilience, India, a few Middle East countries, and Central and Eastern European countries saw rapid growth.

  ◦ ICT services trade grew by 22 percent between 2022 and 2024 (US$1.2 trillion), led by South Asia (SAR; 22 percent, mainly India), the United States (17 percent), and Latin America and the Caribbean (LAC; 14 percent).

  ◦ Digitally deliverable services continue to surge, with LAC (39 percent) and SAR (22 percent) leading growth from 2022 to 2024.

- The expansion of 5G accelerated and the rise of satellite connectivity offers new possibilities.

  ○ *5G expansion.* 5G expanded fastest in LMICs between 2022 and 2024 (30 percentage points of population coverage), but coverage remains minimal in LICs.

  ○ *Satellite connectivity.* Since 2015, the number of communications satellites in orbit deployed for commercial purposes has increased more than 14 times. Low Earth orbit satellites now make up 90 percent of all satellites in orbit providing communications and connectivity services. New business models and price points are increasing the adoption of satellite communications services globally.

- Governments need to create an enabling environment to promote private sector investment in expanding and upgrading digital infrastructure.

  ○ Governments can liberalize restrictions on foreign investment, ensure fair competition, and streamline permitting and rights-of-way processes to reduce delays and costs in network deployment. Clear and stable regulatory frameworks, including spectrum management policies, can reduce investor uncertainty. Promoting infrastructure sharing can improve service affordability.

  ○ Shared internet access points, targeted subsidies, reduced taxes on digital devices, and innovative financing mechanisms could make digital devices more accessible and affordable for low-income families.

Digital infrastructure

Global mobile network coverage has become nearly universal, reaching more than 98 percent of the global population across all regions. As of 2024, only 2 percent of the global population, approximately 170 million people, live without mobile coverage, with the majority residing in low-income countries (LICs). Across all income groups, 5G coverage has increased, with lower-middle-income countries (LMICs) experiencing the fastest expansion between 2022 and 2024, although coverage in LICs remains minimal. More than 90 percent of the population in high-income countries (HICs) and middle-income countries (MICs) were covered by 4G and 5G in 2024. In HICs and upper-middle-income countries (UMICs), 5G has become the predominant technology, reaching more than two-thirds of the population. In LMICs, 5G coverage increased from 5 percent in 2022 to 35 percent in 2024, whereas in LICs, 5G expansion has been minimal, reaching only 4 percent of the population and leaving most users dependent on 3G and 4G networks (refer to figure 2.1).

Nonterrestrial networks (NTNs), especially satellites, play a vital role in filling the connectivity gaps left by traditional terrestrial communications infrastructure. NTNs are wireless communications technologies that broadcast signals, using equipment stationed in the air and in Earth's orbit. These platforms include satellites in low Earth orbit (LEO), medium Earth orbit, and geosynchronous orbit (GSO), as well as high-altitude platform stations and unmanned aerial vehicles. They enhance global communications coverage and services by providing internet connectivity to end users.

FIGURE 2.1 Mobile network coverage, by country income group, 2022 and 2024

Population covered by mobile network (%)

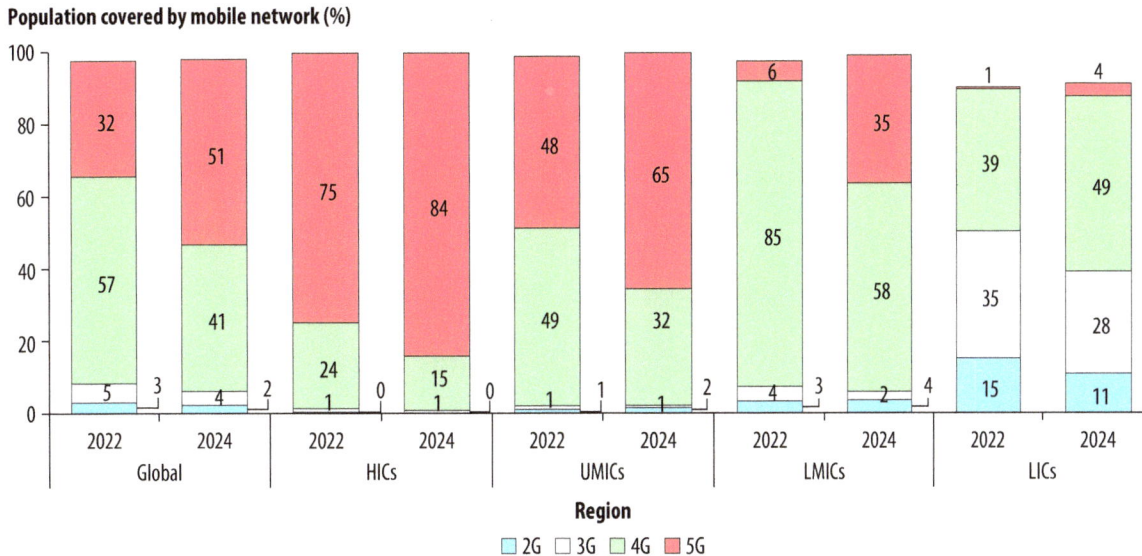

Source: Original figure for this publication using calculations from the International Telecommunication Union (https://datahub.itu.int/).
Note: HICs = high-income countries; LICs = low-income countries; LMICs = lower-middle-income countries; UMICs = upper-middle-income countries.

The recent rise in the availability of satellite internet worldwide has been driven by significant growth in satellite constellations. As of 2023, there were slightly more than 7,560 satellites in orbit, of which approximately 5,300 are commercial communications satellites providing connectivity services in addition to traditional fixed and mobile networks (Sebastian 2005). The presence of large constellations of nongeosynchronous-orbit (NGSO) satellites covering the earth's surface remains the main driver of increased availability of satellite connectivity. Since 2015, the number of communications satellites in orbit deployed for commercial purposes has increased more than 14 times, with LEO satellites constituting the bulk of launches (refer to figure 2.2). LEO satellites now make up 90 percent of all satellites in orbit providing communications and connectivity services.

New business models and price points are increasing the adoption of satellite communications services globally. Although GSO satellites stationed approximately 36,000 kilometers above the Earth's surface have historically provided effective communications services, primarily focused on business and government clients, and played a vital role in enhancing global navigation, backhauling for telecommunications providers, and emergency response capabilities, recent breakthroughs in technology (leading to a significant reduction in launch costs) and business models are changing the landscape of satellite connectivity. NGSO satellite constellations such as Starlink and OneWeb offer solutions with improved speeds, better prices, and reduced latency, making satellite connectivity attractive to end users seeking improved experiences in developing countries. A 2023 study by Ookla found that in Nigeria and Rwanda, SpaceX's Starlink recorded median download speeds almost two times faster than those of other fixed broadband providers.[1] NGSO satellites also provide a viable connectivity solution for rural and remote areas that are hard to reach with terrestrial fixed and mobile networks because of financial, demographic, or geographic constraints, democratizing broadband access to unserved populations. Countries also have their own regulatory processes to decide which providers are best for their own contexts (Stein and Natanson 2025).

FIGURE 2.2 **Growth in commercial communications satellite constellations, by orbital positioning, 2015–23**

Number

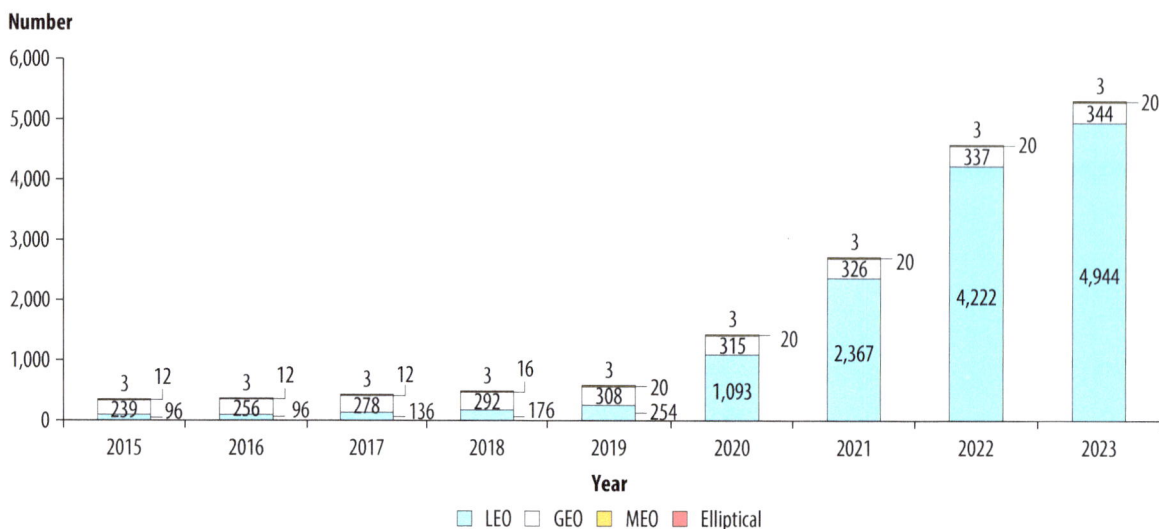

□ LEO □ GEO ▨ MEO ▨ Elliptical

Source: Original figure for this publication calculated using data from the Union of Concerned Scientists (https://www.ucs.org/resources/satellite-database).
Note: GEO = geosynchronous orbit; LEO = low Earth orbit; MEO = medium Earth orbit.

The unique coverage of NGSO satellite constellations makes them integral to a wide range of 4G and 5G use cases. These applications include precision agriculture and Internet of Things (IoT) connectivity.[2] Satellites are increasingly being integrated into development interventions to, for instance, improve infrastructure mapping and quickly restore communications services after a natural disaster. The recent development of a direct-to-cellular/device feature that enables satellites to connect to users' mobile devices, delivering voice, short message service, and data, will bring a wider range of services and use cases.

As communications satellites advance, governments are developing their regulatory responses. Various countries are reforming telecommunications licensing, opening their skies and collaborating for better connectivity to ensure rural access and achieve developmental goals in health education and social services delivery. These policy responses address key satellite challenges such as licensing and coordination (including spectrum and ground stations), high costs that limit affordability, and technical limits such as congestion and bandwidth caps affecting service quality, ensuring integration with terrestrial networks for lower costs and mitigating environmental impacts from launches and deorbiting. The growth of satellite connectivity is also shaped by regulations aiming to create fair competition with the mobile industry, which operates under different rules.

Digital sector development

Global exports of information and communications technology (ICT) goods, which account for 12 percent of global merchandise exports (US$2.5 trillion), declined by 13 percent in 2023 compared with 2022, more than the overall global merchandise trade contraction of 4 percent. The downturn was consistent across all income groups, with HICs maintaining their share of global ICT goods exports at 57 percent. Exports of all ICT subcomponents contracted. This decline was driven by weakening global demand, supply chain imbalances, and trade restrictions.

Among the world's largest ICT goods exporters, China; the Republic of Korea; Hong Kong SAR, China; and Mexico experienced the sharpest declines during 2022–23. Korea experienced the steepest decline, with ICT goods exports falling by 24 percent because of falling semiconductor prices, a delayed recovery in the demand for ICT devices, and an inventory overhang caused by double ordering during the pandemic (Ackerman 2024). Mexico followed with a 14 percent drop, and China and Hong Kong SAR, China, experienced reductions of 10 percent over the same period (refer to figure 2.3). Nevertheless, China remained the world's largest exporter, accounting for nearly 30 percent of global ICT goods exports in 2023. In terms of export destinations, China's ICT goods exports to the United States saw the largest decline because of evolving trade policies and export controls.

FIGURE 2.3 ICT goods exports, 2022–23

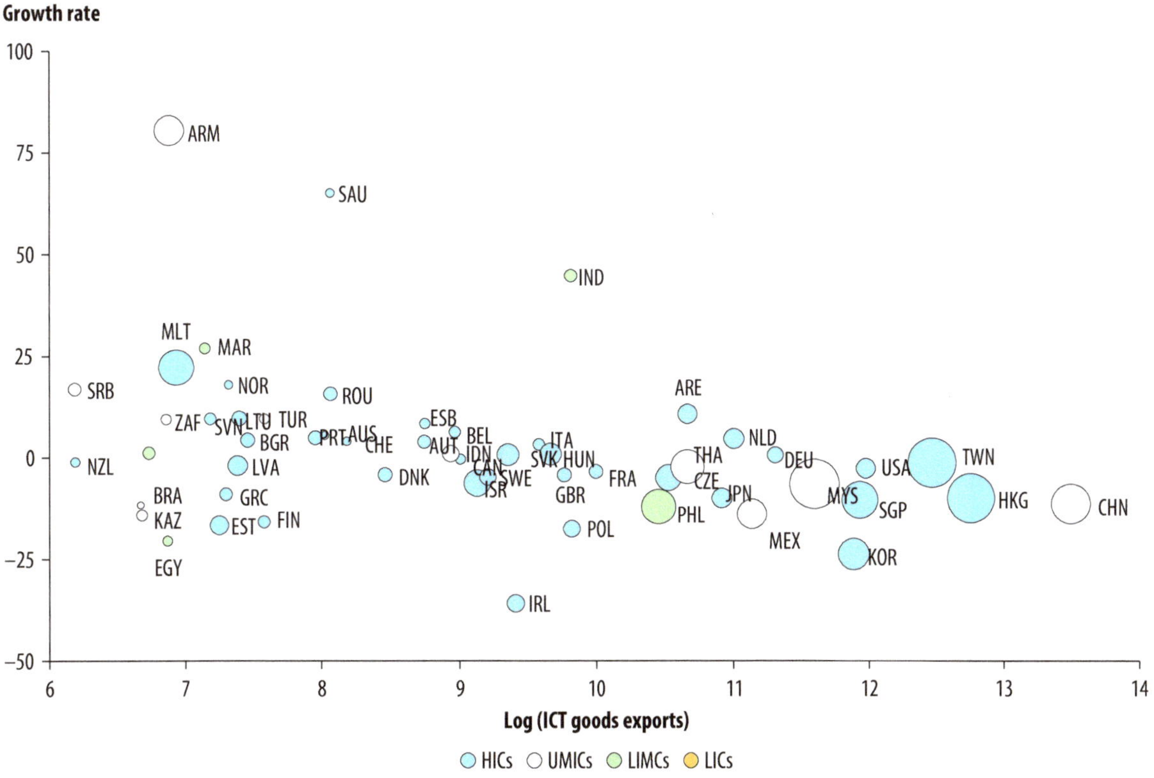

Source: Original figure for this publication calculated using data from the United Nations Trade and Development Stats (https://unctadstat .unctad.org/datacentre/).
Note: Bubble size represents the share of ICT goods exports in a country's total merchandise exports. Countries with shares in total ICT exports more than 0.01 percent are displayed. For a list of country codes, refer to https://www.iso.org/obp/ui/#search. HICs = high-income countries; ICT = information and communication technology; LMICs = lower-middle-income countries; LICs = low-income countries; UMICs = upper-middle-income countries.

As firms diversified sourcing locations to enhance resilience, India, Morocco, Saudi Arabia, the United Arab Emirates, and several Central and Eastern European countries saw surging ICT goods exports in 2022–23. India recorded an exceptional growth of 45 percent. Targeted industrial policies such as the "Make in India" initiative and production-linked incentives bolstered domestic production, with Apple's growing manufacturing presence boosting smartphone exports ("Apple Expands India Manufacturing," 2025). Saudi Arabia's ICT goods exports soared by more than 60 percent. Morocco's ICT goods exports rose by 27 percent as the "Digital Morocco 2030" strategy fostered ICT sector development, driving export gains. Exports also boomed in several Central and Eastern European economies, including Armenia, Bulgaria, Malta, Serbia, Slovenia, and Türkiye, albeit from a low base.

Although exports of ICT goods have declined in recent years, exports of ICT services have continued to grow steadily, increasing by 22 percent between 2022 and 2024. Global ICT services exports reached US$1.2 trillion in 2024, representing 15 percent of global commercial services exports. ICT services exports have largely been driven by IT services, which account for 90 percent of global ICT services exports. From 2022 to 2023, IT services grew by 12 percent, driven by rising demand for cloud computing, software development, and digital services. Within IT services, computer services—which make up 93 percent of IT services exports—grew by 14 percent, whereas information services declined by 9 percent.

Armenia, Cambodia, Georgia, Kazakhstan, and Uzbekistan experienced sizzling growth in IT services exports in 2023. In 2023, Ireland remained the world's largest IT services exporter, accounting for 24 percent of global exports, primarily because of big tech's tax optimization strategies. India followed at 11 percent, with China at 9 percent and the United States at 6 percent. China, India, and Ireland continued to achieve double-digit growth in 2023. Cambodia and Uzbekistan experienced the highest growth in IT services exports, although their global market shares remain below 1 percent (refer to figure 2.4).

Cambodia's IT services market is expanding as demand for software development and outsourcing services rises (Loma Technology 2024), and Uzbekistan has implemented policies requiring that IT firms generating US$8.7 million annually derive at least 10 percent of their revenue from exports, with targets increasing to 50 percent by 2028 (Daryo 2024). Many other MICs in Europe and Central Asia (ECA), Latin America and the Caribbean (LAC), and East Asia and Pacific (EAP) also experienced brisk growth, including Armenia, Brazil, Georgia, Kazakhstan, and Serbia, where growth rates exceeded 30 percent.

More broadly, digital transformation continues to drive the export of digitally deliverable services, which reached US$4.8 trillion in 2024. In 2024, ICT services composed 25 percent of digitally deliverable services, up 1.2 percentage points (p.p.) from 2022. Other categories also posted significant gains. Notably, insurance and pension services surged by 31 percent, and financial services and other business services—which together represent nearly 60 percent of digitally deliverable services exports—expanded by 19 percent and 16 percent, respectively.

The highest growth in digitally deliverable services exports was recorded in ECA and SAR, where exports increased by 39 percent and 22 percent, respectively. HICs remain dominant, accounting for 84 percent of digitally deliverable services exports in 2024, following a 17 percent increase between 2022 and 2024. Digitally deliverable services exports are highly concentrated in some countries, with the United States (15 percent), Ireland (10 percent), the United Kingdom (10 percent), India (6 percent), Germany (6 percent), and China (5 percent) collectively accounting for half of global digital services exports.

FIGURE 2.4 Growth of IT services exports, by country income group, 2022–23

Growth rate

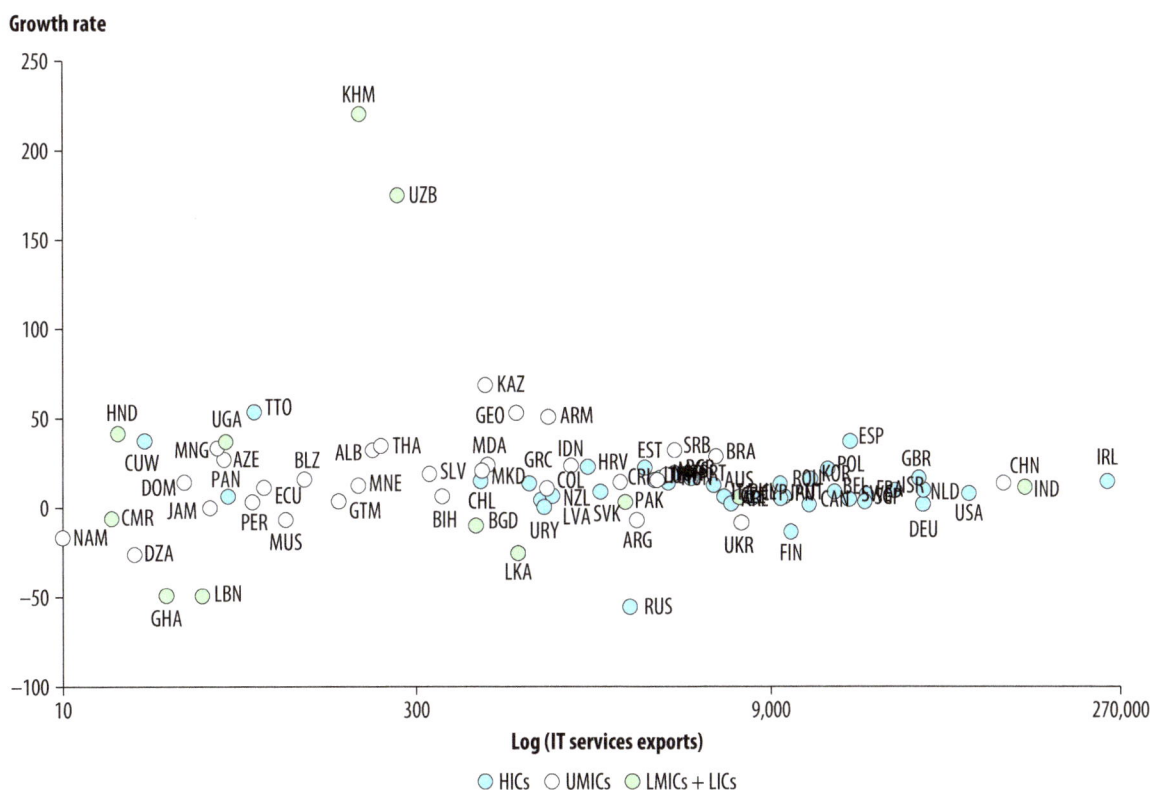

Source: Original figure for this publication calculated using data from the World Trade Organization (https://stats.wto.org/).
Note: Bubble size represents the share of IT services exports in a country's total commercial services exports. Countries with export shares in total IT services exports of more than 0.01 percent are displayed. For a list of country codes, refer to https://www.iso.org/obp /ui/#search. HICs = high-income countries; IT = information technology; LICs = low-income countries; LMICs = lower-middle-income countries; UMICs = upper-middle-income countries.

Among developing countries, all regions saw strong growth. In ECA, Türkiye drove much of the increase, with exports soaring by 65 percent, now accounting for 30 percent of the region's exports. Türkiye's growing prominence in digital services exports can be attributed to its robust technology system, skilled workforce, strategic geographic position, and supportive government policies ("Information Technology Sector Sets Higher Targets for 2025"). In SAR, India contributed 96 percent of the region's exports and achieved 22 percent growth between 2022 and 2024. LAC recorded a 17 percent growth rate, with Brazil, Costa Rica, and Mexico each exceeding 15 percent. The Arab Republic of Egypt (15 percent) in the Middle East and North Africa (MENA), Indonesia (48 percent) in EAP, and South Africa (23 percent) in Sub-Saharan Africa (SSA) also saw their exports surge between 2022 and 2024. In contrast, LICs continue to lag, with exports remaining below US$1 billion.

Digital adoption

Internet penetration expanded steadily during 2022–24, reaching 68 percent of the global population, largely driven by LMICs. Among the 400 million newly connected users, nearly half originated from LMICs. UMICs accounted for approximately 129 million new users, with internet penetration exceeding 80 percent (refer to figure 2.5). LICs experienced a modest increase of 3.4 p.p. since 2022, which raised internet penetration to just over one-quarter of their populations. Internet penetration neared saturation in HICs at 93 percent, contributing only 35 million new users between 2022 and 2024.

UMICs led the growth in fixed broadband penetration (subscriptions per 100 people), whereas LMICs and LICs saw minimal growth. Fixed broadband penetration increased by 4 p.p. in UMICs, reaching 32 percent in 2024. Fixed broadband penetration reached only 4.8 percent in LMICs and less than 1 percent of population in LICs.

Growth in mobile broadband penetration in LMICs and LICs in 2022–24 also lagged their richer peers. In HICs and UMICs, mobile broadband penetration rose by 8 and 5 p.p., respectively, during 2022–24 (refer to figure 2.6). Penetration increased only 4 p.p. in LMICs and LICs, indicating persistent constraints in expanding mobile broadband usage, potentially because of the affordability of mobile internet services and smartphones.

It is important to note that broadband subscription data do not directly reflect the number of internet users. In wealthier countries, higher penetration may reflect multiple subscriptions per user, increased business and IoT subscriptions, or temporary use by tourists—factors less common in LMICs and LICs. In contrast, in poorer countries, a single mobile subscription often supports multiple users through shared access within households or communities.

FIGURE 2.5 Internet penetration, globally and by income group, 2022 versus 2024

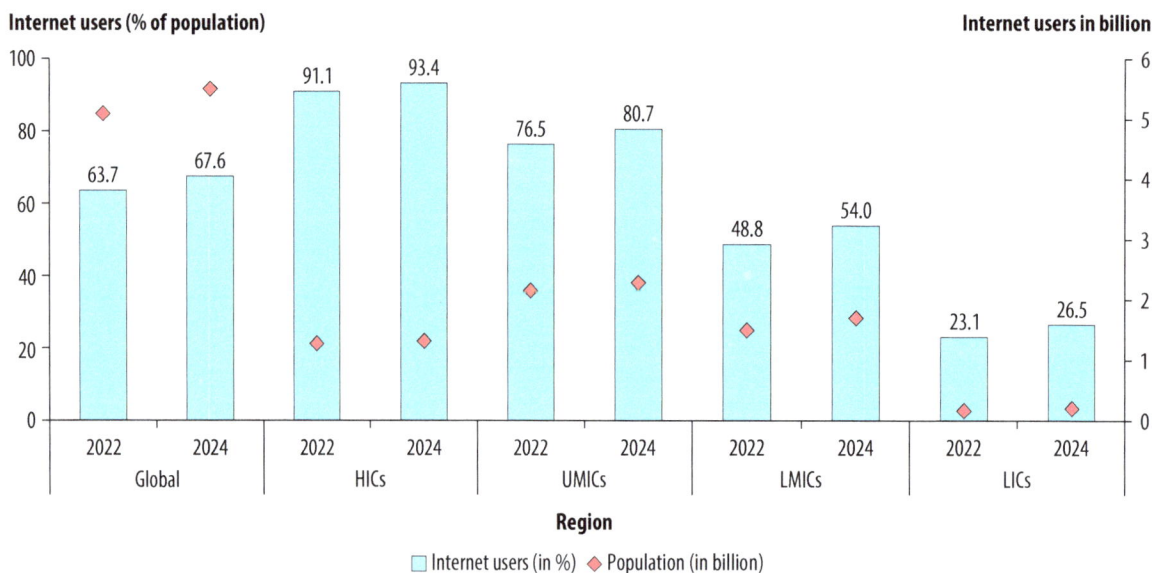

Source: Original figure for this publication using calculations from the International Telecommunication Union (https://datahub.itu.int/).
Note: HICs = high-income countries; LICs = low-income countries; LMICs = lower-middle-income countries; UMICs = upper-middle-income countries.

FIGURE 2.6 Fixed and mobile broadband penetration, globally and by income group, 2022 and 2024

% point gap

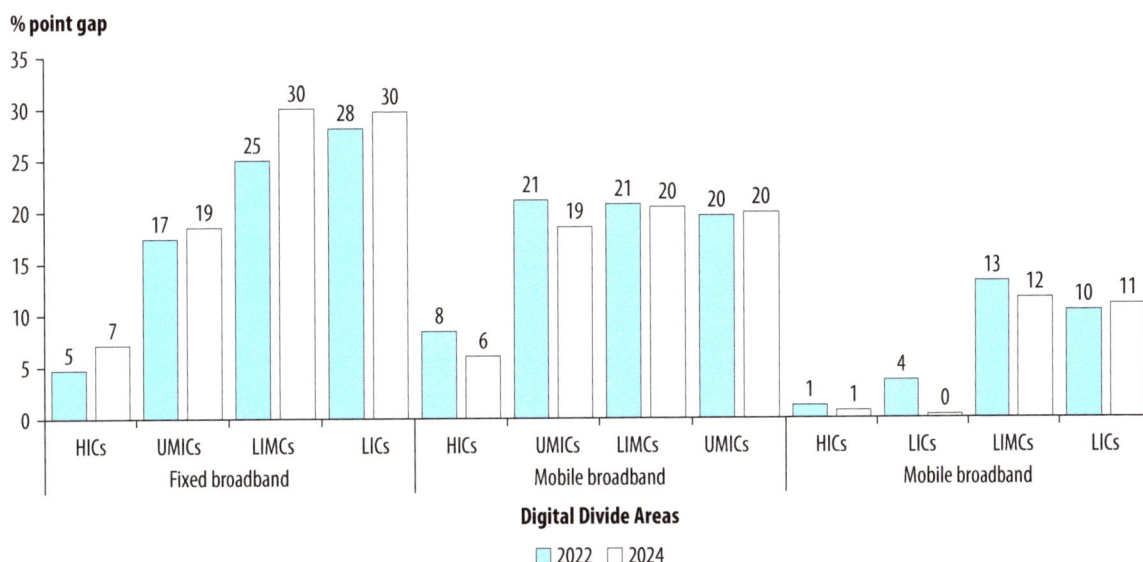

Source: Original figure for this publication based on calculations from the International Telecommunication Union (https://datahub
.itu.int/).
Note: HICs = high-income countries; LICs = low-income countries; LMICs = lower-middle-income countries; UMICs = upper-middle
-income countries.

Despite these gains in internet connectivity, 2.6 billion people, representing one-third of the global population, remained offline in 2024, primarily in rural areas in LICs and LMICs. Among this offline population, 1.8 billion lived in rural areas, and 800 million resided in urban areas. The urban-rural digital divide widened across all income groups between 2022 and 2024, as urban internet adoption outpaced rural expansion. Disparities in internet access persist across gender and age groups, although they generally continue to narrow, except in LICs where the gender gap widened slightly. Gender parity has nearly been achieved in HICs and UMICs, whereas in LMICs and LICs internet access rates among male users exceed those among female users by more than 10 p.p., largely reflecting preexisting gender divides. Age-related disparities also diminished, especially in HICs and UMICs.

Affordability of both fixed and mobile broadband has improved significantly among LMICs and LICs in recent years, but it remains a major obstacle in LICs. In LICs, median fixed broadband costs fell by 18 percent and mobile broadband costs declined by 8 percent in purchasing power parity terms between 2022 and 2023, yet fixed broadband remains nearly 5 times as expensive as mobile broadband. A 5-gigabyte fixed broadband subscription consumed 29 percent of average monthly income in LICs in 2024—a figure that is 5 times higher than in LMICs and 30 times higher than in HICs. Broadband services in HICs and UMICs are generally affordable, with costs below 3 percent of monthly income and affordability improving marginally. In LMICs, mobile broadband costs are similarly low, falling below 3 percent of income. This is close to the affordability threshold of 2 percent of monthly income established by the International Telecommunication Union.

Internet speed increased significantly in HICs and UMICs between 2023 and 2024, whereas speed in LMICs and LICs stagnated. Median fixed internet speeds in HICs and UMICs increased by more than 50 percent. In LMICs and LICs, marginal improvements kept median download speeds below 25 megabits per second for both mobile and fixed broadband in 2023 and 2024 (refer to figure 2.7). The disparity in internet speed translates into substantial differences in download times.

Within-country disparities in broadband speeds generally narrowed from 2019 to 2024 but remain pronounced, especially in SSA. The authors created a coefficient of variation (CV) of the logarithm of download speeds as a measure of within-country internet speed inequality.[3] Within-country speed inequality tends to be higher in LICs (refer to figure 2.8). In 2024, fixed broadband inequality was most pronounced in MENA, SAR, and SSA, with median CV values exceeding 0.15. Mobile speed inequality was highest in LAC and SSA. Although median inequality has generally declined, mobile broadband speed inequality rose in LAC and MENA. This reflects ongoing infrastructure projects that initially benefit certain areas, as seen in Cuba, where the introduction of the Arimao cable in early 2023 coincides with an inequality exceeding 0.5.

Gaps in data consumption across country income groups continue to widen, with HICs increasingly leaving others behind. In HICs and UMICs, annual fixed broadband traffic per capita is nearly 10 times the mobile traffic per capita (refer to figure 2.9). Total data traffic per capita in HICs reached nearly 1,400 gigabytes (GB) in 2023, around 400 GB in UMICs, 100 GB in LMICs, and only 5 GB in LICs.

FIGURE 2.7 **Median fixed and mobile download speed, by country income group, 2023 and 2024**

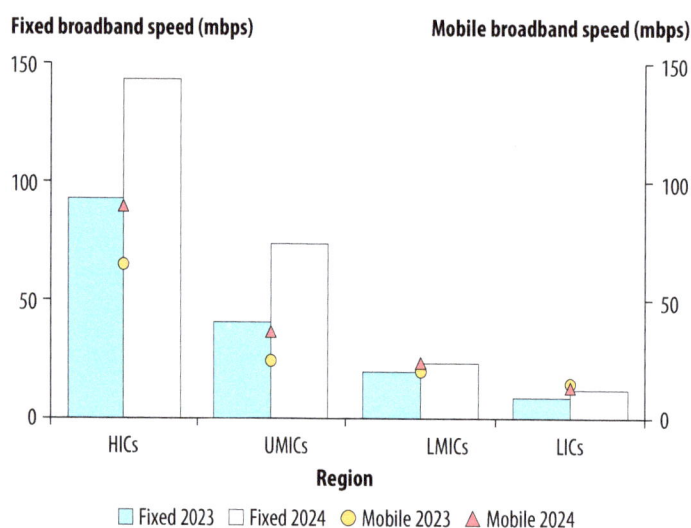

Sources: Original figure for this publication calculated using data from Ookla (https://www.speedtest.net/global-index).
Note: HICs = high-income countries; LICs = low-income countries; LMICs = lower-middle-income countries; mbps = megabits per second; UMICs = upper-middle-income countries.

FIGURE 2.8 **Within-country internet speed inequality, 2019 Q1 and 2024 Q4**

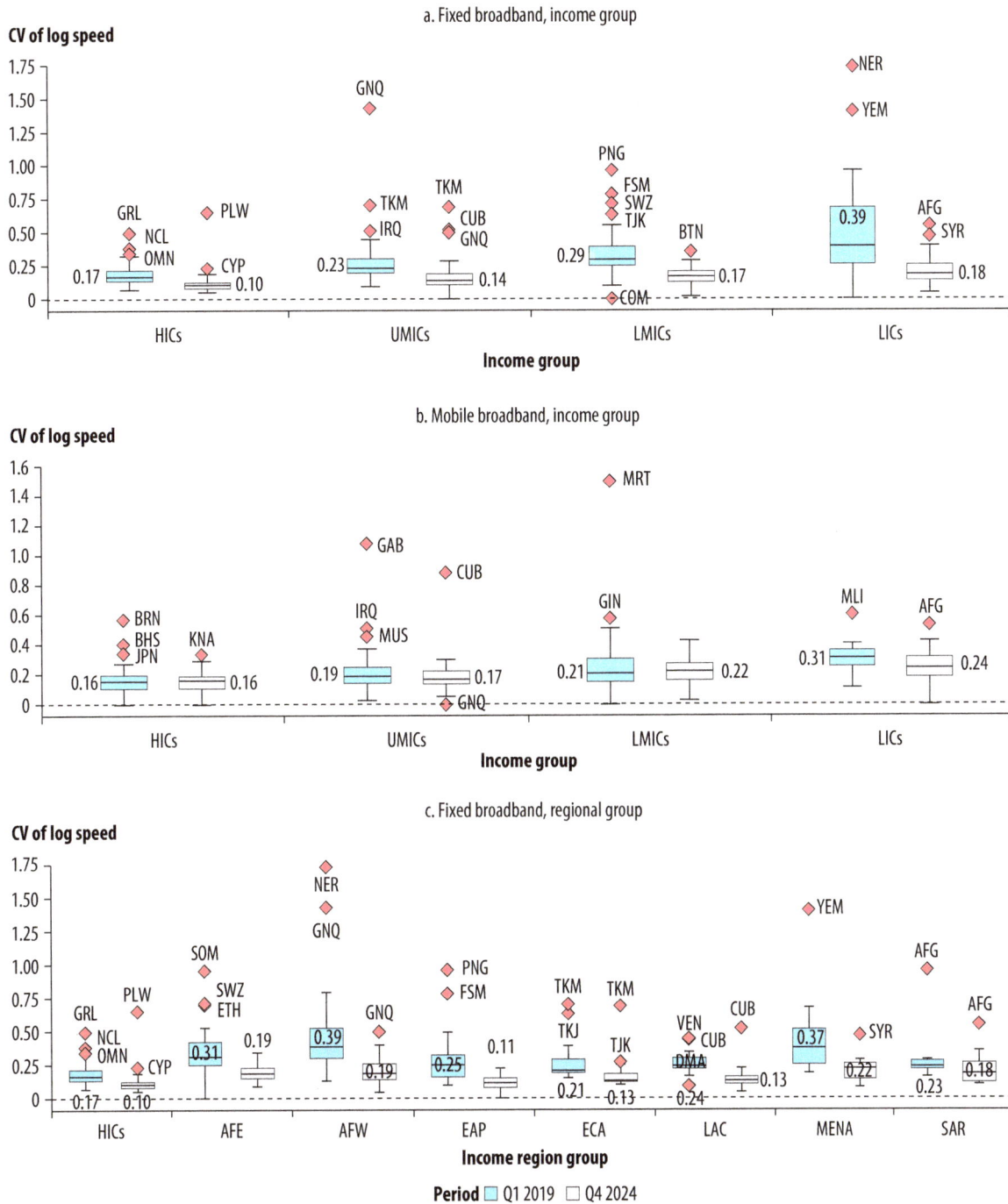

a. Fixed broadband, income group

b. Mobile broadband, income group

c. Fixed broadband, regional group

Period ☐ Q1 2019 ☐ Q4 2024

(Continued)

FIGURE 2.8   **Within-country internet speed inequality, 2019 Q1 and 2024 Q4 (*Continued*)**

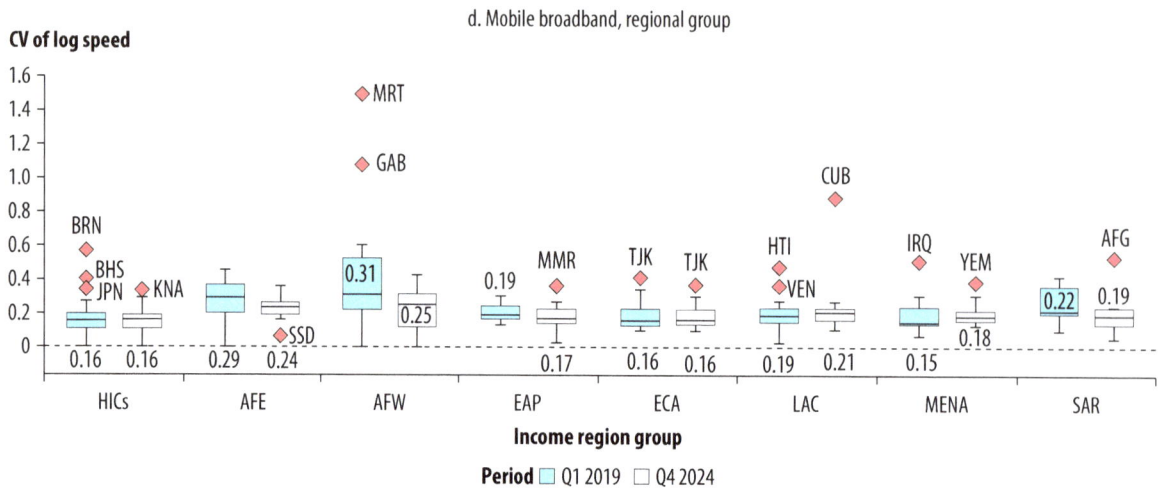

d. Mobile broadband, regional group

Source: Original figures for this publication calculated using data from the Ookla Open Data Initiative (https://www.ookla.com/ookla-for-good/open-data).

Note: Within-country inequality is measured as the CV of the log of download speeds. The analysis includes areas of 610.8 meters × 610.8 meters with at least 20 speed tests. For a list of country codes, refer to https://www.iso.org/obp/ui/#search. AFE = Eastern and Southern Africa; AFW = Western and Central Africa; CV = coefficient of variation; EAP = East Asia and Pacific; ECA = Europe and Central Asia; HICs = high-income countries; LAC = Latin America and the Caribbean; LICs = low-income countries; LMICs = lower-middle-income countries; MENA = Middle East and North Africa; UMICs = upper-middle-income countries; Q1 = first quarter; Q4 = fourth quarter; SAR = South Asia.

FIGURE 2.9   **Median fixed and mobile broadband traffic, by country income group, 2022 and 2023**

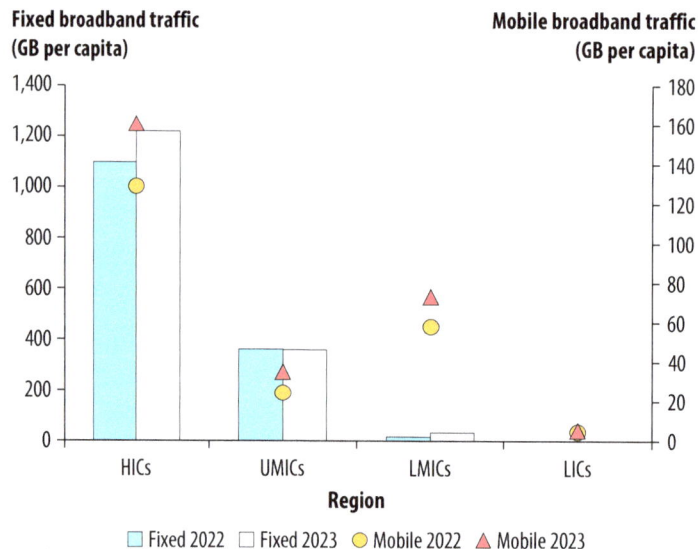

Source: Original figure for this publication based on calculations from the International Telecommunication Union (https://www.itu.int/en/ITU-D/Statistics/pages/facts/default.aspx).

Note: GB = gigabytes; HICs = high-income countries; LICs = low-income countries; LMICs = lower-middle-income countries; UMICs = upper-middle-income countries.

How to ensure digital connectivity and adoption

Governments in countries that are less ready for artificial intelligence (AI) should prioritize creating an enabling environment for the private sector to expand and upgrade broadband infrastructure. Facilitating device access and ownership is also key to increasing AI adoption. An enabling environment remains key to attracting, retaining, and expanding private sector investment in telecommunications infrastructure. Governments can liberalize restrictions on foreign investment, ensure fair competition, and streamline permitting and rights-of-way processes to reduce delays and costs in network deployment.

Clear and stable regulatory frameworks, including spectrum management policies, can reduce investor uncertainty. Promoting infrastructure sharing can improve service affordability. Public policy can promote coinvestment in fiber optic networks by requiring all operators to share deployment plans with competitors and facilitate the use of rights of way. Regulators can also use financial incentives to support infrastructure sharing by reducing universal service requirements when voluntary sharing is undertaken with market competitors.

Finally, policies can also support cross-sector infrastructure sharing, although governance risks need to be carefully managed (Strusani and Houngbonon 2020). Opening the market for foreign and nontraditional satellite providers and simplifying and fast-tracking licensing for satellite operators and ground station installations can unlock the potential of satellite technology to close the digital divide—especially in hard-to-reach places. Shared internet access points, targeted subsidies, reduced taxes on digital devices, and innovative financing mechanisms could make digital devices more accessible and affordable for low-income families.

For countries with higher AI readiness, governments need to promote local digital sector development to ensure widespread digital adoption, paving the way for AI adaptation and innovation. Governments play a vital role in fostering local digital ecosystems by facilitating access to funding, information, markets, and skills. They can attract foreign venture capital (VC), offer grants and loan guarantees, and establish incubators to help entrepreneurs while also developing a robust domestic VC market. To combat information asymmetry, governments can connect start-ups with buyers and investors, both domestically and internationally, and enhance digital skills through training and by attracting foreign talent via streamlined visa processes.

Furthermore, market harmonization through trade agreements and international coordination is essential to remove cross-border barriers such as data localization and inconsistent technical standards, promoting holistic market openness and interoperability. As the digital sector matures, governments must also address intellectual property protection, competition, taxation, and innovation policies to counteract winner-takes-most dynamics and ensure a fair, dynamic, and competitive digital market.

Notes

1. Although satellite internet performs better than fixed-line internet in developing countries, fiber typically outperforms satellite internet on speed because fiber delivers higher bandwidth to users, especially in HICs and UMICs that have a more-developed fixed broadband infrastructure.
2. These applications enable real-time data collection and analysis from various sensors deployed in the field for precision agriculture and asset tracking, remote monitoring, and environmental sensing for IoT connectivity.

3. The CV for log download speeds is computed for each country using the data recorded at a spatial resolution of 610.8 meters × 610.8 meters (called *tiles*), considering only tiles with at least 20 speed tests. It is calculated as the ratio of the standard deviation to the mean of the natural logarithm of download speeds. It standardizes dispersion relative to the mean, making relevant comparisons across countries with different average download speeds.

References

Ackerman, K. 2024. "Excess Electronic Component Inventory to Remain a Challenge in the First Half of 2024." *Sourceability,* January 25, 2024. https://sourceability.com/post/excess-electronic-component-inventory-to-remain-a-challenge-in-the-first-half-of-2024.

"Apple Expands India Manufacturing." *Financial Times,* February 20, 2025. https://www.ft.com/content/35266a4f-e296-45c5-a578-df1fccda318e.

Daryo. 2024. "Uzbekistan's IT Industry Adopts New Export Requirements." May 31, 2024. https://daryo.uz/en/2024/05/31/uzbekistans-it-industry-adopts-new-export-requirements.

"Information Technology Sector Sets Higher Targets for 2025." 2025. *Daily News*, June 30, 2025. https://www.hurriyetdailynews.com/information-technology-sector-sets-higher-targets-for-2025-210907.

Loma Technology. 2024. "IT Outsourcing in Cambodia Southeast Asia Digital Potential." https://lomatechnology.com/blog/it-outsourcing-cambodia/4276.

Ookla. 2023. "New Speedtest Data Shows Starlink Performance Is Mixed—But That's a Good Thing." https://www.ookla.com/articles/starlink-hughesnet-viasat-performance-q2-2023.

Sebastian, K. A. 2005. "USC Satellite Database." Union of Concerned Scientists. December 8, 2005, updated May 1, 2023. https://www.ucs.org/resources/satellite-database.

Stein, J., and H. Natanson. 2025. "U.S. Pushes Nations Facing Tariffs to Approve Musk's Starlink, Cables Show." *Washington Post,* May 7, 2025. https://www.washingtonpost.com/business/2025/05/07/elon-musk-starlink-trump-tariffs/?utm_campaign=wp_main&utm_source=facebook,twitter&utm_medium=social.

Strusani, D., and G. V. Houngbonon. 2020. *Accelerating Digital Connectivity through Infrastructure Sharing*. Note 79. Washington, DC: International Finance Corporation. https://www.ifc.org/content/dam/ifc/doc/mgrt/emcompass-note-79-digital-infrastructure-sharing.pdf.

Compute | 3

KEY MESSAGES

- Compute is foundational for artificial intelligence (AI), but low-income countries (LICs) and middle-income countries (MICs) have very limited resources.

  ○ *AI chips and servers.* In 2024, the United States dominated supply and access to AI chips and hosted 50 percent of global secure internet servers, and other high-income countries (HICs) accounted for another 41 percent, leaving just 9 percent for the rest of the world. On a per capita basis, the United States has 200 times more servers than typical MICs and 20,000 times more than LICs.

  ○ *High-performance computing (HPC) systems.* As of June 2025, HICs hosted 86 percent of the world's top 500 HPC systems and 97 percent of their capacity. Excluding China and India, MICs host only 3 percent of these 500 HPC systems and account for 1 percent of the capacity, despite representing 15 percent of global gross domestic product and 48 percent of the world's population.

  ○ *Data centers.* As of June 2025, HICs accounted for 77 percent of global co-location data center capacity (proxied by total megawatts); upper-middle-income countries (UMICs), 18 percent; lower-middle-income countries (LMICs), 5 percent; and LICs, less than 0.1 percent.

- Compute is highly tradable across borders. Governments must weigh the cost and benefits of promoting investments in domestic data centers on the basis of country context to ensure viability, sustainability, and cost-effectiveness.

  ○ *Growth of cloud computing exports.* The United States is estimated to account for 87 percent of global cloud computing exports, with a staggering 23 percent compound annual growth rate in 2006–23. Most countries rely heavily on US cloud services, although Chinese cloud providers have gained traction in recent years, especially in East Asia and Pacific.

  ○ *Cloud computing disparities.* In 2023, HICs accounted for an estimated 84 percent of US cloud computing exports, followed by 14 percent by UMICs, 2 percent by LMICs, and 0 percent by LICs. Information and communication technology services (79 percent), financial services (73 percent), and professional services (67 percent) industries led cloud integration because of their high degree of digitalization.

  ○ *Weighing costs and benefits.* Well-planned local data center investment can boost economic growth, jobs, and digital sovereignty, but it requires high-quality and affordable energy and digital infrastructure and large volumes of local demand, can strain power grids, can raise land costs, and can affect the environment.

- Governments should create an enabling environment to facilitate access to compute resources, catalyzing AI adoption, adaptation, and innovation:

  ○ *Key barriers and externalities.* High entry costs, energy and digital infrastructure constraints, limited local demand, regulatory uncertainty, lack of cloud expertise, and coordination failures often deter private investment in compute infrastructure. Compute infrastructure generates positive externalities (for example, cross-sector spillovers that boost productivity) as well as negative ones (for example, environmental costs and national security vulnerabilities).

  ○ *Public investment and enabling policies.* Targeted interventions such as compute subsidies for small and medium enterprises and researchers, regional data centers, and public-private partnerships (for example, for AI training infrastructure) can lower barriers, spread access, and unlock AI's full potential while managing risks through incentives and regulations on energy efficiency and data governance.

Introduction

With a simple prompt such as "a squirrel wearing a tiny business suit, aggressively negotiating for acorns with a pigeon in a park," generative AI (GenAI) tools can immediately conjure a photorealistic image with an almost unsettling speed and detail. This magical capability of AI does not materialize from nowhere. Although AI technology is intangible, it relies on a massive physical infrastructure encompassing AI chips, data storage devices, servers, and hyperscale data centers. Whether it is traditional AI or cutting-edge GenAI, these technologies require enormous data storage and computing power to analyze and predict patterns in the data.

This chapter delves into the compute infrastructure that underpins the AI revolution. It begins by analyzing the supply side of the market, highlighting its high concentration among a small handful of big tech firms and sustainability issues. It then discusses demand patterns, comparing different options for accessing storage and compute infrastructure and the factors affecting the tradability of compute across borders. The "Compute Divide" section takes stock of compute capacity across countries, analyzes the digital divide in compute, and examines factors that affect countries' performance. The final section discusses market failures and barriers for low-income countries (LICs) and middle-income countries (MICs) to access compute, the role of the government, and the pros and cons of governments' existing approaches to address the compute barrier.

Supply: Market structure, growth, and sustainability

The compute layer of the artificial intelligence (AI) ecosystem consists of many interrelated hardware, software, and data communication components. The market segments and supply chains are highly complex and constantly evolving because of rapid technological advancements and diverse application needs. New players, products, and business models regularly emerge, and the interplay between hardware advancements and software optimization adds layers of intricacy. This report defines *compute* as the ability to store, process, and transfer data at scale (Tony Blair Institute for Global Change 2023).

Figure 3.1 shows the market segments and key companies involved in compute. Compute is monopolized at key points in the supply chain by one or a small handful of firms. Industry concentration acts as a shaping force in how computational power is manufactured and accessed.

At the heart of AI hardware lies processor chips—the brain that carries out the computations. The term *AI chip* is broad; it includes many kinds of chips designed for the demanding compute environments required by AI tasks. Examples of popular AI chips include graphics processing units (GPUs), tensor processing units, neural processing units, field-programmable gate arrays, and application-specific integrated circuits.

The AI processor chip market has experienced rapid growth in recent years and is projected to expand 10-fold over the next decade, fueled by surging demand for AI-powered technologies across industries (Edge AI + Vision Alliance 2024). The AI chip market is highly concentrated, although competition is intensifying. NVIDIA controls 70–95 percent of the market for AI chips (Leswing 2024). It leads the data center GPU market by a long shot, with a staggering 92 percent market share as of 2023. NVIDIA's enduring leadership can be attributed to its first-mover advantage, as well as its well-established and optimized CUDA software ecosystem that provides a comprehensive development environment for GPU-accelerated computing. However, both large and small businesses are actively searching for alternatives to diversify their AI chip options.

The public cloud computing sector is dominated by "hyperscalers" such as Alibaba Cloud, Amazon Web Services (AWS), Google Cloud Platform, IBM Cloud, and Microsoft Azure. These providers offer a variety of cloud-based solutions, enabling businesses and governments to rapidly scale their operations and access cutting-edge technologies without significant upfront investments in hardware and infrastructure. For organizations preferring more control over their cloud environments, private cloud solutions are available from vendors such as VMware and the open-source OpenStack project. These solutions provide alternatives for on-premises or dedicated cloud deployments.

FIGURE 3.1 AI compute market segments and key companies

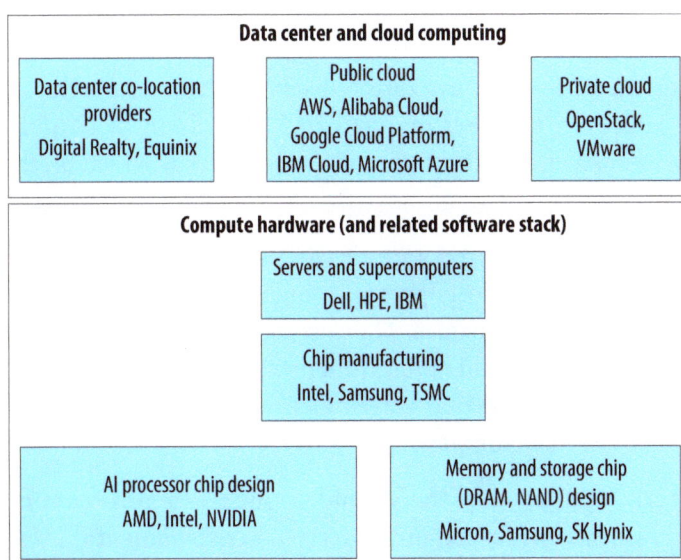

Source: Original figure for this publication.
Note: AI = artificial intelligence; DRAM = dynamic random-access memory; NAND = not and.

An increasingly common approach is the hybrid cloud, which combines public and private cloud resources to balance scalability, cost-efficiency, and control. Effective hybrid cloud strategies often involve collaboration between public and private cloud vendors, enabling interoperability, unified management tools, and shared innovation pipelines that give organizations greater flexibility and resilience.

The global cloud market is similarly experiencing rapid expansion and consolidation, bringing both benefits and challenges to the AI ecosystem. Goldman Sachs (2024) estimated that the cloud computing market will expand with a 22 percent annual growth rate from 2024 to 2030, reaching US$2 trillion by the end of the decade. AWS, Microsoft Azure, and Google Cloud collectively command two-thirds of the market share (Richter 2025). High entry barriers, network effects, and economies of scale jointly result in high market concentration, which can produce effects that are both socially beneficial and harmful.

The size and sophistication of leading cloud providers benefit their customers through improved efficiency, seamlessly integrated platforms, and advanced cybersecurity capabilities, including for incident detection and response. However, high market concentration may also reduce competition, create vendor lock-in, give unfair privileges to first-party applications over third-party equivalents, and pose systemic risks to vital sectors.

The computational resources required for AI models have been growing explosively. The amount of compute used is measured in floating point operations, and compute performance is measured in floating point operations per second. Before the deep learning era, the amount of compute used to train AI models doubled in about 24 months; when deep learning took hold around 2010, the amount of compute required started doubling every 6 months ("The Race Is On to Control the Global Supply Chain for AI Chips" 2024). Larger training data sets, more complex model architecture, and parallel processing all require a growing scale of training computation within AI, despite improvements in computing efficiency brought by new generations of chips. Once trained, applying a learned model to make predictions or decisions on new, unseen data, called *inference,* could eventually require even more compute as usage grows over time.

Provisioning the immense compute infrastructure at the scale required for leading AI research is expensive in both upfront capital expenditures and ongoing operating costs, raising questions about the sustainability of current AI development directions. New Street Research estimates that Alphabet, Amazon, Meta, and Microsoft together invested US$104 billion in building AI data centers in 2024. When spending by smaller tech firms and other industries is added in, the total AI data center investment between 2023 and 2027 could reach US$1.4 trillion ("What Could Kill" 2024).

The training process for GPT-4 incurred an estimated cost of more than US$100 million (Vipra and West 2023). The hefty training costs present a high barrier to entry in the AI model market, favoring large and well-founded companies. The cost may eventually translate to higher prices for users of generative AI (GenAI) tools and application programming interfaces. However, the Chinese start-up DeepSeek has demonstrated that training costs for advanced AI models can be slashed substantially through optimized techniques.

If not managed properly, the growing energy and cooling demand from compute could strain existing energy and water infrastructure and exacerbate environmental impacts. As the compute demand grows, the energy consumed to train models increases accordingly. It is estimated that a single ChatGPT query consumes 25 times more energy than a Google search query (Brussels Times Newsroom 2024).

The training and application of these massive AI models also generates a prodigious heat output that poses cooling challenges. A lot of water is used in cooling the servers that run AI applications. Half a liter of water evaporates for each ChatGPT conversation of about 29–50 queries (Brussels Times Newsroom 2024). These GenAI tools are used billions of times every month, so the water usage quickly adds up to huge amounts.

The private sector has undertaken various efforts to mitigate the environmental impacts of AI. These include improving the energy efficiency of hardware, optimizing training data (algorithms) to reduce computational requirements, and increasing the use of renewable energy sources. Companies are ramping up investments in renewable energy and developing energy-efficient data centers. Some companies are also exploring nuclear power as part of a broader energy mix to meet growing demand. However, views differ on whether nuclear power can scale quickly enough to address the sharp rise in energy needs anticipated this decade (Norton 2024).

Governments are also closely monitoring the development of data centers and contemplating regulations to address sustainability issues. Ireland, the Netherlands, and Singapore have temporarily paused new data center construction to reduce the strain on power grids. Singapore rolled out a new sustainability standard in 2023 as a means of lowering energy consumption (JLL n.d.). In 2024, the European Union (EU) adopted an EU-wide scheme for rating the sustainability of data centers (European Commission 2024).

Organizations operating data centers in EU nations will be required to file reports detailing water and energy consumption, as well as steps they are taking to reduce it. This scheme is intended to increase transparency and potentially to promote new designs and efficiency developments in data centers that can not only reduce energy and water consumption but also promote the use of renewable energy, increase grid efficiency, or the reuse of waste heat in nearby facilities and heat networks.

Demand: Compute access modality and trade-offs

Two ways exist to access compute infrastructure: purchasing or renting. Some organizations, particularly leading AI companies such as Alphabet, Meta, Microsoft, OpenAI, and XAI that provide foundational AI models, choose to purchase AI chips outright to train AI models. A key advantage is having exclusive access to cutting-edge hardware as soon as it becomes available. However, the upfront capital costs of procuring hardware and building and expanding data centers are massive.

Significant operational complexity also is involved in managing clustered resources, scheduling jobs, and so forth. Frequent hardware refresh cycles are required, given the rapid pace of innovation. Furthermore, owned infrastructure lacks the flexibility to easily burst to additional capacity during demand spikes. Organizations must manage their own backup and disaster recovery strategies.

For most other organizations, the primary option is to rent compute and storage capacity from cloud providers on a pay-as-you-go basis. Public cloud offerings provide multitenant shared infrastructure delivered as a service. Private clouds keep the environment dedicated, and they can be hosted internally or by a vendor. Hybrid clouds allow combining private and public cloud with data and application portability between them.

One primary benefit of cloud is low upfront costs. Scalability to instantly burst to higher capacity is another key advantage. The cloud provider manages the underlying infrastructure. Geographic flexibility is enabled through global data center footprints, reducing latency. Cloud computing also reduces management overhead and offers access to advanced services and tools that can be easily integrated into applications. Potential downsides of cloud include high costs at hyperscale over long periods, concerns about vendor lock-in to proprietary services, limited control and customization, and data egress charges for high-volume workloads.

Different types of users have distinct demands for data storage and compute. Purchasing is often favored by organizations with strict regulatory compliance, unique performance demands, stable and predictable workloads, and the resources to manage their own infrastructure. These typically include leading foundational AI model developers and researchers with heavy AI workloads.

Cloud computing is generally recommended for businesses seeking flexibility, scalability, cost-efficiency (especially for variable workloads or experimentation), rapid deployment, access to advanced AI services, and reduced operational overhead. Large enterprises and government agencies often require substantial computing power to manage and process vast amounts of data, run AI applications, and support daily operations. They often leverage hybrid, dynamic models, mapping different workload profiles to the optimal deployment model to balance agility, cost, control, data security, and performance.

For individual workers, consumers, and small businesses, AI is primarily accessed through software platforms and cloud services such as ChatGPT and Microsoft Copilot. As end users, their experience is highly dependent on their internet speed, these platforms' hardware, and data center proximity. AI application providers such as OpenAI rely on cloud providers for hosting AI models and services on a global scale. This allows seamless access for individuals worldwide.

However, latency remains a factor—the farther a user is from a data center, the slower and more degraded their AI experience may be. For applications requiring real-time responsiveness, such as live speech recognition or robotics control, users will get a smoother experience when they are geographically close to the AI system's hosting region. Major cloud providers are continuing to build out larger global data center footprints to reduce these proximity constraints over time. Increasingly, individuals and small businesses can also access AI on their edge devices, such as smartphones, wearables, cars, and smart home devices.

Compute divide

Data on countries' performance on AI chip ownership, data center capacity, and cloud adoption are scarce because of several factors. First, the rapid pace of technological advancement and competitive nature of the AI and cloud industries lead companies to closely guard detailed information about their infrastructure and capabilities as proprietary and strategic assets. Second, standardized reporting and measurement frameworks across countries and organizations are lacking, making it difficult to aggregate and compare data consistently. Third, geopolitical considerations and national security concerns may limit the transparency and availability of information, because nations view technological prowess in AI and cloud computing as critical to their strategic interests. Finally, the nascent and evolving nature of these technologies means that comprehensive data sets and tracking mechanisms are still developing, resulting in fragmented and incomplete data availability on a global scale.

This section combines data on supercomputers from TOP500, co-location data center capacity data from TeleGeography, and cloud computing adoption data to shed light on countries' performance on data storage and compute infrastructure. Given the incomplete information described previously, the findings presented here are just indicative, although the simple stocktaking still reveals a highly uneven distribution of compute access.

The United States has the highest raw compute capacity and the most-powerful supercomputers, is the global leader in AI chip production and access, and dominates the global cloud computing market. As of June 2025, the United States hosted 175 of the top 500 high-performance computing (HPC) systems, the largest number in the world, and accounts for about 50 percent of TOP500 supercomputing capacity,[1] 50 percent of global secure internet servers, 26 percent of co-location data centers, and nearly 40 percent of co-location data center capacity (refer to figure 3.2), relative to its 27 percent of global gross domestic product (GDP) and 4 percent of population. It dominates GPU production and use, accounting for nearly half of NVIDIA's global revenue in the fiscal year ending in January 2025. US big tech companies such as Google, Meta, Microsoft, and XAI, own millions of AI chips, including NVIDIA's H100 chips, dwarfing the ownership of any other company in the world (Tony Blair Institute for Global Change 2023).

FIGURE 3.2 Compute capacity, by country income group and region

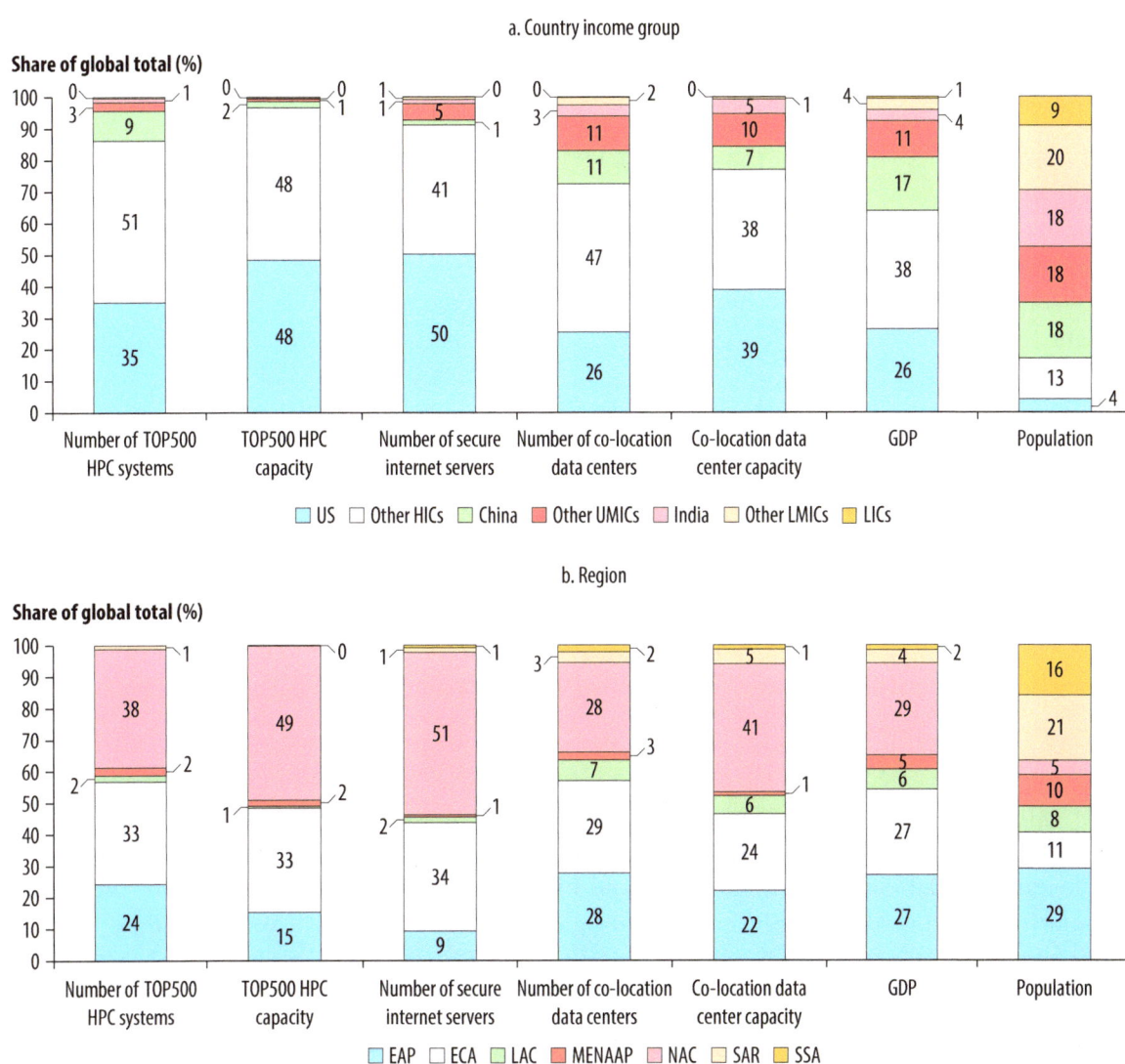

Sources: Original figures for this publication using June 2025 TOP500 data (https://top500.org). HPC compute capacity is measured with Rmax in tera floating point operations per second. Secure internet server data are from the World Development Indicators, World Bank (2024; https://databank.worldbank.org/source/world-development-indicators). Co-location data center data are from TeleGeography (June 2025; https://www2.telegeography.com/). Co-location data center capacity is measured with total megawatts.
Note: EAP = East Asia and Pacific; ECA = Europe and Central Asia; GDP = gross domestic product; HICs = high-income countries; HPC = high-performance computing; LAC = Latin America and the Caribbean; LICs = low-income countries; LMICs = lower-middle-income countries; MENAAP = Middle East, North Africa, Afghanistan, and Pakistan; NAC = North America; SAR = South Asia; SSA = Sub-Saharan Africa; UMICs = upper-middle-income countries; US = United States.

European countries, notably France, Germany, Italy, the Netherlands, and the United Kingdom, also boast substantial computing power, although they face a scarcity of large domestic cloud providers and AI chip vendors. Central Asia and Europe host one-third of global HPC systems, capacity, and internet servers, along with 28 percent of co-location data centers and 22 percent of data center capacity, relative to their 27 percent share in global GDP and 11 percent of the global population. Most of these compute resources are concentrated in EU countries, particularly the five mentioned. Germany alone is home to 41 of the top 500 HPCs, 10 percent of secure internet servers, and 5.5 percent of co-location data centers.

Despite this robust infrastructure, European countries have limited large public cloud providers and AI chip vendors. OVHcloud, a French company and the largest public cloud firm, reported an annual revenue of US$1 billion in 2024, which pales in comparison with the revenues of global giants such as Alibaba Cloud (US$16 billion), Google Cloud Platform (US$49 billion), Microsoft Azure (US$107 billion), and AWS (US$117 billion). Europe also lacks its own AI accelerator chips (Hawkins, Lehdonvirta, and Wu 2025).

China's compute capacity is strong and growing. China hosts 47 HPC systems—9 percent of the world's total—and 2 percent of supercomputing capacity, although this figure is likely an underestimate. China accounts for only 1 percent of global internet servers, 11 percent of co-location data centers, and 7 percent of co-location data center capacity, compared with its 17 percent of GDP and population share. China also accounted for 13 percent of NVIDIA's revenue in fiscal year 2024/25, although that share has been falling because of trade frictions with the United States.

Excluding China, LICs and MICs host a mere 3 percent of the 500 HPC systems, 1 percent of the supercomputing capacity, 7 percent of the secure internet servers, 17 percent of co-location data centers, and 16 percent of corresponding capacity, despite being home to 65 percent of the world's population and contributing 19 percent of global GDP. High-income countries (HICs) account for 86 percent of the top 500 HPC systems and a staggering 97 percent of the capacity. Among MICs, Brazil hosts 9 of the leading HPC systems, India hosts 6, and Thailand and Türkiye each host 2. Argentina, Morocco, and Viet Nam also recorded entries in the TOP500 list in 2025. However, the performance of supercomputers in MICs lags significantly behind frontier systems.

Beyond HPCs, Brazil, India, Indonesia, the Islamic Republic of Iran, Malaysia, South Africa, and Türkiye also have a decent number of secure internet servers and co-location data centers. Many of these nations serve as regional compute hubs, with thriving local digital economies, large market size, and business environments that attract data center investments. The compute situation is challenging for Sub-Saharan Africa (SSA) and LICs. SSA accounts for 16 percent of the global population but contributes only 2 percent of global GDP, 1 percent of secure internet servers and co-location data center capacity, and 0 percent of HPC systems. Nine percent of the world's population resides in LICs, where they account for 0.3 percent of global GDP and 0 percent of compute capacity.

Among the 4Cs (connectivity, compute, context, competency), compute is currently the most-traded element. International broadband connectivity and cloud computing offer a partial substitute for domestic data centers, creating a trade-off influenced by several factors. These include the specific technical design of the compute resources, internet latency, data transmission costs, and crucial privacy and data sovereignty considerations.

The United States contributes 87 percent of global cloud computing and data storage services exports, and during 2006–23 its exports grew annually at 23 percent. On the basis of cloud computing trade data compiled from corporate annual reports, the United States consistently accounted for 87 percent of global exports during 2016–21. China's cloud computing exports have experienced a 10-fold increase from 2016 to 2021, and its share in global exports jumped from 1 percent in 2016 to 6 percent in 2021, whereas Germany's share declined from 10 percent to 6 percent. Except for these three countries, all other economies combined account for only 1 percent of global cloud computing exports.

On the basis of World Trade Organization statistics, US cloud computing and data storage services exports grew 23 percent annually since 2006, reaching US$8.3 billion in 2023. However, this amount only represented 4 percent of the three big cloud providers' revenue.[2]

US cloud computing exports are predominantly destined for HICs (approximately 84 percent), where demand concentrates. LICs and MICs, particularly in Latin America and the Caribbean (LAC), represent a growing, although still small, market. The combined imports of France, Germany, and the United Kingdom alone rival the total share of all developing countries. Upper-middle-income countries contributed 14 percent of US cloud computing exports in 2023, whereas lower-middle-income countries contributed 2 percent and LICs, 0 percent.

In the developing market, LAC stands out as the leading destination for US cloud computing exports, exhibiting the highest import growth rate between 2019 and 2023 (refer to figure 3.3). Brazil and Mexico together account for a substantial one-third of all US cloud computing exports to developing countries. This is largely driven by LAC's relatively mature digital economy, which fuels demand for cloud computing, and its geographical proximity to the United States. Notably, China represents just 2 percent of US cloud exports, largely because of the dominance of domestic cloud providers such as Alibaba Cloud, Huawei Cloud, and Tencent Cloud.

FIGURE 3.3 **US cloud computing exports, by destination country income group and region, 2019–23**

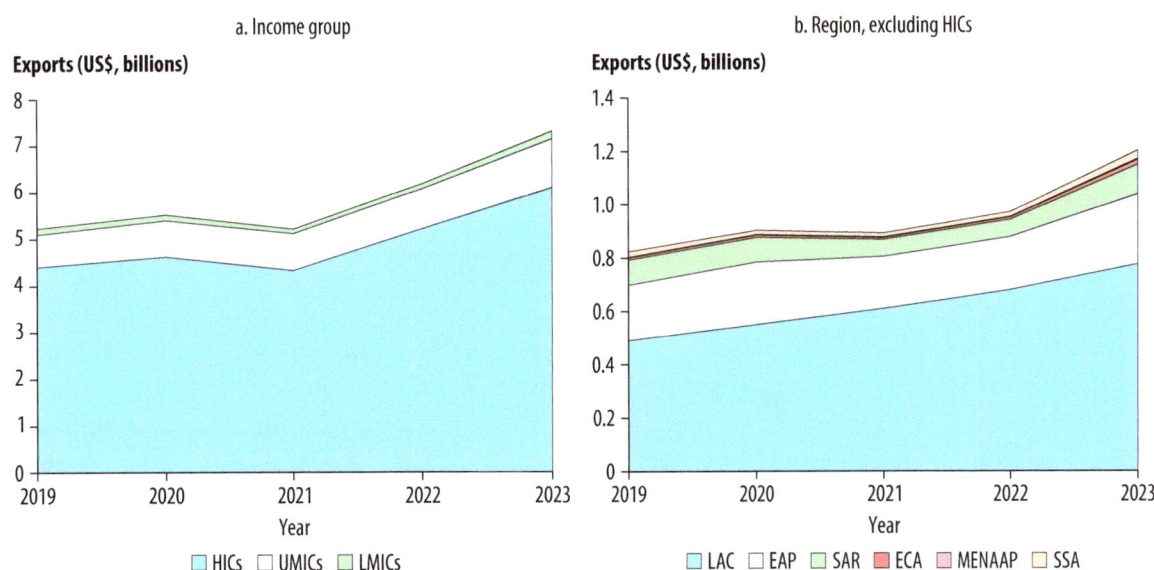

Source: Original figures for this publication, based on calculations using World Trade Organization stastistics (https://stats.wto.org/).
Note: The sum of exports by income group is below US total cloud computing exports, as bilateral exports below certain value thresholds are not reported. EAP = East Asia and Pacific; ECA = Europe and Central Asia; HICs = high-income countries; LAC = Latin America and the Caribbean; LMICs = lower-middle-income countries; MENAAP = Middle East, North Africa, Afghanistan, and Pakistan; SAR = South Asia; SSA = Sub-Saharan Africa; UMICs = upper-middle-income countries.

Governments must weigh whether promoting local data center investment—through incentives, public–private partnerships (PPPs), or other measures—offers better value than relying on regional hubs or international cloud services.

Well-planned domestic data centers can drive local economic development, create jobs, catalyze structural transformation, and boost tax revenues. Northern Virginia, the densely populated area located just outside of Washington, DC, the US capital, has the highest concentration of data centers in the world, with around 200 data centers built and 117 in the development pipeline (Turner 2025). The data center industry in Virginia created nearly 15,000 direct jobs, US$1.9 billion in associated pay and benefits, and $4.5 billion in economic output in 2018 alone. Considering the economic ripple effects generated by direct investment generated, the job creation amounts to more than 45,000, with US$3.5 billion in associated pay and benefits and US$10.1 billion in economic output. Moreover, data centers generated US$600.1 million in state and local tax revenue (Northern Virginia Technology Council 2020).

In China, the mountainous province of Guizhou in the southwest has become a pioneer in China's big data industry. Guizhou, a city with one of the largest number of super-large data centers globally, had 37 big data centers in operation or under construction as of early 2023. Data center investments have powered Guizhou's digital economy development, achieving a top growth rate in China for 7 consecutive years since it became the big data pilot area in 2016.

However, these gains come with trade-offs. Data centers are highly capital and energy intensive, placing heavy demands on local power grids and land markets. Supporting data centers through tax exemptions could attract investment but might also affect electricity prices and tax revenues, potentially crowding out economic activity in labor-intensive sectors (Johansson and Kriström 2021). With the rising prices that result from demand for data center land, nearby commercial real estate and housing become less affordable for residents.

In Frankfurt, Germany, co-location data centers led to increased demand for commercial spaces, causing price hikes (Savvas 2021). To address this issue, in 2022 Frankfurt published an updated plan for commercial developments and constrained data center construction to certain areas (Judge 2022).

For developing countries, the challenge is to ensure that such investments are sustainable, wellutilized, and aligned with broader development goals. Viability depends on stable and affordable electricity, high-quality internet connectivity, competitive operating costs, and sufficient domestic demand. Other key factors include the scale and growth potential of the digital economy, the robustness of information and communication technology (ICT) skills and maintenance capacity, legal and security requirements for certain data sets, the types of data and workloads to be hosted locally, and the potential for integration with regional or global cloud networks. Careful planning, competitive neutrality, and clear sustainability strategies are essential to ensure that domestic data centers serve as enablers of the digital economy rather than costly, underused infrastructure.

How can countries achieve secure, equitable, and sustainable access to compute?

Compute has become a key bottleneck in both the training of large-scale AI models and the deployment of AI across sectors. Compute power will play a crucial role in the future economy by supporting AI, automation, and data-driven innovation, enhancing productivity and efficiency across industries. The market alone cannot ensure equitable access or distribution, because compute supply is currently tightly controlled by a few dominant players, creating significant barriers to entry and innovation (Azoulay, Krieger, and Nagaraj 2024).

LICs and MICs often lag in access to compute, through either domestic data centers or cloud computing, limiting their ability to train and deploy AI models at scale. This section summarizes key barriers and market failures in LICs and MICs in developing local compute capacity and accessing compute and discusses different approaches to address these challenges and the pros and cons of each approach.

High market concentration, high cost, and supply constraints

High upfront costs associated with procuring AI chips and establishing data centers are prohibitive for many LICs and MICs. Cutting-edge AI chips, such as NVIDIA's Blackwell GPUs, cost between $30,000 and $40,000 per unit (Kim 2024). Large-scale AI data centers can reach costs in billions of US dollars (Haranas 2024). Those who need to access cutting-edge compute in developing countries but cannot afford to buy AI chips often turn to cloud computing, but even this option is pricey and often unavailable. For instance, AWS charges US$98 per hour to rent a virtual machine powered by an NVIDIA H100 chip, compared with US$0.004 per hour for its least-expensive non-AI virtual machines.

These exorbitant costs are compounded by limited access to investment capital in developing countries. Domestic investors may lack the resources to fund compute infrastructure, and foreign investors are often deterred by perceived risks, including political instability, economic uncertainty, and regulatory unpredictability.

The challenges of supply and affordability are deeply intertwined with the concentration of the compute supply chain. The production of AI chips is dominated by a few companies with highly specialized expertise, and the entire supply chain—from chip design to fabrication and distribution—is controlled by a few key players. Network effects, increasing returns on scale and scope, and winner-takes-most dynamics also entrench leading AI chip and cloud providers' advantage and make it challenging for new players to enter. This concentration not only limits supply but also reinforces pricing power, keeping AI chips out of reach for many developing countries.

Encouragingly, emerging models such as DeepSeek demonstrate that high AI performance can be achieved with lower compute demands, and their open-source approach offers potential to democratize access. This could reduce costs and make AI development more feasible for resource-constrained countries.

Negative externalities: Environmental costs and national security

Data centers consume huge amounts of electricity and water. This usage contributes to carbon emissions and strains local resources, and the costs are not fully reflected in service prices. E-waste from server turnover can also be substantial. Control over AI chips has become a major geopolitical tool and source of friction. Countries that rely on foreign data centers also subject the data of their citizens and organizations to foreign laws and regulations, including sensitive information, increasing the risks of unauthorized foreign access, surveillance, and national security.

Positive externalities: Research and development and cross-sector innovation

Investments in compute infrastructure can unlock broad innovation benefits—improving productivity across sectors, boosting research capacity, and supporting local start-ups. Yet these public goods characteristics mean private investors may underinvest without public support, especially in markets where returns are uncertain or long-term.

Underdeveloped energy and internet infrastructure, coordination failure, and limited demand

In many developing countries, limited or unreliable energy and internet connectivity restricts the potential utilization of cloud services, diminishing the incentive for investment. In addition, either energy infrastructure is unreliable or the cost of energy is prohibitively high, making it challenging to operate data centers efficiently. A study by the International Energy Agency (2020) found that more than 60 percent of developing countries face significant energy security challenges. This can lead to increased costs, downtime, and even project cancellations. Slow digital transformation due to coordination failures, small market size, and low purchasing power in some developing countries may not justify significant investments in data centers, especially when compared with potential returns in higher-income markets.

Lack of technical expertise and brain drain

The scarcity of local technical expertise in cloud technologies and data center management exacerbates the challenge. Talent requirements grow as compute complexity and costs grow, because specialized knowledge is needed to make the most of scarce hardware, and much of this knowledge is tacit. Yet, many developing countries lack the resources needed to cultivate a robust pool of local talent, because students often face limited access to advanced technical training, underresourced educational institutions, and insufficient digital infrastructure.

Moreover, even when local talent is developed, these countries face intense competition from advanced economies, often resulting in brain drain as trained professionals seek better opportunities abroad. This lack of technical expertise can lead to difficulties in maintaining and managing data centers and cloud infrastructure, which can result in downtime, security breaches, and other issues.

Regulatory constraints and uncertainty

Limited regulatory readiness and uncertainty can significantly deter cloud computing investment and adoption in developing countries. Clear, predictable, and modern regulatory frameworks are essential for both accessing cloud services and attracting providers to establish local infrastructure. Policies on cloud or data hosting, and data protection laws that specify legal mechanisms for cross-border data flows, directly affect where and how data can be stored and processed. Without such clarity, cloud service providers (CSPs) face legal and operational risks, and potential users—particularly in regulated sectors such as finance and health care—may be reluctant to migrate to the cloud. Outdated procurement rules can also block public agencies from leveraging cloud offerings, reducing a major source of demand that could anchor local markets.

Beyond access, measures such as intermediary liability frameworks and transparent CSP licensing regimes are important to encourage market entry, ensure a level playing field, and foster competition. In their absence, uncertainty over legal responsibilities, market access, and cost structures can delay investment decisions, limit service availability, and ultimately slow the development of the compute market itself.

How can countries address the compute barrier?

This section provides insights into how countries can address the compute barrier and enable equitable access. It summarizes some existing approaches, discusses their pros and cons, and discusses priorities for countries at various levels of AI readiness.

Large countries and countries relatively advanced in AI

Countries at the forefront of AI development need to secure adequate computing resources to maintain their competitive advantage, foster continued innovation, safeguard national security, and drive economic growth. Governments can invest in national supercomputers and AI research facilities to provide a shared infrastructure for researchers and companies to access HPC resources. For example, the United Kingdom has announced £300 million in funding for two supercomputers to promote AI research (Reuters 2023).

However, hefty costs and lack of expertise often constrain governments' ability to build their own supercomputers in developing countries. To secure adequate compute for a thriving AI ecosystem and facilitate cutting-edge research, governments can partner with leading technology companies. For instance, India has collaborated with NVIDIA to establish the NVIDIA AI Technology Center and support the country's AI research efforts ("IIT Hyderabad, NVIDIA Establish First AI Research Center in India" 2020). The Indian government is also planning to partner with NVIDIA to offer affordable GPUs to local start-ups, researchers, and academic institutions (Vivek 2024). Such PPPs provide AI start-ups and researchers with access to compute resources, accelerating innovation.

Several countries have implemented compute voucher initiatives to provide free or subsidized cloud computing credits to AI researchers and start-ups. The Republic of Korea's AI Computing Cloud Voucher program is a notable example, granting start-ups up to US$33,000 worth of credits on local cloud platforms (Ministry of Science and ICT, Republic of Korea 2020). Multiple Chinese city governments have also pledged to provide computing vouchers worth the equivalent of US$140,000–US$280,000 to subsidize AI start-ups facing rising data center costs. These can be used for time in AI data centers to train and run the companies' large language models and to perform other tasks ("China Offers AI Computing 'Vouchers' to Its Underpowered Start-ups" 2024).

Although PPPs and targeted subsidies can help democratize access to compute to a certain degree, such programs are costly to scale and maintain over time. Although such initiatives can alleviate financial pressures on AI start-ups and researchers, they effectively transfer the financial burden to government budgets and, ultimately, taxpayers. Given that public funds are often constrained by competing priorities, these compute access programs risk being underfunded or inconsistently supported. The eligibility criteria for these programs are typically stringent, potentially skewing benefits toward well-established start-ups, prestigious universities, and communities that already have some level of compute access. Moreover, these measures do not directly tackle the underlying issue of scarcity. As such, subsidies and PPPs are only short-term strategies rather than long-term solutions to the compute scarcity problem.

No consensus exists on whether the market concentration in several segments of the compute ecosystem is too high. However, concerns are growing about how the dominant firms are limiting opportunities for newcomers. Big tech companies are aggressively pursuing investments and alliances with AI start-ups through their cloud computing arms, raising regulatory questions over their role as both suppliers and competitors in the battle to develop AI ("Big Tech Companies Use Cloud Computing Arms to Pursue Alliances with AI Groups" 2023). AI start-ups that need to train models have little choice but to rush into the arms of large companies offering essential cloud computing. Big tech companies may use their power in compute services to stifle competition in AI by giving discriminatory preference to their own AI products over new entrants and competitors.

It is critical for regulators to monitor competition dynamics in various segments of the compute market, scrutinize vertical integration, and ensure market contestability and nondiscrimination. In 2022, the US Federal Trade Commission prevented NVIDIA's proposed acquisition of Arm to stimulate innovation. The United Kingdom's Ofcom is also investigating concentration in the cloud market. France, Japan, Korea, and the Netherlands are also exploring antitrust cases in cloud computing (Vipra and West 2023).

Governments should conduct thorough cost-benefit analyses to evaluate the economic impact of data center incentives against factors such as job creation, tax revenues, and long-term digital transformation benefits. Regulatory oversight is needed to prevent data center proliferation from excessively straining electricity grids. Policy makers must strike a balance between fostering innovation and controlling energy costs. Robust climate policies are also essential to ensure sustainability targets are met as AI infrastructure grows.

Small countries with good digital infrastructure

Small nations can achieve economies of scale and risk diversification by collaborating on shared regional data center facilities, cloud platforms, and connectivity infrastructure. Concepts such as data embassies allow countries to maintain legal control over data hosted abroad. Estonia established a data embassy at a data center located in Luxembourg in 2017. The two nations struck an agreement to afford the facility the same rights as a conventional embassy. Estonia owns the hardware and uses it as a backup for its digital services and critical data sets (Meyer 2022). Monaco created a data embassy in Luxembourg in 2021 because Monaco's territory is too small to diversify the risk of natural disaster. Australia is also exploring a data embassy for Pacific nations so that these small island nations, who are unable to attract private sector investment in data centers, can use Australian data centers without compromising their sovereignty (Sharwood 2024).

However, challenges with diplomacy, data sovereignty, geopolitics, and equitable cost sharing must be navigated. Establishing more data embassies will require either a change to the Vienna Conventions that govern diplomatic and consular relations or bilateral agreements. To date, only the latter have been created. Deep trust is required among home and host governments, the private sector company, and the country in which the provider is headquartered to ensure the success of data embassies. Comprehensive risk assessments should be conducted to establish acceptable risk tolerance and associated requirements.

Accelerating government cloud adoption can stimulate local demand for AI services. This not only advances e-governance initiatives but also signals policy priorities, incentivizes private sector adoption, and creates opportunities for domestic cloud providers to emerge over time. For example,

Thailand's Ministry of Higher Education, Science, Research, and Innovation partnered with AWS in 2023 to accelerate the migration of its government's workload to the cloud. AWS will also provide training programs to upskill public servants (AWS Sector Blog Team 2023).

To fully realize the benefits of cloud computing, governments need to invest in building local cloud expertise and skills. Although hyperscalers often offer cloud credits—targeting start-ups, researchers, or government innovation programs—these resources frequently go underused in developing countries. A key reason is the widespread shortage of technical cloud skills needed to design, deploy, manage, and scale AI or other data-intensive workloads. Effective use of cloud infrastructure requires expertise in areas such as cloud architecture, cybersecurity, data governance, application migration, and cost optimization. Without this capacity, organizations may lack the confidence or ability to integrate cloud services into their operations, leaving credits unused and opportunities missed.

Governments can help close this gap by integrating cloud skills into national digital skills strategies, supporting specialized training for ICT professionals, and creating hands-on learning opportunities in partnership with cloud providers. Building a pool of cloud-literate engineers, developers, and policy makers ensures that financial incentives such as cloud credits translate into real adoption, innovation, and economic impact.

Governments can promote cloud computing investment and adoption by strengthening and modernizing their regulatory frameworks, with a focus on clarity, predictability, and alignment with international good practices. Robust data governance frameworks—covering data classification, privacy, security, and mechanisms for cross-border data flows—provide certainty for both CSPs and users, especially in sectors that handle sensitive information. Clear and transparent CSP regulations, including licensing processes, service quality standards, and security requirements, help ensure a competitive and trusted marketplace while reducing entry barriers for providers. Modernizing related areas, such as public procurement rules, can enable government agencies to leverage cloud services directly, creating anchor demand that can stimulate local market growth. In parallel, adopting intermediary liability frameworks and streamlined compliance processes can further encourage CSP investment. By combining legal clarity with pro-competition policies and safeguards for privacy and security, governments can build the trust and market conditions necessary for a thriving cloud ecosystem.

Countries lacking basic digital infrastructure

For nations lacking foundational connectivity infrastructure, prioritizing investment in high-speed broadband access for households and businesses is crucial. This enables cloud service adoption for individual users and small and medium enterprises, allowing them to access AI applications without major domestic data center investment upfront. Fiber optic networks that provide diverse paths supporting high-capacity bandwidth and low-latency and resiliency requirements are critical in enabling AI adoption in these countries. In Africa, although a growing number of underwater cables connect the continent with the wider world, a dearth of onshore lines to carry data inland leaves much of that internet capacity wasted.

Although the paths vary depending on existing capabilities, a proactive, collaborative multistakeholder approach involving governments, industry, and global institutions is critical for countries to ensure sufficient compute resources while mitigating risks and negative effects.

Notes

1. TOP500 has compiled a list of the world's 500 fastest supercomputers twice a year since 1993. The performance of a supercomputer is measured by the number of tera floating point operations it can carry out per second. The sum of the performance of all supercomputers in a country is typically used to measure the country's supercomputer capacity.

2. The cloud computing exports from balance-of-payments data could be significantly underestimated because of several factors: (1) Statistical agencies struggle to accurately capture the value of cloud computing services because of a lack of standardized definitions and reporting frameworks; (2) determining the true location of the transaction and thus export when data are stored in distributed data centers across the globe and accessed by users worldwide is challenging; (3) cloud computing is often embedded within other services or products; and (4) multinational cloud providers often have subsidiaries and data centers in multiple countries. Transactions between these entities may not be fully captured in export statistics, even though they represent cross-border service provision. Also, some cloud services are offered for free or in exchange for data.

References

AWS Sector Blog Team. 2023. "Ministry Collaborates with AWS to Boost Innovation and Upskill Public Servants." *AWS Blog*, February 1, 2023. https://aws.amazon.com/blogs/publicsector/thailands -higher-education-science-research-innovation-ministry-collaborates-aws-boost-innovation-upskill -public-servants/.

Azoulay, P., J. L. Krieger, and A. Nagaraj. 2024. "Old Moats for New Models: Openness, Control, and Competition in Generative AI." Working Paper 32474, National Bureau of Economic Research, Cambridge, MA.

"Big Tech Companies Use Cloud Computing Arms to Pursue Alliances with AI Groups." 2023. *Financial Times*, February 5, 2023. https://www.ft.com/content/5b17d011-8e0b-4ba1-bdca-4fbfdba10363.

Brussels Times Newsroom. 2024. "ChatGPT Consumes 25 Times More Energy Than Google." *Brussels Times*, May 12, 2024. https://www.brusselstimes.com/1042696/chatgpt-consumes-25-times-more -energy-than-google.

"China Offers AI Computing 'Vouchers' to Its Underpowered Start-ups." 2024. *Financial Times*, March 4, 2024. https://www.ft.com/content/9d67cda3-b157-47a0-98cb-e8e9842b2c90.

Edge AI + Vision Alliance. 2024. "AI Chip Market to Grow 10x in the Next 10 Years and Become a $300 Billion Industry." *Market Analysis,* April 30, 2024. https://www.edge-ai-vision.com/2024/04/ai-chip -market-to-grow-10x-in-the-next-ten-years-and-become-a-300-billion-industry/.

European Commission. 2024. "Commission Adopts EU-Wide Scheme for Rating Sustainability of Data Centres." News Release, March 15, 2024. https://energy.ec.europa.eu/news/commission-adopts-eu -wide-scheme-rating-sustainability-data-centres-2024-03-15_en.

Goldman Sachs. 2024. "Cloud Revenues Poised to Reach $2 Trillion by 2030 Amid AI Rollout." *Insights*, September 4, 2024. https://www.goldmansachs.com/insights/articles/cloud-revenues-poised-to-reach -2-trillion-by-2030-amid-ai-rollout.

Haranas, M. 2024. "Microsoft and OpenAI Plan $100B AI-Centric Data Center: Report." *CRN*, April 1, 2024. https://www.crn.com/news/data-center/microsoft-and-openai-plan-100b-ai-centric-data-center -report.

Hawkins, Z., V. Lehdonvirta, and B. Wu. 2025. "AI Compute Sovereignty: Infrastructure Control across Territories, Cloud Providers, and Accelerators." Preprint, posted June 24, 2025. https://papers.ssrn .com/sol3/papers.cfm?abstract_id=5312977.

Kim, T. 2024. "NVIDIA CEO Says Blackwell GPU Will Cost $30,000 to $40,000." *Barron's*. https://www.barrons.com/livecoverage/nvidia-gtc-ai-conference/card/nvidia-ceo-says-blackwell-gpu-will-cost-30-000-to-40-000-l0fnByruULe4RAdr4kPE.

"IIT Hyderabad, NVIDIA Establish First AI Research Center in India." July 9, 2020. https://www.ndtv.com/education/iit-hyderabad-nvidia-establish-first-ai-research-centre-in-india-2259850.

International Energy Agency. 2020. *World Energy Outlook 2020*. https://www.iea.org/reports/world-energy-outlook-2020/outlook-for-energy-demand.

JLL. n.d. "How Government Initiatives Are Impacting Data Centers." *Insights*. https://www.us.jll.com/en/trends-and-insights/cities/how-government-initiatives-are-impacting-data-centers.

Johansson, P.-O., and B. Kriström. 2021. "The Costs and Benefits of Supporting Data Centers: A General Equilibrium Analysis." Preprint, posted December 9, 2021. https://papers.ssrn.com/sol3/papers.cfm?abstract_id=3981376.

Judge, P. 2022. "Frankfurt Updates Its Plans for Environmental Data Center Zoning." *Data Center Dynamics*, July 27, 2022. https://www.datacenterdynamics.com/en/news/frankfurt-updates-its-plans-for-environmental-data-center-zoning/.

Leswing, K. 2024. "NVIDIA Dominates the AI Chip Market, but There's More Competition Than Ever." *CNBC*, June 2, 2024. https://www.cnbc.com/2024/06/02/nvidia-dominates-the-ai-chip-market-but-theres-rising-competition-.html.

Meyer, T. 2022. "How Data Embassies Can Strengthen Resiliency with Sovereignty." *Google Cloud Blog*, November 11, 2022. https://cloud.google.com/blog/products/identity-security/data-embassies-strengthening-resiliency-with-sovereignty.

Ministry of Science and ICT, Republic of Korea. 2020. "Data Dam Project Begins, Being Key to Digital New Deal." Press Release, September 2, 2020. https://www.msit.go.kr/eng/bbs/view.do?sCode=eng&mId=4&mPid=2&pageIndex=&bbsSeqNo=42&nttSeqNo=453&searchOpt=&searchTxt=.

Northern Virginia Technology Council. 2020. *The Impact of Data Centers on the State and Local Economies of Virginia*. Falls Church, VA: Northern Virginia Technology Council. https://biz.loudoun.gov/wp-content/uploads/2020/02/Data_Center_Report_2020.pdf.

Norton, K. 2024. "AI Is Fueling a 'Nuclear Renaissance.' Bill Gates and Jeff Bezos Are in the Mix." *Investor's Business Daily*, July 12, 2024. https://www.investors.com/news/artificial-intelligence-ai-data-centers-demand-nuclear-energy/.

Reuters. 2023. "Britain to Invest 300 Million Pounds in AI Supercomputing." November 1, 2023; updated November 2, 2023. https://www.reuters.com/technology/britain-invest-300-million-pounds-ai-supercomputing-2023-11-01/.

Richter, F. 2025. "The Big Three Stay Ahead in Ever-Growing Cloud Market." https://www.statista.com/chart/18819/worldwide-market-share-of-leading-cloud-infrastructure-service-providers/.

Savvas, A. 2021. "Growth of Data Centers in Frankfurt to Now Be Controlled." *Capacity*, May 13, 2021. https://www.capacitymedia.com/article/29ot42ikril15nn8s4bvd/news/growth-of-data-centres-in-frankfurt-to-now-be-controlled.

Sharwood, S. 2024. "'Data Embassies' Promise Bubbles of Digital Sovereignty, but India Just Cooled on the Idea." *The Register*, July 24, 2024. https://www.theregister.com/2024/07/24/data_embassies.

"The Race Is On to Control the Global Supply Chain for AI Chips." 2024. *The Economist*, July 30, 2024. https://www.economist.com/schools-brief/2024/07/30/the-race-is-on-to-control-the-global-supply-chain-for-ai-chips.

Tony Blair Institute for Global Change. 2023. *State of Compute Access: How to Bridge the New Digital Divide*. London: Tony Blair Institute for Global Change. https://www.institute.global/insights/tech-and-digitalisation/state-of-compute-access-how-to-bridge-the-new-digital-divide.

Turner, M. 2025. "Loudon County, Virginia: Data Center Capital of the World." https://www.loudoun .gov/ArchiveCenter/ViewFile/Item/13979.

Vipra, J., and S. M. West. 2023. *Computational Power and AI.* New York: AI Now Institute. https:// ainowinstitute.org/publication/policy/compute-and-ai#b443b50d-b935-4687-a7fc-415a5cacfcb6.

Vivek, S. 2024. "India Eyes NVIDIA Partnership for Affordable AI Chips: Report." *India Today,* updated April 17, 2024. https://www.indiatoday.in/business/story/india-nvidia-partnership-affordable-ai -chips-at-subsidised-rates-report-2528346-2024-04-17.

"What Could Kill the \$1trn Artificial-Intelligence Boom?" 2024. *The Economist,* July 28, 2024. https://www.economist.com/business/2024/07/28/what-are-the-threats-to-the-1trn-artificial-intelligence -boom.

Context: Training Data and AI Model Adaptation | 4

KEY MESSAGES

- *Data power artificial intelligence (AI).* The quantity, quality, and diversity of data are essential to making AI systems effective and adaptable, enabling them to evolve and perform reliably in diverse real-world scenarios.

- *The data divide grows as the AI training data industry booms globally, yet private sector investment in low-income countries and middle-income countries remains negligible.* In 2023, cumulative venture capital investments in the AI training data industry reached US$32 billion, predominantly concentrated in advanced economies—56 percent in the United States, 15 percent in the European Union, and 2 percent in the United Kingdom. China and India contributed 17 percent and 3 percent, respectively, with the rest of the world making up the remaining 6 percent.

- *The dominance of English in text data affects the usefulness of generative AI models in non-English-speaking countries, while opportunities in nontext data are expanding.*

  - English is spoken by 19 percent of the global population, but it makes up 45 percent of global URLs, 56 percent of open-source data sets on the leading AI development platform Hugging Face, and nearly 98 percent of scientific papers.

  - For nontext data, the language distribution tends to be more diverse, offering opportunities for non-English-speaking countries. Only 21 percent of YouTube videos are estimated to be in English, with Hindi and Spanish accounting for 7.6 percent and 6.7 percent, respectively.

- *Market failures highlight the need for government intervention to bridge the data divide.*

  - Although the private sector is adopting innovative approaches such as synthetic data to fill data gaps, market failures such as reusability, vague property rights, and challenges in valuing data often lead to underinvestment and undersharing.

  - Governments play a critical role in addressing these gaps by curating and publishing government data, facilitating secure and ethical data exchange, and developing and promoting interoperable data formats and taxonomies. Civil societies can contribute to enhancing AI data diversity through open-source data sets and community involvement.

- *Open-source AI is proliferating and allows developing countries to adapt global solutions to their local needs.*

  ◦ Developing countries could face challenges in adopting AI because models are misaligned with local needs. Open-source AI models can lower the barrier to entry for developing countries, enabling them to adapt and customize AI solutions to local needs without incurring high licensing costs.

  ◦ Open-source models are growing rapidly and narrowing the performance gaps with proprietary models: Among the 308 notable AI models published from 2022 to June 2025, around half have open weights, and a quarter have both open weights and open-source training code. Open-source models are also increasingly challenging proprietary models in terms of performance.

Introduction

Data are the cornerstone of artificial intelligence (AI) development, profoundly influencing the capabilities and performance of AI models. Three key aspects—quantity, quality, and diversity—are critical in determining how effective and adaptable AI systems are across different applications. Addressing market failures and externalities in training data production is crucial for fostering AI development and digital inclusion. Market failures stem from the positive spillovers and reusability of data, vague property rights, challenges in assessing the value of data, and privacy and security concerns. Although private firms play a key role in training data generation, they often underinvest as market failures diminish their potential returns, particularly for small and medium enterprises (SMEs) in developing economies. Public intervention is essential to address these failures.

For many developing countries, the challenge is not just obtaining large, high-quality data but also adapting AI models to their specific economic, cultural, and institutional contexts. Some countries are exploring local AI models that are better suited to their unique needs. However, the process is often costly and sometimes not feasible because of less-advanced countries' limited resources and expertise. Open-source AI models are more accessible and cost-effective, but they may require more technical resources that countries may lack. The advantages and challenges of developing proprietary systems or adapting open-source models vary depending on each application's requirements, the technological capabilities, and the specific needs, underscoring the importance of a tailored approach to AI development and deployment.

This chapter analyzes the availability and quality of AI training data, particularly text data in developing countries, and explores how various stakeholders can address training data gaps. It also examines the adaptability of AI models in diverse country contexts and governments' considerations between open-source and proprietary AI models.

Effective AI models hinge on training data

The capability of AI is fundamentally shaped by the data used to train the model, much as how the books a person reads deeply influence their thinking. In AI, the term *training* refers to the process by which a model learns from data, adjusting the parameters and structures of algorithms to improve the performance of specific tasks such as classification or prediction. A training data set is comparable to a textbook, providing the foundation for AI models to learn and shaping their ability to recognize patterns, generate content, or make decisions.

AI models heavily rely on the quantity, quality, and diversity of the training data, which we summarize as the three pillars of effective training data.

- *Quality* encompasses factors such as accuracy, completeness, granularity, timeliness, intensity of information, being error-free, and ensuring fairness while minimizing bias in the data.
- *Quantity* refers to the scale or size of the data set used for training, which directly affects the model's ability to learn and generalize from data.
- *Diversity,* or *representativeness,* refers to the data's ability to reflect the social, economic, institutional, cultural, and linguistic diversity of populations, aligning with the specific contexts in which AI is applied.

The AI training data industry is growing rapidly. *Fortune Business Insights* (2025) estimated that the market value was approximately US$2.26 billion in 2023, with projections of US$17.04 billion by 2032, representing a compound annual growth rate of 22 percent. In addition, venture capital (VC) investments in data have surged in recent years. The cumulative VC investments from 2012 to 2023 reached US$32 billion, with a significant acceleration after 2020, according to OECD. ai (https://oecd.ai/en/). This influx of capital demonstrates the evolution in the AI training data industry, where vendors strategically respond to the escalating demand for AI capabilities.

The process of obtaining high-quality AI training data involves a comprehensive data production chain. Data, as a vital asset in the AI industry, flow through several key stages: sourcing, collection, processing, brokerage, and usage (refer to figure 4.1). The process begins with sourcing data from various origins, such as open-source, commercialized, or private data, followed by collection through crawling or purchasing. The data then undergo processing, where they are cleaned, filtered, deduplicated, formatted, and sometimes labeled to enhance quality and meet the requirements of AI models. Developers have the option to manage these stages in house or acquire data from brokers who have already processed them. During the usage phase, data are refined by AI developers to fit specific AI models, and this process often loops back to dynamically adjust data production for continuous improvement.

At each step, opportunities and challenges emerge as the industry evolves dynamically. Data sourcing and collection, the pivotal initial steps in AI model development, often involve navigating complex legal and ethical landscapes, especially when using web-crawled content from media sources or

FIGURE 4.1 Production chain for training data

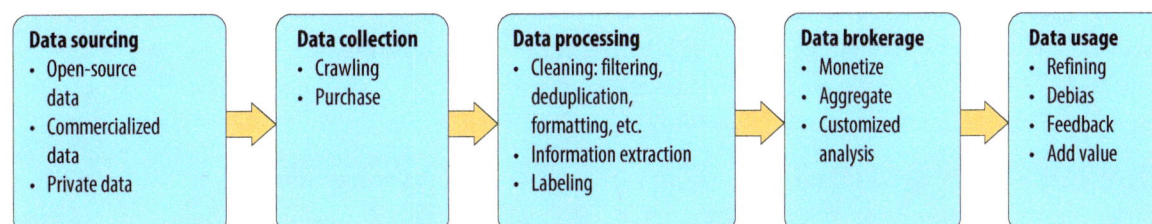

Source: Original figure for this publication.

even private data. The vast amount of text, images, audio, and videos available on social media and traditional media present substantial opportunities for AI training. However, web crawling these sources raises concerns over data ownership, copyrights, use rights, and privacy, underscoring the importance of careful legal and ethical consideration in the sourcing process to maintain the integrity and trustworthiness of AI technologies.

In the era of generative AI (GenAI), data communities have become a key source for AI training data. Unlike private entities, these communities offer valuable data sets as public goods at no cost, with platforms such as Hugging Face hosting data sets comparable in size to those used to train models such as GPT-4 and Llama 3.1. These contributions are often overlooked in traditional market estimates.

Data communities vary widely, from global networks such as OpenStreetMap and Wikipedia, which engage hundreds of thousands of contributors, to localized initiatives such as CocôZap in Brazil and Dakshina in India, advocating for local issues. These communities not only supplement the data sets typically provided by the private sector but also offer diverse, real-world data that enhance AI models' robustness and applicability (Massey, Narayan, and Simperl 2024). Although open-source data are accessible, they frequently lack the economic incentives necessary for comprehensive development and may not meet specific requirements, leading to a demand for customized data solutions.

Data labeling, part of the broader business process outsourcing industry, thrives in low-income countries (LICs) and middle-income countries (MICs) because of low labor costs. *Data labeling* refers to marking or classifying data, such as identifying objects in images or transcribing speech, to enhance machine learning model performance. Data labeling typically requires an intermediate level of education and provides employment opportunities for women, youth, and disabled workers. The earnings are often comparable to, or even more than, those in traditional industries, and these jobs offer flexible work arrangements, driving rapid growth of data labelers in countries such as India, Kenya, and the Philippines.

Companies integrated into the global data production chain in LICs and MICs often enhance their employees' digital skills through targeted training programs. These programs equip employees with the necessary digital skills, covering foundational digital literacy, data processing, and even more advanced technical skills, tailored to meet the demands of outsourcing partners. Integrating local businesses and the workforce into the global AI industry enhances developing countries exposure to advanced technologies and information and communication technology sectors, potentially supporting national industry upgrades and fostering innovation.

However, the rise of GenAI poses a challenge to relatively simple tasks in the data production chain. Although demand is increasing for training data production because of the rise of GenAI, AI systems are also increasingly used to automate repetitive tasks, which complicates the outlook in this industry. These AI applications cut down on labor-intensive work. As a result, more specialized skills are needed for managing complex labeling tools and overseeing quality control. This shift underscores the need for developing countries to invest in higher-level digital skills and adapt to the evolving demands of the AI-driven economy.

Despite the challenges in data transactions, the growing need for efficient data exchange has catalyzed the development of a distinct market. Issues such as defining property rights, monitoring usage, and verifying data quality distinguish data from traditional commodities and complicate standardization (World Bank 2021). Consequently, a standardized, publicly accessible platform for data trading is lacking, with transactions predominantly occurring bilaterally between data users and providers for specific and customized needs.

Within this evolving framework, specialized firms such as Appen and Scale AI play crucial roles by offering customized data solutions that encompass data collection, enhancement, and labeling. In addition, large technology companies such as Google enhance the efficiency and scope of AI applications by integrating outsourced services into their broader data management and AI development strategies, further illustrating the intricate dynamics of data transactions in the AI industry.

Data divide across countries and languages

Developing countries face a shortage of local data providers, reflected in their marginal share of VC investments and start-up activities in the training data industry. The bulk of VC investments in the training data industry flow to advanced economies, except for China and India (refer to figure 4.2). In 2023, the United States alone reached US$18 billion in VC investments in training data (56 percent of the global total), and the European Union and United Kingdom together attracted US$5.5 billion (17 percent). Outside of this group, China and India emerged as significant players, with investments of US$5.5 billion (17 percent) and US$1.0 billion (3 percent), respectively, with the rest of the world making up the remaining 6 percent.

FIGURE 4.2 **Training AI in a data desert: VC investments in training data, by country and region**

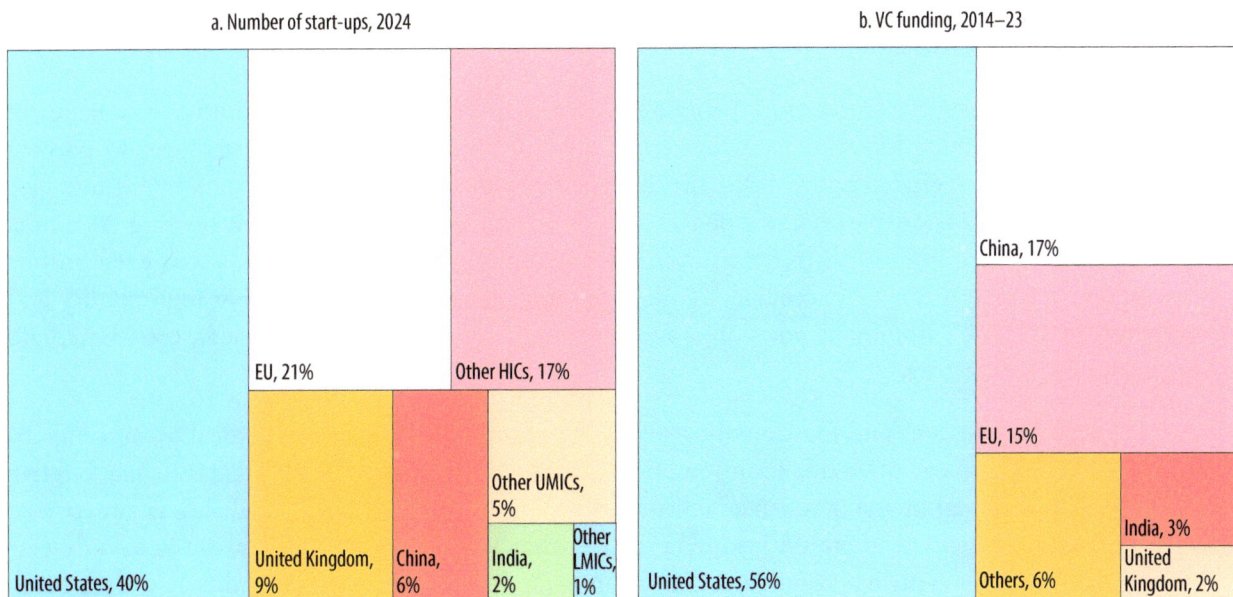

a. Number of start-ups, 2024

United States, 40%; EU, 21%; Other HICs, 17%; United Kingdom, 9%; China, 6%; India, 2%; Other UMICs, 5%; Other LMICs, 1%

b. VC funding, 2014–23

United States, 56%; China, 17%; EU, 15%; Others, 6%; India, 3%; United Kingdom, 2%

Sources: Original figures for this publication using calculations from OECD.AI (https://oecd.ai/en/data?selectedArea=investments-in-ai-and-data&selectedVisualization=vc-investments-in-data-start-ups-by-country) and CB Insights (https://www.cbinsights.com/); data extracted in September 2024.
Note: Start-ups in the training data sector were selected because the keywords *data management, data collection,* or *data tracking* were present in their company descriptions. EU = European Union; HICs = high-income countries; LMICs = lower-middle-income countries; UMICs = upper-middle-income countries; VC = venture capital.

Notably, these figures are highly disproportionate relative to their share of global gross domestic product (GDP)—especially for the United States, which accounts for roughly one-quarter of global GDP yet commands more than half of these investments. Similarly, measured by the distribution of start-ups in the training data sector, the United States leads with 40 percent, and China and India trail behind with 6 percent and 2 percent, respectively. This lack of investment not only constrains innovation but also restricts these countries' participation in the burgeoning data economy.

Global data holders, particularly social media platforms, face challenges in regions with limited internet penetration, where low digital engagement restricts the availability of valuable text and nontext data. Social media platforms such as Facebook, TikTok, and YouTube offer abundant resources—text, images, audio, videos, and location data—but poor internet coverage, slow speeds, high costs, and limited digital skills in less-developed countries result in lower computer and smartphone ownership and fewer online activities (World Bank 2024).

This scarcity of digital footprints hinders data collection in less-advanced economies. The challenge is even more acute in countries with small populations, where the lack of country-specific data compounds the problem. Moreover, although social media provide significant digital footprints, the data are controlled by platforms headquartered largely in the United States, complicating access for developing countries.

The global distribution of spoken languages among populations is uneven, and this natural disparity affects the development and adoption of AI models. More than 7,000 languages are spoken worldwide, with the 20 largest being the native tongues of more than 3.6 billion people, 44 percent of the global population. English, the most-spoken language, is spoken by 1.5 billion people, or 19 percent of the global population (refer to figure 4.3, panel a), and 390 million of these people consider English their first language. The second largest language is Mandarin Chinese, spoken by 15 percent of the global population, followed by Hindi (7.6 percent) and Spanish (6.9 percent).[1]

This uneven distribution is more prominent on the internet and in AI training. A handful of languages dominate most internet content, and English makes up the largest share, 45 percent of global URLs (refer to figure 4.3, panel b). The imbalance in text training data is pronounced. As of April 2024, 56 percent of open-source data sets on Hugging Face, a leading AI model repository, were in English (refer to figure 4.3, panel c). This trend is consistent even among larger data sets; of the 50 exceeding 1 trillion tokens, 28 are English-based. For high-quality text sources, English's dominant position is more pronounced because of historical, economic, and technological factors.

The United Kingdom and the United States have historically led in technological advancements. Their technological prowess, economic heft, and cultural influence have established English as the primary language of science, culture, business, and technology. English has functioned as a lingua franca, or common bridge language, that facilitates communication across diverse linguistic groups. This has resulted in a disproportionate amount of high-quality text data being generated and available in English. Nearly 98 percent of scientific papers are estimated to be written in English, even by researchers from countries in which English is not the native language (Gordin 2015).

FIGURE 4.3 Predominance of English in online content

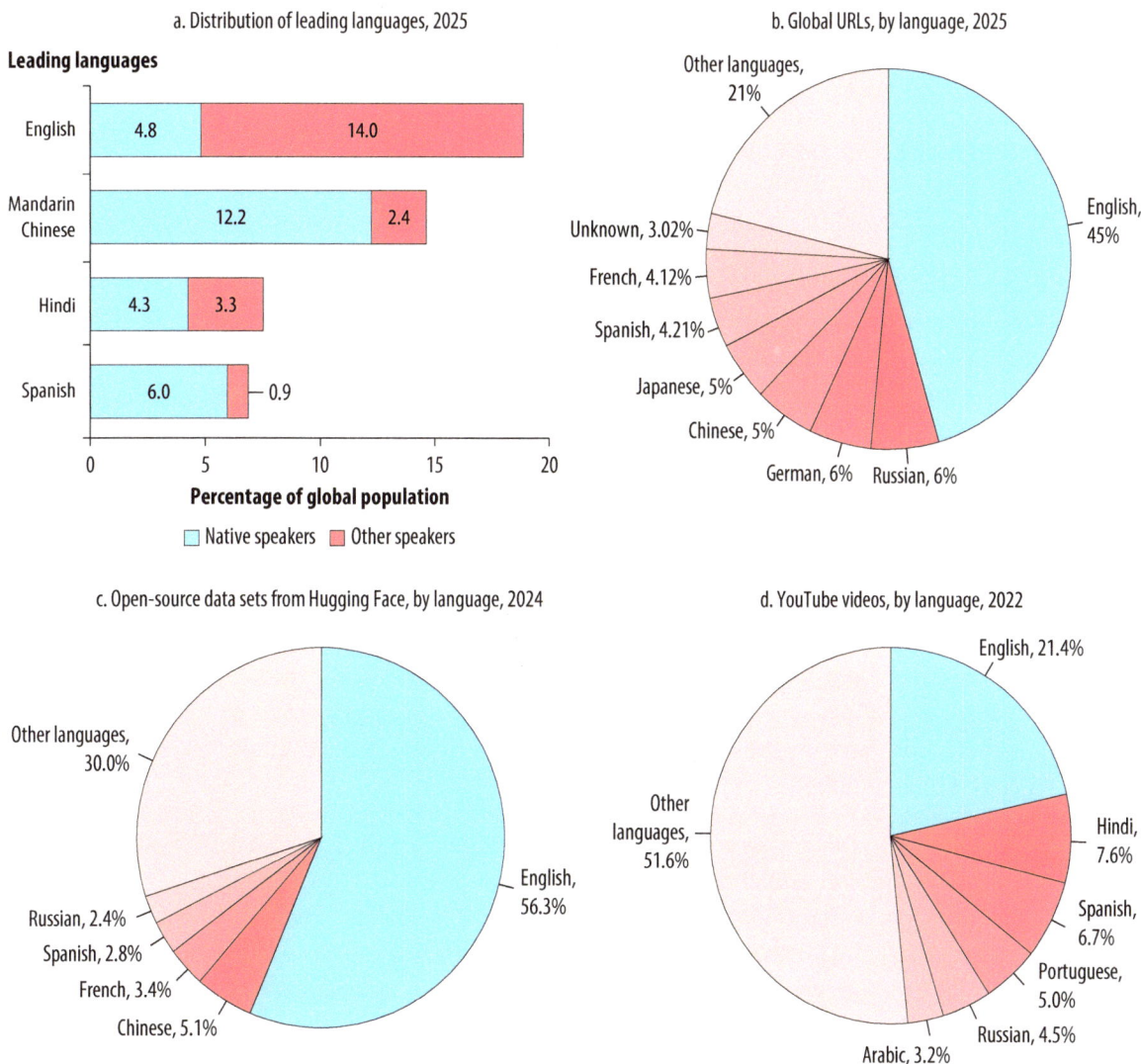

a. Distribution of leading languages, 2025

Leading languages

b. Global URLs, by language, 2025

c. Open-source data sets from Hugging Face, by language, 2024

d. YouTube videos, by language, 2022

Sources: Original figures for this publication based on calculations using Ethonologue 2025 data (https://www.ethnologue.com/); CommonCrawl data accessed in July 2025 (https://commoncrawl.org/); OECD.AI data updated on April 22, 2024 (https://oecd.ai/en/); and Figure 18 in McGrady et al. 2023.
Note: AI = artificial intelligence.

For nontext data, the language distribution tends to be more diverse, offering opportunities for non-English-speaking countries. The deepened penetration of mobile internet, increased internet speeds, and widespread use of mobile devices have fueled the fast growth of video-based social media in this decade. This trend has made it easier to produce and share video content on platforms such as TikTok and YouTube, which serve as rich sources of training data for video GenAI. Unlike text-based data and websites, the language distribution on video platforms is more diverse. For instance, only 21 percent of YouTube videos are estimated to be in English, with Hindi and Spanish accounting for 7.6 percent and 6.7 percent, respectively (refer to figure 4.3, panel d). Such diversity presents the potential to mitigate language and cultural biases in training data for nontext GenAI models.

Technology innovation, such as synthetic data, offers promising solutions to bridging data gaps in GenAI models. *Synthetic data* refers to artificially generated data that mimic the characteristics and patterns of real-world data but are created through algorithms, generative models, or simulations (Liu et al. 2024). These data can be used to supplement real-world data or to develop new training data sets altogether. Synthetic text from one large language model (LLM) can train another, potentially mitigating data depletion issues.

For instance, Amazon's multilingual language models have leveraged synthetic data to better understand and generate text across different languages, enhancing model performance where real data are scarce. This approach allows AI systems to function more equitably across various linguistic contexts, reducing the bias inherent in traditional data sets. Another example application of synthetic data is using LLM to write a math proof, with one AI generating multiple initial steps and a helper AI selecting the best one (Luo et al. 2023), where the feedback loop acts as synthetic data and refines the model.

However, this approach also has challenges. Models trained primarily on synthetic data risk "model collapse," in which performance degrades with repeated training on generated outputs (Shumailov et al. 2023). In addition, applying synthetic data in fields such as health care and education is also challenging because of the need for domain-specific knowledge. Nonetheless, ongoing research addresses these challenges to make synthetic data more applicable to AI training. For example, accumulating synthetic data alongside real data during training, rather than replacing them, has the potential to solve model collapse (Gerstgrasser et al. 2024), and physics models have been used to generate synthetic coronavirus disease 2019 lung images to incorporate domain knowledge into AI training (Zhao, Fong, and Bell 2024).

Addressing the data divide across countries and languages requires concerted efforts from the private sector, public sector, and civil societies. The private sector plays a pivotal role in bridging training data gaps by research and investment in collecting and curating data with innovative approaches. The private sector, especially leading tech companies, uses its scale, financial resources, and technological expertise to drive the development of inclusive AI data systems. These efforts, in turn, enable companies to create more inclusive AI models, expanding their reach and effectiveness in global markets.

For instance, Amazon's MASSIVE data set includes more than 1 million utterances in 51 languages, enhancing AI models' multilingual capabilities by incorporating diverse linguistic inputs. Similarly, platforms such as Facebook and Google invest heavily in multilingual data sets and partner with local content creators to enrich their language resources. In addition, firms specializing in providing high-quality training data services, such as Appen and Lionbridge, are emerging as new and promising forces in the AI training data landscape by leveraging global crowdsourcing to gather diverse data sets across various languages and contexts. The sustainability of these efforts relies on collaboration with other stakeholders, including governments and civil societies, to ensure data privacy and ethical standards.

However, market failures and externalities in the production and sharing of high-quality, localized training data arise from several intrinsic characteristics that discourage private investment. First, one special attribute of data is the ability to be reused by multiple parties without diminishing its value, thereby generating positive externalities that the investing firm cannot fully capture. Second, ambiguous property rights and difficulties in valuing data also result in underinvestment and sharing. Third, producing high-quality data involves substantial fixed costs for collection and curation, which can be prohibitively expensive—especially for SMEs in developing economies.

Fourth, although localized data offer significant societal benefits and positive spillover effects for targeted communities and beyond, their direct profitability is often limited, further disincentivizing private investment. Finally, a shortage of necessary skills and digital infrastructure—essential public goods for effective data production—creates additional barriers in many regions. Collectively, these factors highlight the urgent need for public intervention to address these market failures and stimulate investment in high-quality, diverse, localized training data.

Governments can adopt strategic measures to enhance data accessibility and governance. First, by enhancing data governance to ensure privacy and security, governments can create a trustworthy environment that supports the growth of the data sector. For example, initiatives such as the UK Data Service and Health Data Research UK provide secure access to health and social science data to foster innovation (Health Data Research UK n.d.). Second, governments can prioritize the digitization of nondigital records to unlock valuable resources. The Digital India program is another notable example that has significantly increased the accessibility of public records. Third, introducing financial support in the form of subsidies and vouchers can help SMEs access high-quality data for AI training and tools. Programs such as the European Union's Horizon 2020 illustrate how such incentives support a competitive environment for AI developers.

Fourth, fostering international collaboration between countries, and between countries and major tech firms, is crucial. Examples include the Global Partnership on AI, which involves multiple countries working together to guide the responsible adoption of AI, and partnerships between governments and tech giants such as Google and IBM to leverage advanced AI technologies for public sector innovation. In addition, measures to enhance digital infrastructure and skills, as discussed in chapters 2 and 6, are needed to complement efforts to address market failures in data production.

Civil society can contribute to enhance AI data diversity through open-source data sets and community involvement. Engaging diverse communities in AI development ensures language data with fewer biases and blind spots that can arise from homogeneous data sets. This empowers marginalized groups and incorporates their linguistic and cultural nuances into AI systems. Open-source communities such as Hugging Face play a crucial role in diversifying data sharing, a practice that should be encouraged to further enhance data accessibility. Initiatives such as Masakhane (https://www.masakhane.io/), which gathers linguistic data from African speakers, and Universal Dependencies (https://universaldependencies.org/), which offers data sets for nonstandard languages, showcase how community-driven efforts can improve language diversity in training data.

However, investing in AI training data sets for some low-resource languages may not always be financially wise or sustainable. Several factors influence the future of a language, including the size and growth of the population and economy where the language is spoken and its use in academia, business, government, and media. If a language is not widely used in these domains, it may face challenges in attracting and retaining speakers, particularly among younger generations.

In addition, the cost of developing, maintaining, and updating low-resource language data sets can be substantial. As more people learn and use English or other widely spoken languages for online communication, the demand for digital resources in low-resource languages may decline, making it difficult to justify large-scale investments in training data. If the potential benefits of low-resource language data sets do not outweigh the costs, it might be more practical to focus on languages with larger speaker populations and more established digital infrastructure.

Regions with less-available linguistic data have been relying on translation for AI applications. This option will likely be the most feasible, although it comes with caveats. For example, in India, some AI models use a two-step translation process in which user input is first translated into English and then back into the local language. Efforts such as Project Bhashini and AI4Bharat are working to enhance AI technology for Indian languages, aiming to reduce reliance on English as an intermediary and improve the quality of AI translations across diverse linguistic contexts (AI4Bharat 2025). This method leverages the robustness of English-based models to improve accuracy and consistency. However, these approaches have some drawbacks, such as the loss of cultural nuances, increased risk of errors, and additional computation costs.

Adaptation of AI models to the national context

AI models developed in a few leading economies may not address the unique contexts and needs of developing countries, despite their global reach. This mismatch stems from several factors in addition to data limitations, including economic and societal priorities, resource constraints, and divergent AI use cases. Sector-specific challenges further complicate AI adoption: Precision farming models may require significant adjustments for smallholder farmers and different crops; public service AI solutions often do not account for infrastructure gaps and informal economies; and applications in health care, education, and legal services need substantial customization to local protocols and cultural norms.

As Alami et al. (2020) noted, most AI-based health care applications are developed in high-income countries, resulting in a lack of robust adaptations for low-resource settings and making it challenging to tailor decision-making to local needs. These factors collectively highlight the need for context-specific AI development or significant adaptation of existing models to ensure their relevance and effectiveness in developing economies, where the application of AI technologies may be limited without proper customization to accommodate local conditions and constraints.

The development of AI models is characterized by two distinct approaches: open source and closed source or proprietary. For businesses and governments seeking to integrate AI into their operations, open-source and proprietary AI models have pros and cons (refer to the following sections for more information).

Open-source AI models make their underlying code or model parameters and weights accessible to the public, allowing for broad collaboration and innovation. Notable examples include DeepSeek, Meta's Llama 3.1, and Stability AI's Stable Diffusion. These open-source models empower developers to adapt and enhance AI applications for diverse needs, offering transparency, flexibility, and cost-effectiveness. In contrast, closed-source models, such as Anthropic's Claude, Google's Gemini, and OpenAI's GPT-4, keep their code and weights proprietary, offering optimized performance and integrated security for specific business applications.

Although the term *open source* implies full accessibility, in practice, the level of access can differ significantly. Open-source AI not just involves the sharing of code but can also include model architecture, parameters (or weights), training process, training data, application programming interface, and even hardware. Some projects offer complete access, including training data and model weights, and others may share the code but restrict access to essential components, such as training data or model weights, requiring users to exert significant effort to effectively use the AI (Gent 2024; Shrestha, von Krogh, and Feuerriegel 2023). In addition, open-source licenses can vary, imposing restrictions ranging from very permissive to limiting commercial use, potentially involving licensing fees (Liesenfeld and Dingemanse 2024).

Open-source models are growing rapidly and narrowing the performance gaps with proprietary models. Among the 308 notable AI models published from 2022 to June 2025, around half have open weights, and a quarter have both open weights and open-source training code. Open-source models are also increasingly challenging proprietary models in performance. This progress is driven by community-led development, readily available tools such as Hugging Face, and the increasing accessibility of powerful open-source models such as DeepSeek and Meta's Llama series. Although proprietary models still hold an edge in overall capabilities and scale, open-source models are gaining ground and offering compelling alternatives, particularly in areas such as flexibility, transparency, and cost-effectiveness.

For AI solution providers, the choice between open-source and proprietary AI models depends on various strategic, business, and technical considerations and whether they prioritize rapid adoption and community-driven innovation or control, monetization, and competitive differentiation. Open-source models offer broader adoption and a robust ecosystem but require creative monetization strategies, whereas proprietary models allow tighter control over revenue and user experience at the cost of openness.

Open-source models

For open-source models, the pros are as follows:

- *Customization.* Open-source models offer significant opportunities for adaptation; the level of customization goes beyond what is typically achievable with commercial off-the-shelf products, allowing for more targeted applications.
- *Portability.* Often vendor-agnostic, open-source models reduce the risk of vendor lock-in and remain flexible to the changing needs of businesses and governments.
- *Model transparency and risk mitigation.* Their open-source nature allows for a more comprehensive study of their limitations, such as bias, relevancy, and potential degradation. Understanding these issues is crucial for implementing AI responsibly and mitigating risks.

For open-source models, the cons are as follows:

- *High adoption barriers and development costs.* Fine-tuning open-source models for specific contexts requires substantial expertise and access to quality data. This issue can pose a challenge for organizations that may not have the necessary technical capacity or resources in house. Model adaptation also comes with high costs in development and support.
- *Security vulnerabilities.* Open-source code may be more susceptible to security exploits if it is not properly reviewed and maintained.
- *Hidden costs.* Despite being labeled *open source,* many models are not entirely free, with complex licensing requirements that can limit usage and impose costs (Stephens et al. 2024).

- *Potentially lower performance.* Open-source models generally have fewer parameters compared with limited-access and no-access models, which often correlates with a simpler architecture. Although this simplicity can make open-source models more accessible and easier to train and deploy, it also suggests that these models may offer lower performance potential compared with their parameter-richer counterparts.

Proprietary models

For proprietary models, the pros are as follows:

- *High performance.* Proprietary models have superior optimization for complex tasks. For instance, proprietary models such as Google's Gemini and OpenAI's GPT-4 have been widely adopted in sectors requiring robust performance and seamless integration with existing systems.
- *Enhanced security.* Businesses involved in finance, health care, and enterprise-level operations typically opt for proprietary models because of their superior optimization, enhanced security measures, and the ability to handle complex sensitive data securely (Ahmad 2023).
- *Comprehensive support.* Proprietary models provide access to dedicated technical support and updates, ensuring reliable performance and integration.
- *Tailored collaborations.* For governments, collaborating with big technology firms enables low-resource nations to rapidly adopt advanced AI technologies and tailor them to their national needs.

For proprietary models, the cons are as follows:

- *Reliance on external providers.* Such reliance may pose risks to national sovereignty and data security and potentially limit long-term innovation capacity and the ability to independently evolve the technology.
- *High costs.* Such collaborations require significant investment and resources to establish and maintain, which can be a considerable burden for low-resource nations.
- *Limited customization.* Customization is often restricted, and these models may not be as flexible as open-source alternatives.

Conclusion

As AI regulators, governments should promote a balanced approach and avoid unnecessary restrictions on open-source AI. The contours of open and closed systems are fluid, and society benefits from the broad array of constantly evolving systems along that spectrum. The development of more open systems—even when not completely open—is crucial to keep proprietary providers on their toes by infusing more competition and choice into digital systems.

AI regulations should focus on responsible use, promoting innovation while mitigating risks, regardless of whether AI models are open source or proprietary. Policies can encourage open-source AI development to foster wider scrutiny and collaboration. A mix of multistakeholder processes, iterative standards, and existing regulatory remedies could be used to address problems arising from open-source AI. Excess restrictions on open-source AI may slow innovation and curtail options for users.

Open-source AI models can lower the barrier to entry for developing countries, enabling them to adapt and customize AI solutions to local needs without incurring high licensing costs. To capitalize on this, governments should invest in digital infrastructure, promote AI education and skills development, and foster collaborative ecosystems that encourage local innovation and adaptation of open-source AI.

Note

1. Language statistics are based on the 27th edition of *Ethnologue*. For details, refer to https://www.ethnologue.com/.

References

Ahmad, F. 2023. "The Choice for Businesses between Open-Source and Proprietary Models to Deploy Generative AI." *Towards AI*. Last updated November 8, 2023. https://towardsai.net/p/artificial-intelligence/the-choice-for-businesses-between-open-source-and-proprietary-models-to-deploy-generative-ai.

AI4Bharat. 2025. "The IndicLLMSuite—Blueprint for Creating Pre-Training and Fine-Tuning Datasets for Indic Languages." https://github.com/AI4Bharat.

Alami, H., L. Rivard, P. Lehoux, et al. 2020. "Artificial Intelligence in Health Care: Laying the Foundation for Responsible, Sustainable, and Inclusive Innovation in Low- and Middle-Income Countries. *Global Health 16* (52). https://doi.org/10.1186/s12992-020-00584-1.

Fortune Business Insights. 2025. "AI Training Dataset Market Size, Share and Industry Analysis, by Type (Text, Audio, Image, Video, and Others), by Deployment Mode (On-Premises and Cloud), by End-Users (IT and Telecommunications, Retail and Consumer Goods, Healthcare, Automotive, BFSI, and Others), and Regional Forecast, 2025–2032." Last updated August 25, 2025. https://www.fortunebusinessinsights.com/ai-training-dataset-market-109241.

Gent, E. 2024. "The Tech Industry Can't Agree on What Open-Source AI Means. That's a Problem." *MIT Technology Review*.

Gerstgrasser, M., R. Schaeffer, A. Dey, R. Rafailov, H. Sleight, J. Hughes, T. Korbak, et al. 2024. "Is Model Collapse Inevitable? Breaking the Curse of Recursion by Accumulating Real and Synthetic Data." Preprint, last revised April 29, 2024. https://arxiv.org/abs/2404.01413.

Gordin, M. D. 2015. *Scientific Babel: How Science Was Done Before and After Global English*. Chicago: University of Chicago Press.

Health Data Research UK. n.d. "Our Strategy." https://www.hdruk.ac.uk/about-us/our-strategy/.

Liesenfeld, A., and M. Dingemanse. 2024. "Rethinking Open Source Generative AI: Open-washing and the EU AI Act." In *Proceedings of the Seventh Annual ACM Conference on Fairness, Accountability, and Transparency*, 1–14. Association for Computing Machinery, New York.

Liu, R., J. Wei, F. Liu, C. Si, Y. Zhang, J. Rao, S. Zheng, et al. 2024. "Best Practices and Lessons Learned on Synthetic Data for Language Models." Preprint, last revised August 10, 2024. https://arxiv.org/abs/2404.07503.

Luo, H., Q. Sun, C. Xu, P. Zhao, J. Lou, C. Tao, X. Geng, et al. 2023. "WizardMath: Empowering Mathematical Reasoning for Large Language Models Via Reinforced Evol-Instruct." Preprint, last revised June 4, 2025. https://arxiv.org/abs/2308.09583.

Massey, J., V. Narayan, and E. Simperl. 2024. "How Can We Empower Data Communities in the Era of Generative AI?" Open Data Institute (blog). https://theodi.org/news-and-events/blog/how-can-we-empower-data-communities-in-the-era-of-generative-ai/.

McGrady, R., K. Zheng, R. Curran, J. Baumgartner, and E. Zuckerman. 2023. "Dialing for Videos: A Random Sample of YouTube." *Journal of Quantitative Description: Digital Media* 3.

Shrestha, Y. R., G. von Krogh, and S. Feuerriegel. 2023. "Building Open-source AI." *Nature Computational Science* 3 (11): 908–11. https://doi.org/10.1038/s43588-023-00540-0.

Shumailov, I., Z. Shumaylov, Y. Zhao, Y. Gal, N. Papernot, and R. Anderson. 2023. "The Curse of Recursion: Training on Generated Data Makes Models Forget." Preprint, last revised April 14, 2024. https://arxiv.org/abs/2305.17493.

Stephens, M., M. Esposito, R. Awamleh, T. Tse, and D. Goh. 2024. "Unraveling Open Source AI." *California Review of Management* 66 (4). https://cmr.berkeley.edu/2024/06/unraveling-open-source -ai/.

World Bank. 2021. *World Development Report 2021: Data for Better Lives.* Washington, DC: World Bank. https://doi.org/10.1596/978-1-4648-1600-0.

World Bank. 2024. *Digital Progress and Trends Report 2023.* Washington, DC: World Bank. https://openknowledge.worldbank.org/handle/10986/40970.

Zhao, L., T. C. Fong, and M. A. L. Bell. 2024. "Detection of COVID-19 Features in Lung Ultrasound Images Using Deep Neural Networks." *Communications Medicine* 4 (1): 41.

Competency: Digital Skills | 5

KEY MESSAGES

- The demand for artificial intelligence (AI) and generative AI (GenAI) skills has surged since 2021. Although primarily concentrated among information and communication technology (ICT) professionals, GenAI skills are increasingly sought in roles related to content creation, marketing, and research.

  - From 2021 to 2024, job postings requiring AI skills grew by 2 percent in high-income countries (HICs), 16 percent in upper-middle-income countries (UMICs), and 11 percent in lower-middle-income countries (LMICs). Still, only 1.5 percent of all online vacancies globally required AI skills during this period. In 2024, more than 70 percent of these postings were based in HICs.

  - Vacancies specifically requiring GenAI skills rose ninefold from 2021 to 2024, reaching 0.2 percent of all online job postings in 2024. Although demand remains concentrated in ICT professions, it is rapidly permeating into content creation, design, marketing, research and development, education, and health care.

- Significant gaps in the supply of digital and AI skills exist in lower-income countries (LICs), creating barriers to AI adoption, inclusive growth, and economic convergence across geographies.

  - Less than 5 percent of the population in LICs possess basic digital skills, compared with 21 percent in LMICs, 38 percent in UMICs, and 66 percent in HICs. Similarly, less than 15 percent of the population in LMICs have intermediate digital skills, compared with around 26 percent in UMICs and 57 percent in HICs.

  - China, India, and the United States together account for 57 percent of ICT specialists globally. Of these specialists, 53 percent reside in HICs, 29 percent in UMICs, 17 percent in LMICs, and less than 1 percent in LICs. Women represent only 24 percent of ICT specialists worldwide.

  - The supply of AI and GenAI skills largely aligns with demand, with more than one-quarter of GenAI talent concentrated among ICT professionals, along with significant shares in business, marketing, research, engineering, and teaching roles as of June 2025.

  - The number of tertiary graduates in ICT programs has expanded globally since 2000, but it remains insufficient to meet current demand. The expansion of technical and vocational education and training programs, coding bootcamps, and online courses has been notable, with GenAI course enrollments on platforms such as Coursera increasing 12-fold from 2023 to 2025. However, women make up only 30 percent of GenAI learners.

- Migration and brain drain further complicate AI development in LICs and middle-income countries.
  - Countries such as Bangladesh, Lebanon, Nigeria, and Ukraine experience outflows of digital talent that are 3–4 times higher than their inflows.
  - The brain drain challenge is especially acute for top-tier AI researchers. In 2022, 28 percent of the world's most-elite AI researchers originated from the United States, followed by 26 percent from China and 7 percent from India. However, 57 percent of these top AI researchers eventually worked in the United States.
- Governments play a crucial role in building and retaining digital talent to unlock AI's full potential.
  - Externalities and coordination failures result in underinvestment in digital skills; education systems often lag behind industry needs, firms hesitate to invest in training because of fears of poaching by competitors, and brain drain pulls top talents abroad.
  - To address these barriers, governments can integrate digital skills into formal education curricula, collaborate with educational technology providers to expand access, align training programs with labor market demands, subsidize training for underserved populations and small and medium enterprises, and implement policies to attract and retain digital talent, including streamlined visa processes.

Introduction

The rapid advancements in artificial intelligence (AI) are reshaping labor markets and raising demand for diverse digital skills related to AI usage, integration, and development. Digital transformation has already increased the demand for digital skills across economies, industries, and occupations. Now, with the rise of generative AI (GenAI), intuitive human-machine interactions are accelerating widespread AI adoption.

Consequently, digital and AI skills are no longer confined to specialized roles; they are becoming essential across three key dimensions. AI adoption demands basic digital and AI literacy to use consumer-facing tools such as ChatGPT. AI adaptation necessitates intermediate to advanced digital skills for embedding AI into business workflows. AI innovation requires highly specialized expertise in creating and refining AI models.

This chapter develops a taxonomy of digital skills to assess the supply-demand dynamics in the context of labor market transformations driven by AI, particularly with the rise of GenAI. In this chapter, digital skills are categorized into three levels: basic, intermediate, and advanced (refer to figure 5.1):

- *Basic digital skills* are essential for accessing information and services, participating in the modern workforce, and using AI-powered tools. These skills are often assumed rather than explicitly mentioned in current online job postings, reflecting their ubiquity across roles (Sostero and Tolan 2022).
- *Intermediate digital skills* are often required for most white-collar and professional jobs and are essential for integrating digital and AI tools into professional and business functions.
- *Advanced digital skills* are divided into AI skills and other advanced digital skills. *AI skills* involve developing and customizing AI algorithms and models. *Other advanced digital skills* mainly involve programming, software development, data science, cybersecurity, and so forth.

FIGURE 5.1 Classification of digital skills

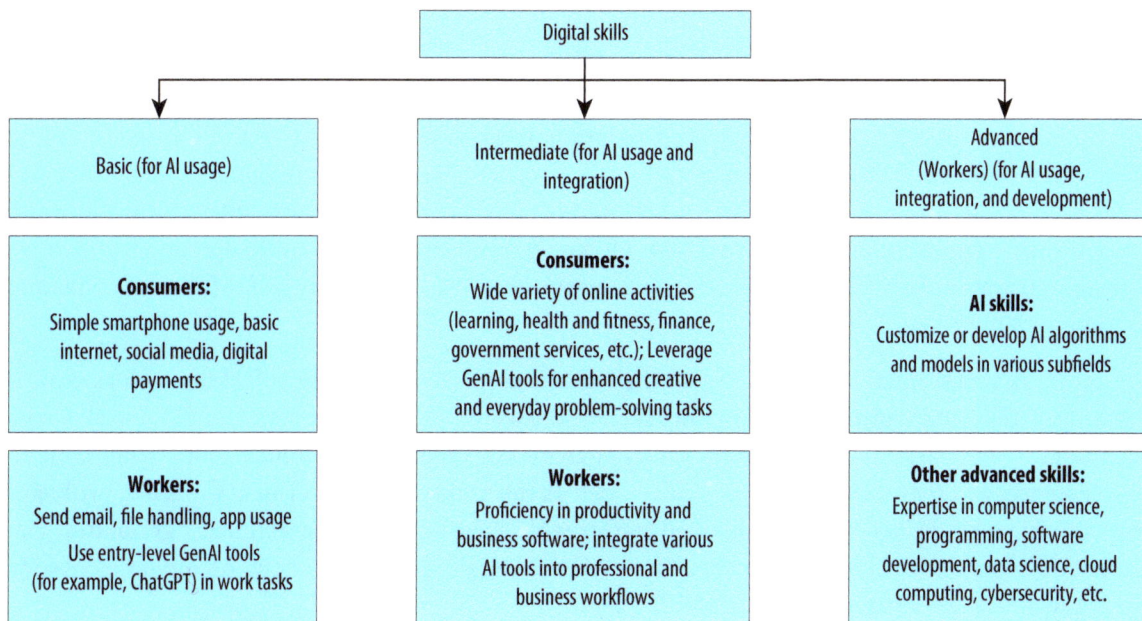

```
                              ┌─────────────────┐
                              │  Digital skills │
                              └─────────────────┘
         ┌───────────────────────────┼───────────────────────────┐
         ▼                           ▼                           ▼
┌──────────────────┐    ┌──────────────────────┐    ┌──────────────────────┐
│ Basic (for AI    │    │ Intermediate (for AI │    │ Advanced             │
│ usage)           │    │ usage and            │    │ (Workers) (for AI    │
│                  │    │ integration)         │    │ usage, integration,  │
│                  │    │                      │    │ and development)     │
└──────────────────┘    └──────────────────────┘    └──────────────────────┘
```

Basic (for AI usage)	Intermediate (for AI usage and integration)	Advanced (Workers) (for AI usage, integration, and development)
Consumers: Simple smartphone usage, basic internet, social media, digital payments	**Consumers:** Wide variety of online activities (learning, health and fitness, finance, government services, etc.); Leverage GenAI tools for enhanced creative and everyday problem-solving tasks	**AI skills:** Customize or develop AI algorithms and models in various subfields
Workers: Send email, file handling, app usage Use entry-level GenAI tools (for example, ChatGPT) in work tasks	**Workers:** Proficiency in productivity and business software; integrate various AI tools into professional and business workflows	**Other advanced skills:** Expertise in computer science, programming, software development, data science, cloud computing, cybersecurity, etc.

Source: Original figure for this publication.
Note: AI = artificial intelligence; GenAI = generative artificial intelligence.

Although digital transformation and AI advances fuel demand for digital skills, a stark global imbalance exists, posing barriers to inclusive growth and economic convergence across geographies. Many economies struggle to train a sufficiently digitally savvy workforce, particularly in developing countries, where even basic digital skills are scarce, limiting AI adoption and its potential benefits. Existing digital divides—characterized by inadequate infrastructure, limited access to digital devices, and weak educational systems—exacerbate these challenges, particularly in small communities and vulnerable populations. A few countries dominate the global demand for advanced digital skills, leading to a brain drain of digital talents in many other economies. This chapter explores the digital skills gap from both demand and supply perspectives.

The chapter is structured as follows: The "Digitalization of Occupations" section examines the growing digital transformation across occupations and the complementary skills required along with digital expertise. The "Demand for Digital Skills" section analyzes digital skills demand using job vacancy data, with a focus on AI-related skills. The "Supply of Digital Skills" section examines the supply of digital skills, and the "Policy Insights to Bridge the Digital Skills Gap" section identifies key barriers for individuals to acquire digital skills and for firms to retain digital talents in developing countries and summarizes policy trends and insights to help bridge the digital skills gap.

Digitalization of occupations

Almost all occupations have become more digitalized over the past decade, with an especially rapid increase in the previously least-digitalized roles. As digitalization transforms how people work, digital skills have become a prerequisite in most occupations.

O*NET offers comprehensive insights into the tools and technologies used across various occupations, serving as an umbrella for all available digital resources. In addition, the growing integration of AI technology into these tools has simplified complex tasks and broadened their scope of application, further transforming day-to-day workflows.

Figure 5.2 shows the usage of digital technology (refer to panel a) and digital tools (refer to panel b) across International Standard Classification of Occupations 1-digit occupations in 2015 and 2024 using O*NET data. High-skilled occupations consistently report greater usage of digital technologies and tools than medium- and low-skilled occupations.[1] Professionals hold the most-digitalized occupations, making use of more than 60 percent of all the available digital tools and 90 percent of digital technologies in 2024. However, middle- and low-skilled occupations have seen the largest increases, with their roles now requiring greater integration of digital tools and technologies in the workplace.

Digital skills are essential in the AI era, but their role is amplified by strong soft skills such as critical thinking, intellectual curiosity, communication, and teamwork, which remain fundamental across occupations. The fast pace of technological change makes specialized technical skills vulnerable to obsolescence, whereas transversal soft skills—such as the ability to learn, critical thinking, problem-solving, and adaptability—are durable and transferable across roles.[2] Postsecondary graduates who lack strong foundational and transversal skills often struggle to adapt to new job demands despite having technical expertise (World Bank 2025).

FIGURE 5.2 Exposure to digitization through the use of technologies and IT tools, by occupation, 2015 and 2024

a. Ratio of technology used compared to all available digital technologies

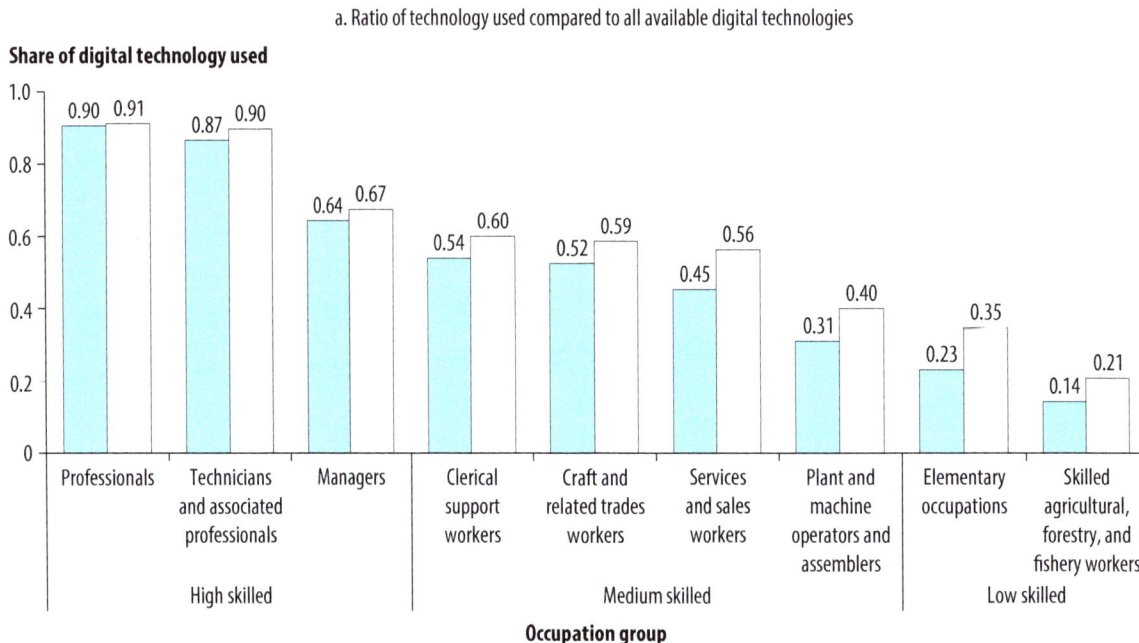

Share of digital technology used

Professionals: 0.90, 0.91
Technicians and associated professionals: 0.87, 0.90
Managers: 0.64, 0.67 — High skilled
Clerical support workers: 0.54, 0.60
Craft and related trades workers: 0.52, 0.59
Services and sales workers: 0.45, 0.56
Plant and machine operators and assemblers: 0.31, 0.40 — Medium skilled
Elementary occupations: 0.23, 0.35
Skilled agricultural, forestry, and fishery workers: 0.14, 0.21 — Low skilled

Occupation group

(Continued)

FIGURE 5.2 **Exposure to digitization through the use of technologies and IT tools, by occupation, 2015 and 2024 (*Continued*)**

b. Ratio of digital tools used compared to all available digital tools

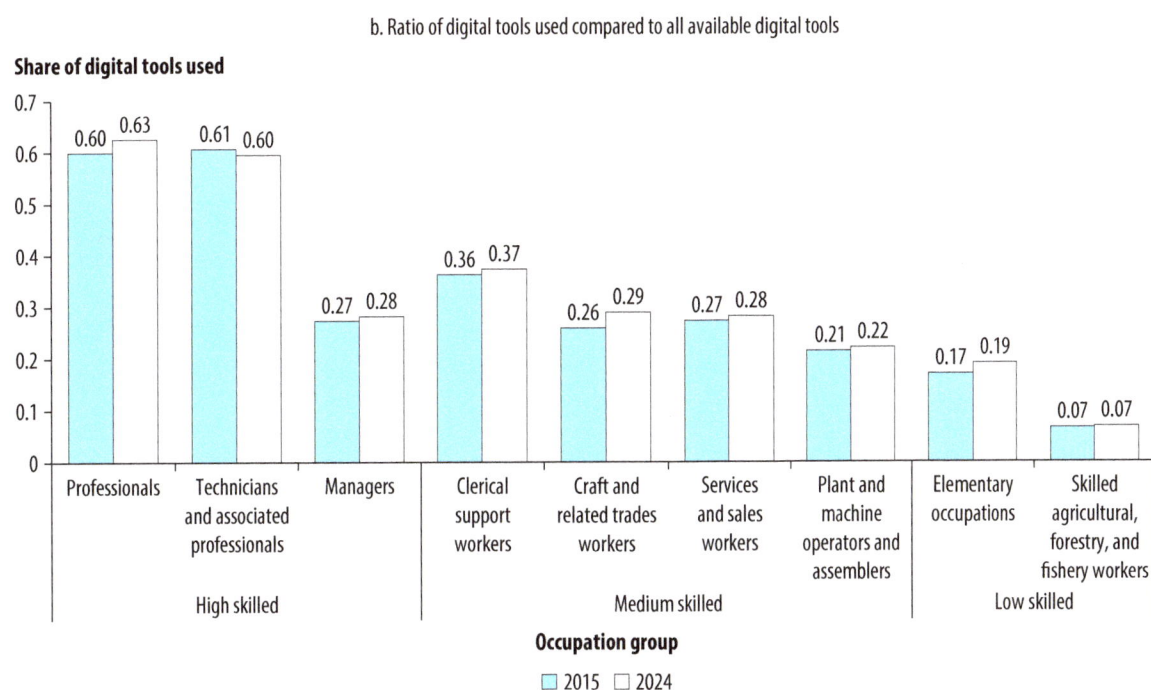

Share of digital tools used

Source: Original figures for this publication using calculations based on O*NET data (https://www.onetonline.org/).
Note: IT = information technology.

Demand for digital skills

This section uses online job posting data from Lightcast to analyze the demand for digital skills, with a focus on advanced digital skills and AI skills. Lightcast searches major job posting websites such as Glassdoor, Indeed, and LinkedIn across economies and provides real-time information on labor demand, including company names, industry affiliations, locations, job titles, job descriptions, qualifications, and other relevant details. Specifically for digital skills, the data offer detailed information on the software, programming languages, and technical competencies sought by employers, providing a level of granularity far beyond traditional labor force surveys.

However, these data have some limitations. Biases arise because of the nature of online job postings, because many roles—particularly in occupations or regions reliant on traditional hiring practices—are not advertised online. For example, nearly half of mining, shipping, and machinery manufacturing candidates in the United States still rely on local newspapers (Resources for Employers 2023; Zojceska 2019), making such roles underrepresented. Consequently, the coverage of online job postings tends to be skewed toward big cities, high-skilled industries, and white-collar occupations, reducing representativeness, especially in developing countries and for non-white-collar roles.

The reliance on English and European language-searching results in a severely incomplete picture of the job market in non-Western-language countries such as China, Japan, the Republic of Korea, and Viet Nam. In addition, the data reflect only active job openings, excluding the broader employment stock, informal sector, and freelance or gig work. Despite these limitations, Lightcast data provide timely and nuanced insights into global digital skills demand. Because low-skilled occupations are often not well-represented in Lightcast data, this chapter focuses on demand in middle- and high-skilled occupations.

Basic digital skills now serve as a minimum requirement across a broad spectrum of occupations.[3] Employers increasingly expect candidates to be proficient in operating digital devices, managing email, entering data, and leveraging social media for marketing or customer engagement. These competencies are also essential in the gig economy, where tasks such as data labeling and content moderation require platform proficiency, and location-based gig workers rely on digital tools for job matching, scheduling, and payment processing.

Intermediate and advanced digital skills are pivotal in driving productivity and fostering innovation. Intermediate digital skills, particularly proficiency in Microsoft Office and various business software applications, are highly valued in roles spanning marketing, project management, finance, professional services, and scientific research.

Demand for intermediate and advanced digital skills is concentrated in high-skilled occupations, especially in information technology (IT), professional services, finance, and insurance industries, and among information and communication technology (ICT) and business professionals, technicians, scientists, and engineers. Globally, around 27 percent and 21 percent of job postings for high-skilled occupations in 2024 required intermediate or advanced digital skills, respectively, compared with 14 percent of job postings for medium-skilled occupations.

The IT services industry is most likely to require advanced digital skills, with 60 percent of job postings requiring such skills, followed by 53 percent in professional services and 44 percent in finance and insurance. Nearly 90 percent of job postings for ICT professionals require advanced digital skills, followed by 62 percent of those for ICT technicians, 60 percent of those for science and engineering professionals, and 45 percent of those for business and administration professionals. The same pattern holds across country income groups and over time.

Global demand for advanced digital skills has fallen since mid-2022, attributed to macroeconomic headwinds, pandemic-era overhiring, and the potential influence of GenAI, with high-income countries (HICs) experiencing the steepest decline. Between 2021 and 2022, HICs witnessed a 40 percent growth in job vacancies requiring advanced digital skills, propelled by the expansion of online services in response to the coronavirus disease 2019 pandemic. Big technology firms such as Alphabet, Amazon, Apple, Meta, and Microsoft nearly doubled their head counts during this period, collectively adding around 1 million employees.

However, in HICs this rapid expansion has reversed since mid-2022. As lockdowns eased and offline activities resumed, demand for digital services slowed (Symon 2024). At the same time, the US Federal Reserve's interest rate hikes between March 2022 and July 2023 pushed borrowing costs above 5 percent, dampening overall hiring activity in the United States with knock-on effects globally (US Bureau of Labor Statistics 2024).

In addition, GenAI is changing the hiring calculus for companies. Companies are increasingly delaying or reducing hiring, opting to experiment with GenAI tools to do more with fewer employees. Increased AI spending is also diverting funds from hiring budgets (Bousquette 2024, 2025). In 2024, vacancies dropped back to nearly 2021 levels in HICs. This contraction in demand for advanced digital skills has also spilled over into other regions, underscoring the interconnectedness of the global labor market.

Demand for advanced digital skills in upper-middle-income countries (UMICs) peaked in 2023 and declined in 2024 but remained well above the 2021 level, whereas demand in lower-middle-income countries (LMICs) remained stable except for an uptick in 2023. UMICs saw a significant surge, with advanced digital skills vacancies doubling between 2021 and 2023, outpacing overall vacancy growth. Although a slight decline occurred in 2024, demand remained 66 percent above 2021 levels. Notably, Brazil and Indonesia experienced a tripling of demand from 2021 to 2024, and Colombia, Malaysia, Mexico, and Serbia nearly doubled their demand.

In LMICs, demand for advanced digital skills rose in 2023 but returned to 2021 levels in 2024, whereas other vacancies grew faster. This trend was largely driven by India, where demand contracted by 30 percent in 2024 after a 2023 increase. Conversely, Kenya, Nigeria, and the Philippines saw a tripling of vacancies by mid-2023, maintaining levels above those of early 2021 despite recent moderate declines.

These demand fluctuations reflect a complex interplay of factors. Initial increases likely resulted from enhanced online labor market data coverage, capturing previously underreported positions. The 2024 decline may indicate spillover effects from weakening demand in HICs and the nascent impact of GenAI.

A notable trend across all income groups is the accelerated demand for advanced digital skills in medium-skilled occupations, outpacing growth in high-skilled occupations. This suggests that digitalization is increasingly transforming the nature of work for previously less-digitalized roles. In HICs, the most-pronounced increase in demand for advanced digital skills was observed among personal service workers, drivers and mobile plant operators, and sales workers. In middle-income countries (MICs), sales workers, customer service clerks, and numerical and material recording clerks experienced the fastest growth in demand for advanced digital skills, reflecting the upskilling trends within the business process outsourcing sector.

HICs consistently drive the global demand for AI skills, excluding GenAI, accounting for roughly 70 percent of all AI vacancies from 2021 to 2024. Global demand has held steady at about 1.7 million annual vacancies, consistently representing around 1.5 percent of total vacancies. HICs, particularly the United States, led a notable surge in 2022. However, AI vacancies have declined since late 2022, following a trend similar to that for advanced digital skills (refer to figure 5.3, panel a). Despite this, the United States still represents 40 percent of all AI vacancies in HICs in 2024. Interestingly, although US AI vacancies decreased by 9 percent between 2021 and 2024, they nearly doubled in Canada, France, Italy, and Japan.

Demand for AI skills, excluding GenAI, in UMICs and LMICs also saw a cool down after 2022 and 2023, although 2024 demand remained above 2021 levels. Brazil, China, Colombia, Malaysia, and Mexico all recorded brisk growth. In UMICs, AI vacancies grew by 16 percent from 2021 to 2024, reaching 225,000 in 2024. In China, vacancies for natural language processing surged by 111 percent in the first half of 2024 compared with the same period in 2023, followed by a 76-percent growth in AI for robotics, a 61-percent growth in deep learning, and a 49-percent growth in autonomous driving (*China Youth Daily* 2024). Brazil recorded around 56,000 AI vacancies in 2024, nearly tripling its 2021 level. Demand also tripled in Indonesia and doubled in Colombia, Malaysia, and Mexico.

Among LMICs, India maintained a stable AI skills demand, consistently hovering around 230,000 vacancies every year. From 2021 to 2024, AI vacancies doubled in the Arab Republic of Egypt, Pakistan, and the Philippines. Demand grew fourfold in Kenya, albeit from a very low base.

The IT industry is most likely to require AI skills across countries, followed by professional services and finance. The IT industry demonstrates the highest probability of AI skills demand across most countries, with around 8 percent of IT industry job postings requiring AI skills globally in 2024. Professional services and finance are the other top industries that require AI skills, with about 4–5 percent of job postings requiring such competencies. Managers and professionals in manufacturing are also increasingly expected to possess AI skills. AI skills are less required in the agriculture industry. In occupations, software developers, database designers and administrators, mathematicians, and physicists are most likely to require AI skills, with more than 10 percent of vacancies requiring them.

FIGURE 5.3 Trends in AI and GenAI skills demand across country income groups, 2021–24

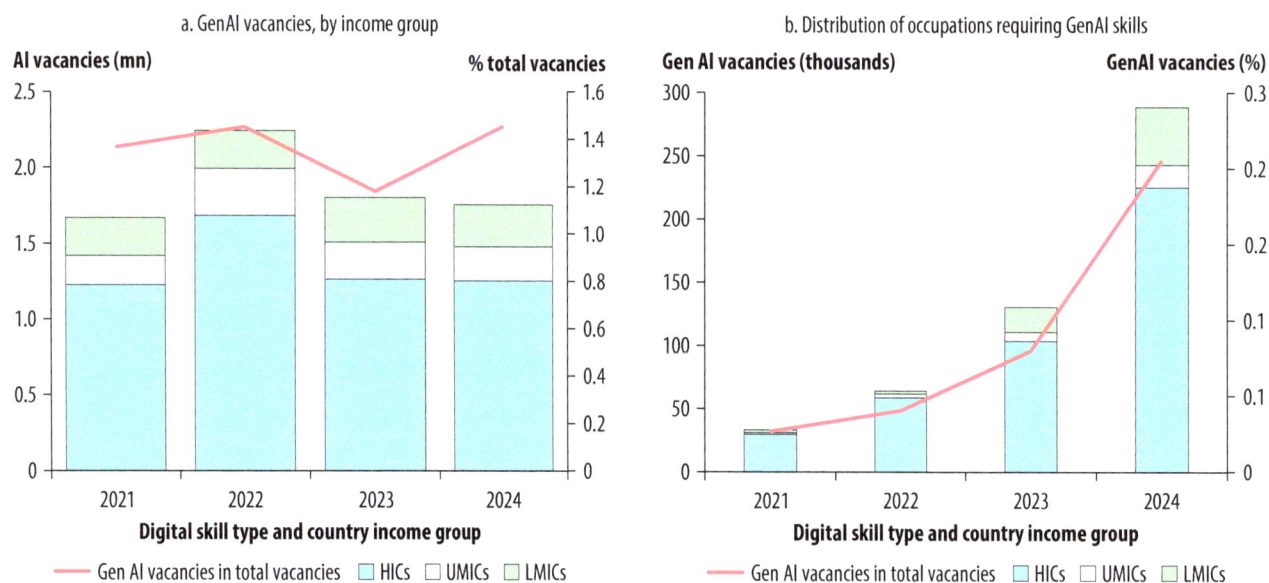

a. GenAI vacancies, by income group

b. Distribution of occupations requiring GenAI skills

Source: Original figures for this publication using computations based on Lightcast data (https://lightcast.io/).

Note: Data for UMICs is severely underestimated due to extremely limited coverage in China. GenAI = generative artificial intelligence; HICs = high-income countries; ICT = information and communication technology; IT = information technology; LMICs = lower-middle-income countries; UMICs = upper-middle-income countries.

AI vacancies stand out for their significantly higher demand for advanced degrees compared with other advanced digital skills roles. In 2024, 51 percent of global AI vacancies required at least a master's degree, a stark contrast to the 27 percent of vacancies demanding advanced digital skills without an AI component. This clearly indicates a higher skill threshold and greater technical specialization for AI roles. The gap is even more pronounced at the doctoral level, with more than 7 percent of AI vacancies requiring a PhD, compared with just 1 percent for other advanced digital skills positions.

Vacancies requiring GenAI skills surged ninefold globally from 2021 to 2024 as companies raced to develop and deploy GenAI solutions (refer to figure 5.3, panel b).[4] Before the release of Chat GPT, GenAI vacancies almost exclusively stemmed from HICs, with a focus on developing GenAI models. After GenAI tools became publicly available, demand shifted toward skills to integrate and use GenAI. GenAI skills also command substantial wage premiums. GenAI development skills are associated with a 7–9 percent wage increase in technical roles, while GenAI literacy skills yield a 25–36 percent premium in nontechnical white-collar roles (Martins Neto et al. 2025).

France and the United States accounted for nearly half of global GenAI vacancies in 2024, excluding China. The United States recorded nearly 84,000 vacancies requiring GenAI skills in 2024, up from 3,000 in 2021, representing 30 percent of global GenAI vacancies. France posted around 53,000 GenAI vacancies in 2024, accounting for another 18 percent of global vacancies, far ahead of other HICs. French start-up Mistral AI has quickly ascended as a notable player in the global GenAI arena and stimulated demand for local GenAI vacancies. Germany and the United Kingdom recorded about 16,000 and 12,000 GenAI vacancies in 2024, respectively.

Among MICs, Brazil, China, India, Malaysia, Mexico, and the Philippines have been leading the surge in GenAI vacancies. Before the release of ChatGPT, UMICs registered fewer than 3,000 GenAI vacancies, but by 2024, vacancies had soared sixfold to nearly 18,000, largely excluding China.

LMICs experienced a 23-fold increase, reaching around 46,000 vacancies by 2024 (refer to figure 5.3, panel b). India experienced a near 22-fold growth in GenAI vacancies between 2021 and 2024, contributing 80 percent of all GenAI vacancies among LMICs. Notably, Brazil and the Philippines saw the most-remarkable expansion, with 82-fold and 115-fold increases, respectively, from 2021 to 2024, significantly propelling growth in East Asia and Pacific (EAP) and Latin America and the Caribbean. Beyond the leading nations, Colombia, Malaysia, Mexico, Pakistan, and South Africa all recorded more than 1,000 GenAI vacancies in 2024, indicating rapid global diffusion of GenAI across major emerging markets.

The data for UMICs and EAP are grossly underestimated because of incomplete data for China. Various GenAI-related vacancies have surged in China, ranging from large language model (LLM) engineers and prompt engineers to GenAI application developers and users across industries. It is estimated that vacancies requiring GenAI skills will exceed 1 million in China by the end of 2025 ("AI Large Language Model-Driven Career Change" 2025).

GenAI vacancies primarily target ICT professionals, particularly in MICs. HICs exhibit a broader occupational distribution, including a notable presence of teaching and health professionals. In HICs, ICT professionals made up 41 percent of all GenAI vacancies in 2024 (refer to figure 5.4, panel a), suggesting that firms are hiring ICT professionals to develop and customize GenAI solutions across industries. In MICs, ICT professionals dominate, accounting for around 60 percent of all GenAI vacancies.

Software developers and systems analysts are most likely to require GenAI skills, with 2–3 percent of global vacancies requiring GenAI skills in 2024. The more even occupational distribution in HICs reflects their rapid adoption and broader integration of GenAI. Business and administrative professionals and administrative and commercial managers are the other two top occupations among GenAI vacancies across income groups, accounting for 10 percent and 7 percent of GenAI vacancies, respectively. Notably, teaching professionals and health professionals each constitute 5–6 percent of GenAI vacancies in HICs but are nearly absent in UMICs and LMICs. This disparity suggests limited integration of GenAI in education and health care in MICs.

FIGURE 5.4 **Top occupations requiring GenAI skills, 2024**

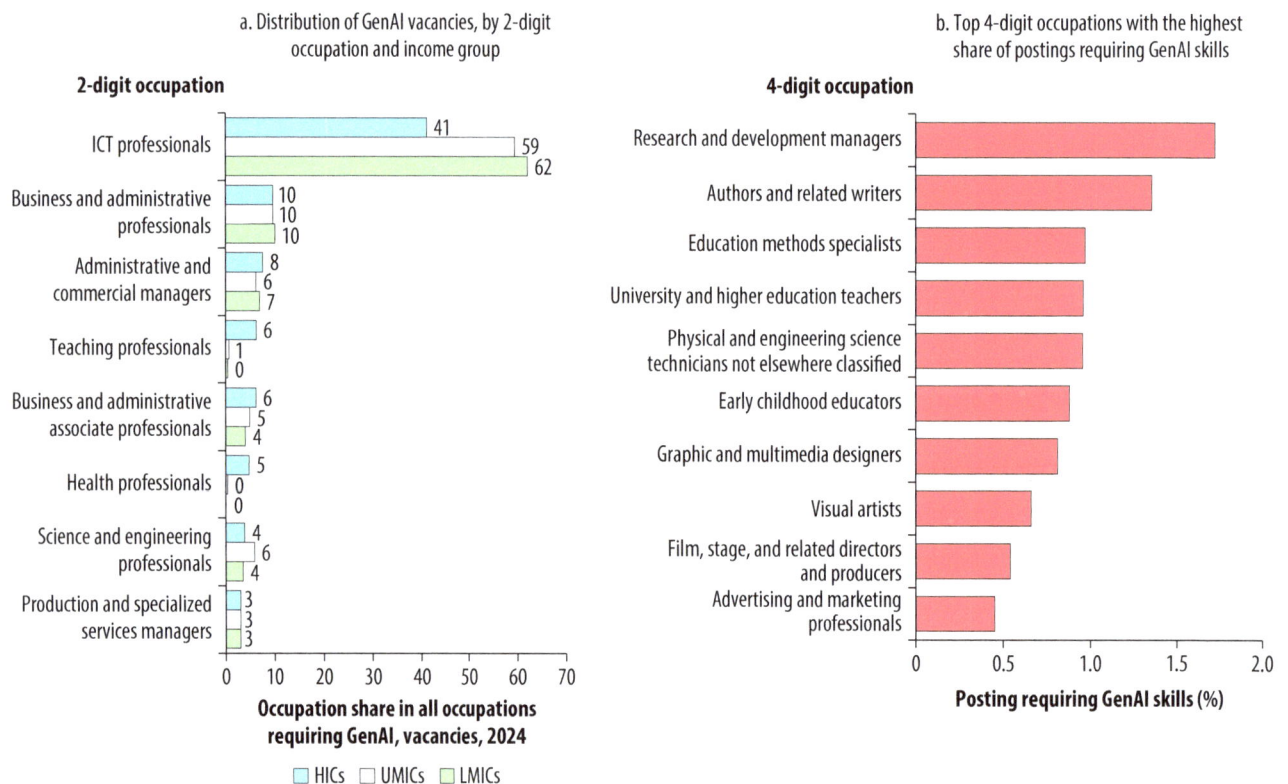

a. Distribution of GenAI vacancies, by 2-digit occupation and income group

b. Top 4-digit occupations with the highest share of postings requiring GenAI skills

Source: Original figures for this publication using computations based on Lightcast data (https://lightcast.io/).

Note: Data for UMICs is severely underestimated due to extremely limited coverage in China. GenAI = generative artificial intelligence; HICs = high-income countries; ICT = information and communication technology; IT = information technology; LMICs = lower-middle-income countries; UMICs = upper-middle-income countries.

The demand for GenAI skills is rapidly extending beyond ICT occupations, permeating research and development (R&D), content creation, design, marketing, and education. Occupations in these areas increasingly require GenAI skills. Globally, R&D managers, authors and writers, education methods specialists, university teachers, graphic and multimedia designers, visual artists, film directors, and advertising and marketing professionals are among the top non-ICT occupations that were most likely to require GenAI skills in 2024, with around 0.5–2 percent of job postings requiring these skills (refer to figure 5.4, panel b). The actual demand is likely much higher because such skills are assumed rather than explicitly listed in job postings.

Despite the rapid expansion, GenAI is still in the early stages of affecting the labor market. It has created new occupations, such as prompt engineers and LLM engineers, but these jobs total only a few thousand globally and have a limited effect on overall job creation. Despite the rapid increase in GenAI vacancies, they accounted for only 0.2 percent of all job postings globally in 2024. Furthermore, GenAI has shown no discernible impact on worker earnings or recorded hours across any occupation, even among those most highly exposed, suggesting its overall labor market effects remain minimal so far (Humlum and Vestergaard 2025).

Supply of digital skills

Although surging demand for digital and AI skills has driven rapid expansion in supply, gaps remain because of rapid technological advances, specialized and evolving skills requirements, outdated curricula, competition for talent and brain drain, infrastructure, and access disparities. This section analyzes the availability of digital skills across countries and examines supply through both formal education and alternative learning pathways.

A significant digital skills gap persists between rich and poor countries across all proficiency levels. Even basic digital skills are notably scarce in low-income countries (LICs), with less than 5 percent of the population possessing them, compared with 21 percent in LMICs, 38 percent in UMICs, and 66 percent in HICs (refer to figure 5.5, panel a). Less than 15 percent of the population of LMICs have intermediate digital skills, compared with around 26 percent in UMICs and 57 percent in HICs.

Advanced digital skills are limited globally, with approximately 1 in 10 people in HICs proficient in them. In LICs, this figure falls below 1 percent. Gender and urban-rural gaps deepen for more advanced digital skills, especially in LICs, where the share of individuals with advanced digital skills is 5 times higher in urban areas than in rural areas. In HICs, gender disparities are modest for basic and intermediate digital skills but widen for advanced digital skills. Urban-rural gaps in HICs also grow with skill levels. In LMICs, the median gender gap begins at 1.21 for basic skills and reaches 1.52 for advanced skills. Urban-rural gaps are more pronounced, soaring to 5.30 for advanced digital skills, indicating a significant concentration of advanced digital skills in urban areas.

UMICs show moderate disparities, with gender gaps rising from 1.05 males per female for basic skills to 1.47 males per female for advanced digital skills, and urban-rural gaps increase from 1.88 to 2.70 urban residents per rural resident for advanced skills (refer to figure 5.5, panel b). These findings highlight the need for targeted interventions to improve digital skills among women and rural populations, particularly in developing countries, to address these persistent inequalities.

FIGURE 5.5 **Supply of digital skills, 2023**

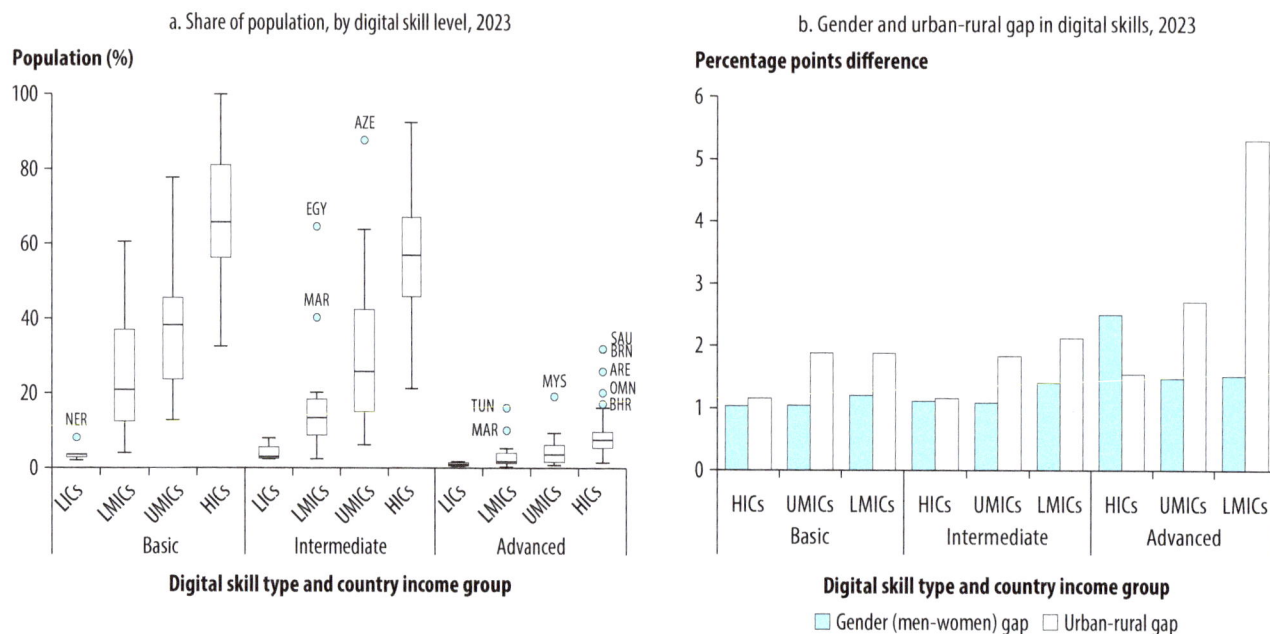

a. Share of population, by digital skill level, 2023

b. Gender and urban-rural gap in digital skills, 2023

Source: Original figures for this publication using data from the International Telecommunication Union (https://www.itu.int/en/ITU-D/Statistics /Documents/intlcoop/sdgs/2025%20SDG%204.4.1_REV.xlsx).
Note: For panel a, data include 5 countries in LICs, 16 in LMICs, 31 in UMICs, and 49 in HICs. For panel b, gender gap data include 11 countries for LMICs, 27 for UMICs, and 46 for HICs; for the urban-rural gap, data include 11 countries for LMICs, 20 for UMICs, and 23 for HICs. Bars indicate minimum and maximum of distribution; dots are outliers. For a list of country codes, refer to https://www.iso.org/obp/ui/#search. HICs = high-income countries; LICs = low-income countries; LMICs = lower-middle-income countries; UMICs = upper-middle-income countries.

The availability of ICT specialists is heavily concentrated in a few countries, with China (21 percent), the United States (21 percent), and India (15 percent) leading, followed by the United Kingdom (5 percent), the Russian Federation (5 percent), and Germany (4 percent) as of 2023. LICs account for less than 1 percent of ICT specialists. ICT specialists also are predominantly male. Switzerland has the highest gender disparity, with a male-to-female ratio of 5.84, followed by Belgium, the Netherlands, Russia, Germany, and Italy, all of which have a ratio above 4.5. Several MICs have a more gender-balanced ICT specialist workforce. The male-to-female ratio among ICT specialists is 1.9 in the Philippines, 2.3 in China, and 2.8 in India.

Responding to rising demand, the proportion of graduates in ICT programs has consistently increased across all income groups since 2010. Despite the rapid expansion of ICT programs, universities struggle to meet the growing demand because of faculty recruitment difficulties, capacity constraints, and curriculum gaps. In Canada and the United States, the number of computer science graduates has tripled, rising from approximately 18,000 in 2010 to 52,000 in 2022. Bachelor's-degree graduates quadrupled from 9,000 to 36,000, master's-degree graduates doubled from 7,000 to 14,000, and PhD graduates saw only marginal growth, increasing from 1,800 to 2,100 (Thormundsson 2025). However, these numbers have fallen short of surging demand.

Universities face several challenges in scaling up ICT programs rapidly. Recruiting qualified faculty is a major challenge, because top-tier professionals often find industry roles far more financially rewarding than academic positions. Expanding ICT programs also requires substantial investment in infrastructure, such as dormitories, classrooms, computer labs, and campus facilities, which cannot be scaled up quickly. Universities also face challenges in staying current with rapid technological advancements. For example, a survey of universities in Africa found that 40 percent have not updated their ICT curricula in more than 5 years, and 3 percent have never done so (World Bank forthcoming). These issues have resulted in a mismatch between the skills graduates possess and the skills employers require.

These challenges are even more acute in LICs, where infrastructure and device access gaps further compound the problem. Limited availability of reliable internet, computers, and AI labs significantly hinders the development of digital skills. Although general computer labs are common in African universities, fewer than 30 percent of institutions have specialized facilities for AI, data science, or computer-aided design (World Bank forthcoming). Moreover, many computer science students in LICs cannot afford personal computers, severely restricting their ability to practice programming and deepen their technical expertise.

Online education has emerged as a critical avenue for acquiring digital skills, driven by its accessibility, affordability, and flexibility compared with traditional university education. These platforms offer high-quality courses from top institutions and industry leaders, often at a fraction of the cost of a university degree. Learners can acquire in-demand skills such as programming, data science, and AI on their own schedules, making online education appealing to working professionals and those in regions with limited access to quality universities. Unlike traditional degrees, which may take years to complete and often lag behind industry trends, online courses are frequently updated to reflect the latest technological advancements. Many platforms also provide hands-on projects, industry-recognized certifications, and pathways to employment, making them a more practical and responsive alternative for acquiring digital skills in today's fast-evolving job market.

A growing share of workers now enroll in online courses, but online learning remains underused by women, especially in science, technology, engineering, and mathematics (STEM) and GenAI courses. As of April 2025, global Coursera learners exceeded 170 million, representing 5 percent of the global workforce. The number of female learners has grown rapidly, reaching 46 percent of users in 2024, up from 43 percent in 2023 (Coursera Global Skills Report 2024). However, the share of female learners in STEM (34 percent) and GenAI (30 percent) courses significantly trails the overall share of female learners.

GenAI courses have seen explosive growth, with enrollments on Coursera skyrocketing 12-fold since the launch of ChatGPT in late 2022 (Coursera 2024, 2025). By April 2025, Coursera had recorded more than 8 million GenAI enrollments across its catalogue of nearly 700 GenAI courses. This surge reflects a global race toward AI literacy and adoption. According to Coursera's 2025 survey, 75 percent of employers prefer hiring less experienced candidates with GenAI skills over more experienced ones without such capabilities.

Workers in richer countries are more likely to report AI and GenAI skills, although interesting patterns emerge across educational attainment. As of June 2025, AI skill availability generally increases with education: Around 1 percent of workers without a bachelor's degree report AI skills, rising to 3 percent for those with a bachelor's degree, 6 percent for those with a master's degree, and 8 percent for those with a doctorate (refer to figure 5.6, panel a). Although PhD holders are most likely to possess AI skills across all income groups, those with master's degrees are most likely to report GenAI skills (0.4–1.4 percent across income groups; refer to figure 5.6, panel b), suggesting that GenAI has lowered the barrier to AI adoption and is increasingly being used by professionals.

FIGURE 5.6 **Share of workers with AI and GenAI skills, by educational attainment, 2024**

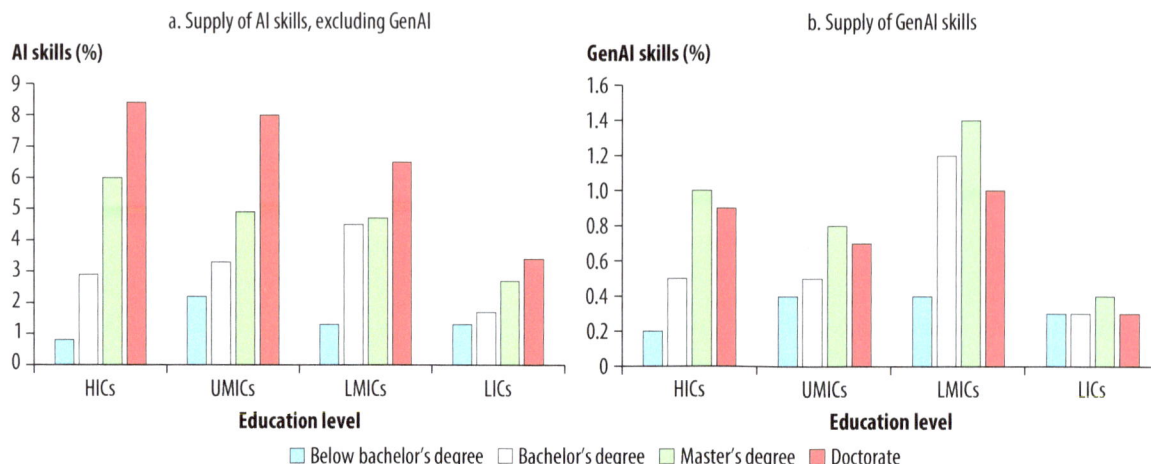

a. Supply of AI skills, excluding GenAI

b. Supply of GenAI skills

Below bachelor's degree Bachelor's degree Master's degree Doctorate

Source: Original figures for this publication using calculations based on data from Lightcast (https://lightcast.io/).
Note: AI = artificial intelligence; GenAI = generative artificial intelligence; HICs = high-income countries; LICs = low-income countries; LMICs = lower-middle-income countries; UMICs = upper-middle-income countries.

However, workers are significantly less likely to claim GenAI skills overall. Notably, workers in LMICs report GenAI skills more frequently than those in UMICs and HICs; this is largely attributable to sample bias, because a more elite segment of the workforce in poorer countries typically uses LinkedIn.

The supply of GenAI skills largely mirrors demand, being concentrated among ICT professionals, followed by administrative and commercial managers and business and administrative professionals across all country income groups. As of June 2025, an analysis of nearly 400 million individual career profiles globally revealed that one-quarter of all users claiming GenAI skills in HICs are ICT professionals. This share rises to one-third in LMICs (refer to figure 5.7, panel a).

The top five broad occupations in which GenAI skills are concentrated include administrative and commercial managers, business and administrative professionals, chief executives, and production and specialized services managers, dovetailing with demand patterns. Among non-ICT occupations, GenAI skills are most likely claimed by R&D managers, policy and planning managers, management and organizational analysts, survey and market research interviewers, human resources professionals, engineers, and advertising and marketing professionals (refer to figure 5.7, panel b). However, GenAI skill penetration in these roles remains low, typically ranging from 0.5 percent to 1.5 percent of all profiles. This limited uptake, even among highly exposed occupations, corroborates earlier findings that GenAI adoption is still in its nascent stages and has had minimal impact on skills demand and supply to date.

FIGURE 5.7 **Top occupations in which workers are most likely to have GenAI skills, 2024**

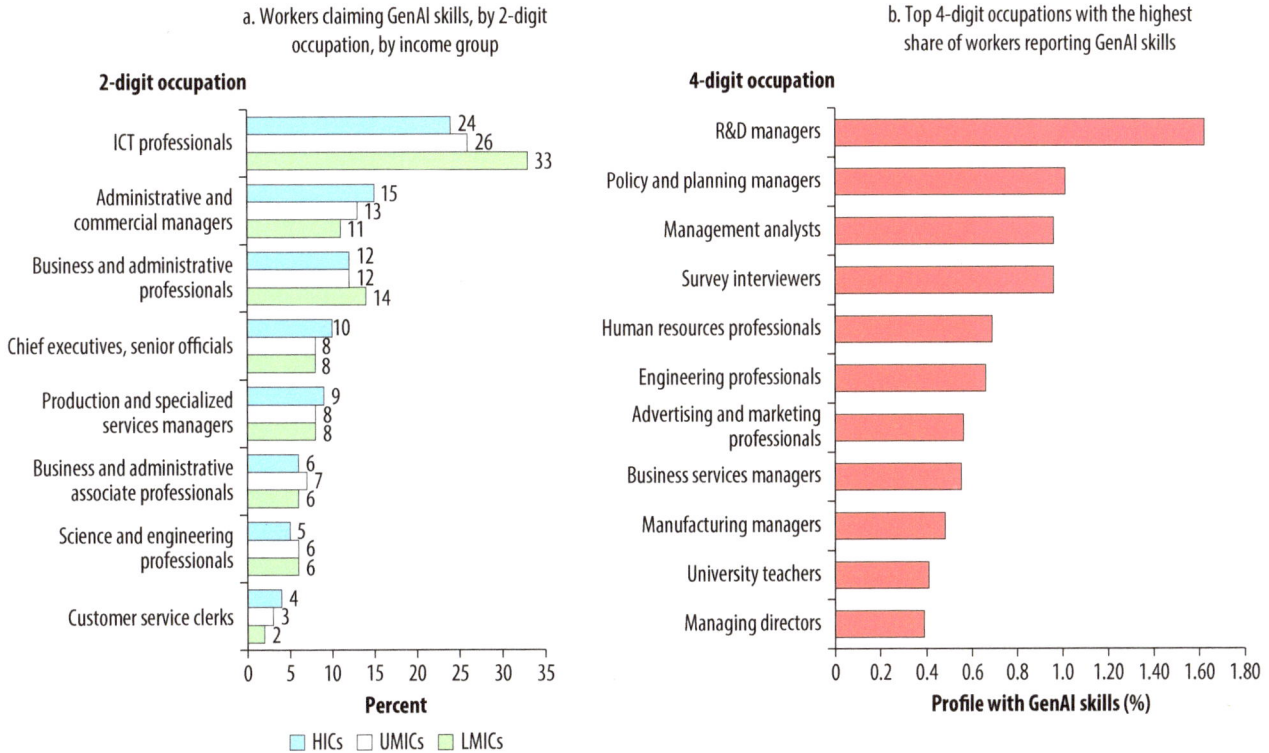

a. Workers claiming GenAI skills, by 2-digit occupation, by income group

b. Top 4-digit occupations with the highest share of workers reporting GenAI skills

2-digit occupation

Occupation	HICs	UMICs	LMICs
ICT professionals	24	26	33
Administrative and commercial managers	15	13	11
Business and administrative professionals	12	12	14
Chief executives, senior officials	10	8	8
Production and specialized services managers	9	8	8
Business and administrative associate professionals	6	7	6
Science and engineering professionals	5	6	6
Customer service clerks	4	3	2

Percent (0, 5, 10, 15, 20, 25, 30, 35)

☐ HICs ☐ UMICs ☐ LMICs

4-digit occupation

Profile with GenAI skills (%) (0, 0.2, 0.4, 0.6, 0.8, 1.0, 1.20, 1.40, 1.60, 1.80)

- R&D managers
- Policy and planning managers
- Management analysts
- Survey interviewers
- Human resources professionals
- Engineering professionals
- Advertising and marketing professionals
- Business services managers
- Manufacturing managers
- University teachers
- Managing directors

Source: Original figures for this publication using calculations based on data from Lightcast (https://lightcast.io/).

Note: AI = artificial intelligence; GenAI = generative artificial intelligence; HICs = high-income countries; ICT = information and communication technology; LMICs = lower-middle-income countries; R&D = research and development; UMICs = upper-middle-income countries.

Highly skilled digital talents enjoy global mobility and often move across borders to seek better job opportunities. This has advantaged HICs while accelerating brain drain in developing countries. LinkedIn data show that in Bangladesh, Lebanon, Nigeria, and Ukraine, talent outflows are 3–4 times higher than inflows. Argentina, Brazil, Colombia, India, Morocco, Pakistan, and South Africa follow with a ratio of outflow to inflow between 2 and 3 times (refer to figure 5.8, panel a). In contrast, countries such as Australia, Canada, and Cyprus attract high-skilled workers at least twice the rate of those leaving. Poland, Portugal, and Switzerland also attract a substantial share of skilled professionals (refer to figure 5.8, panel b).

The United States remains the world's premier destination for AI talents, benefiting from a significant brain gain, particularly from China and India. On the basis of Macro Polo's Global AI Talent Tracker, 28 percent of the most-elite AI researchers globally in 2022 originated from the United States, followed by 26 percent from China and 7 percent from India. However, 57 percent of the top AI researchers eventually work in the United States, followed by 12 percent in China and almost none in India. The pattern highlights both the strength of US academic and research institutions in cultivating AI expertise and the country's ability to offer attractive career opportunities in both academia and industry, underlining the inherent winner-takes-all dynamic of the technology sector. This sustained ability to attract and retain top global AI talent has been instrumental in maintaining US technological leadership and economic competitiveness in the rapidly evolving field.

FIGURE 5.8 **Cross-border migration of high-skilled talent, 2022**

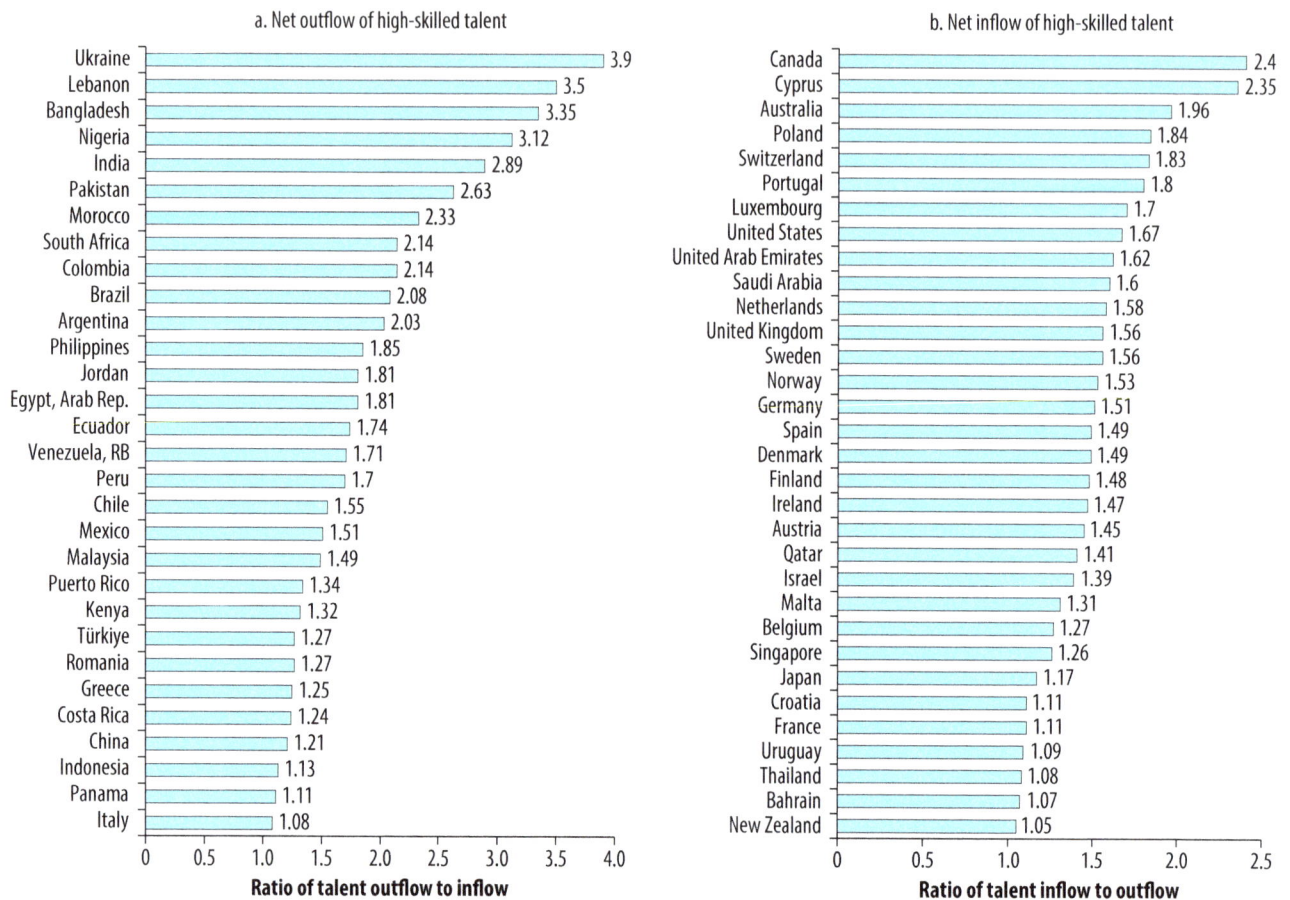

a. Net outflow of high-skilled talent

Country	Ratio of talent outflow to inflow
Ukraine	3.9
Lebanon	3.5
Bangladesh	3.35
Nigeria	3.12
India	2.89
Pakistan	2.63
Morocco	2.33
South Africa	2.14
Colombia	2.14
Brazil	2.08
Argentina	2.03
Philippines	1.85
Jordan	1.81
Egypt, Arab Rep.	1.81
Ecuador	1.74
Venezuela, RB	1.71
Peru	1.7
Chile	1.55
Mexico	1.51
Malaysia	1.49
Puerto Rico	1.34
Kenya	1.32
Türkiye	1.27
Romania	1.27
Greece	1.25
Costa Rica	1.24
China	1.21
Indonesia	1.13
Panama	1.11
Italy	1.08

b. Net inflow of high-skilled talent

Country	Ratio of talent inflow to outflow
Canada	2.4
Cyprus	2.35
Australia	1.96
Poland	1.84
Switzerland	1.83
Portugal	1.8
Luxembourg	1.7
United States	1.67
United Arab Emirates	1.62
Saudi Arabia	1.6
Netherlands	1.58
United Kingdom	1.56
Sweden	1.56
Norway	1.53
Germany	1.51
Spain	1.49
Denmark	1.49
Finland	1.48
Ireland	1.47
Austria	1.45
Qatar	1.41
Israel	1.39
Malta	1.31
Belgium	1.27
Singapore	1.26
Japan	1.17
Croatia	1.11
France	1.11
Uruguay	1.09
Thailand	1.08
Bahrain	1.07
New Zealand	1.05

Source: Original figures for this publication using data from LinkedIn (data development partnership, https://datapartnership.org/about/).

In contrast, Europe tends to have a weaker draw on top AI talents and to lose its most-elite AI talents to the United States (Pal 2024). Most of the top-tier AI talents in Europe end up working for US companies with a major presence in Europe (Macro Polo n.d.). Nonetheless, China, India, and several European countries have improved the attraction and retention of their domestic AI talents in recent years.

Policy insights to bridge the digital skills gap

Developing countries face significant market failures and barriers in cultivating and retaining digital talent, limiting their ability to participate in the digital economy and benefit from AI. Limited access to high-speed internet, modern computing infrastructure, and AI labs restricts hands-on learning opportunities. Another challenge is the lack of quality education and training programs aligned with industry needs, often resulting from weak coordination between universities and the private sector. In addition, high training costs and credit constraints prevent many individuals from acquiring digital skills, and firms underinvest in employee training because of fears of poaching by competitors.

Financial constraints, lower education levels, and sociocultural norms restrict women's access to technology and training, reinforcing gender inequality in digital skills development. Even when talent is developed, brain drain remains a persistent issue, as skilled professionals seek higher wages and better career opportunities abroad. These barriers create a vicious cycle in which a shortage of skilled workers discourages investment in the digital sector, further limiting opportunities for talent development and retention.

Governments in developing countries could consider the following actions to address the digital skills gap. Countries with low AI readiness can target interventions to improve device access and ownership. Governments can reduce taxes on digital devices, introduce targeted subsidies, and partner with device manufacturers and internet services providers to explore innovative financing schemes to promote device access and ownership.

Governments can enhance digital literacy and basic skills for AI use by doing the following:

- *Embedding basic digital skills content into compulsory education.*
- *Encouraging online content generators to teach basic digital skills,* especially for marginalized populations.
- *Tailoring initiatives to local contexts.* For example, the Saya Digital initiative in Malaysia uses native languages and addresses local challenges, enhancing its accessibility and impact.
- *Incorporating critical thinking and communication skills into education.* Overreliance on AI-generated responses may reduce cognitive engagement, leading to intellectual laziness. Digital literacy programs should integrate training on effective questioning, evaluating AI-generated content, and fostering independent problem-solving.

Countries with medium AI readiness can strengthen intermediate and advanced digital skills training and workforce readiness by doing the following:

- *Make digital training more affordable for small and medium enterprises (SMEs).* SMEs often lack the resources to train employees in digital skills, affecting their productivity and competitiveness. Public investment, complemented by industry association support, can fund upskilling programs, ensuring that SME workers gain essential competencies.
- *Address the shortage of digital skills instructors.* Expanding faculty training and incentivizing careers in digital education can improve instruction quality.
- *Promote industry-specific training to address sectoral skills shortages.* Partnerships between industry and educational institutions can help ensure that the training provided aligns with ever-changing market needs. Models such as Korea's Meister schools, which focus on aligning vocational training with labor market requirements, offer valuable lessons for replication.
- *Introduce a framework for regular curriculum updates across education systems.* In a rapidly evolving technological landscape, periodic assessments of digital skills demand and supply are essential. These diagnostics enable policy makers to identify skills gaps, project future needs, and design responsive education and training programs. Such initiatives can improve labor market matching efficiency, reducing unemployment and underemployment by equipping workers with relevant competencies. For example, Singapore's SkillsFuture program leverages big data analytics and industry consultations to update training frameworks swiftly, avoiding delays associated with long-term studies.

- *Ensure quality assurance for AI tools used in education.* Many AI-powered learning platforms operate with proprietary models, raising concerns over accuracy, biases, and long-term skills development. Public oversight and transparent certification processes can ensure AI tools align with educational best practices.

Countries with high AI readiness can support access to AI infrastructure and training data for universities, researchers, and AI start-ups for AI research, innovation, and commercialization. AI research is increasingly dominated by industry instead of academia because state-of-the-art AI models increasingly require vast compute and extensive data sets that universities lack. Empowering universities to remain at the forefront of AI research will be key to realizing AI's long-term potential. Similarly, AI start-ups may also lack access to compute and training data to effectively compete with established giants. Governments can provide targeted subsidies to facilitate access to high-performing computing resources for domestic AI researchers and start-ups.

Investment in cutting-edge AI skills and research capabilities can generate significant positive spillovers. The positive externality of such investments justifies government intervention. Governments can partner with leading technology companies and prestigious universities to offer highly specialized AI courses and training programs in university curricula, especially in PhD programs. Governments can also provide scholarships for AI-related degrees.

To retain and attract digital talent, countries with high AI readiness can do the following:

- *Enhance retention strategies to address brain drain.* Offering competitive salaries in public research institutions, research grants, tax incentives, and career development opportunities could incentivize skilled workers to stay. For instance, China's Thousand Talents Plan has successfully brought back Chinese researchers by offering high salaries, research funding, and leadership roles in AI and semiconductor research, strengthening its innovation ecosystem.

- *Streamline work visas and issue digital nomad visas to help attract foreign digital talents.* Governments can offer streamlined visas, research grants, and tax incentives for AI experts and entrepreneurs, as well as foster international collaborations and AI hubs that position the country as a competitive AI destination.

Addressing the skills gap and safeguarding workers in the age of AI is a complex challenge that requires a multifaceted policy approach. By implementing regular skills assessments; investing in digital infrastructure; enhancing critical thinking, communication, and self-learning skills; and supporting continuous, lifelong learning and reskilling initiatives, countries can create an environment in which both businesses and workers thrive. These strategies not only improve market matching efficiency and empower low-skilled workers but also bolster SMEs and promote inclusive economic growth.

Notes

1. The chapter classifies the 9 broad ISCO occupations into 3 skill levels: (1) *high-skilled occupations* include managers, professionals, technicians, and associate professionals; (2) *middle-skilled occupations* include clerical support workers, services and sales workers, plant and machine operators and assemblers, and craft and related trade workers; and (3) *low-skilled occupations* include skilled agricultural, forestry, and fishery workers and other elementary occupations such as cleaners and domestic helpers.

2. *Transversal soft skills* refer to core competencies that apply across various industries and functions, enabling workers to adapt, collaborate, and resolve challenges effectively.

3. Each job posting in the data set lists the required skills, totaling more than 40,000 unique skills, including around 13,000 digital skills. These digital skills are categorized as basic, intermediate, or advanced. Each job posting's dominant digital skills category is determined by the most-frequent classification.

4. This chapter used the following keywords and their derivatives to identify GenAI skills: *ChatGPT, generative adversarial networks, generative artificial intelligence, Transformer (machine learning model), large language modeling, natural language generation, prompt engineering, variational autoencoders, AWS Bedrock, stable diffusion, Azure OpenAI, AI copywriting, Google Bard/Gemini, Azure AI Studio,* and *DALL-E Image Generator.*

References

Bousquette, I. 2024. "Generative AI Is Changing the Hiring Calculus at These Companies." *Wall Street Journal,* April 12, 2024. https://www.wsj.com/articles/generative-ai-is-changing-the-hiring-calculus-at-these-companies-41a06b88.

Bousquette, I. 2025. "How AI Tools Are Reshaping the Coding Workforce." *Wall Street Journal,* March 4, 2025. https://www.wsj.com/articles/how-ai-tools-are-reshaping-the-coding-workforce-6ad24c86.

China Youth Daily. 2024. "AI Large Language Model Potential Impact on China's Labor Market Research Released" [in Chinese]. https://finance.sina.com.cn/jjxw/2024-09-24/doc-incqfwyt1343038.shtml.

Coursera. 2024. *2024 Global Skills Report.* Mountain View, CA: Coursera. https://www.alejandrobarros.com/wp-content/uploads/2024/06/GSR_2024.pdf.

Coursera. 2025. *2025 Global Skills Report.* Mountain View, CA: Coursera. https://www.coursera.org/skills-reports/global/get-report.

Humlum, A., and E. Vestergaard. 2025. "Large Language Models, Small Labor Market Effects." Working Paper 33777, National Bureau of Economic Research, Cambridge, MA.

Macro Polo. n.d. "Regional Dives: Europe, Asia-Pacific, and Middle East." https://macropolo.org/interactive/digital-projects/the-global-ai-talent-tracker/regional-deep-dives-europe-asia-and-middle-east/.

Martins Neto, A., Y. Liu, S. Khurana, and J. Porras Lopez. 2025. "Click, Code, Earn: The Returns to Digital Skills." World Bank, Washington, DC.

Pal, S. 2024. *Where Is Europe's AI Workforce Coming From? Immigration, Emigration and Transborder Movement of AI Talent.* Berlin: Interface. https://www.stiftung-nv.de/publications/where-is-europes-ai-workforce-coming-from.

Resources for Employers. 2023. "Does Anyone Advertise Jobs in Newspapers Anymore?" September 2023. https://resources.workable.com/stories-and-insights/newspaper-job-ads.

Sostero, M., and S. Tolan. 2022. "Digital Skills for All? From Computer Literacy to AI Skills in Online Job Advertisements." JRC Working Paper 2022/07, Joint Research Centre, Brussels, Belgium. https://publications.jrc.ec.europa.eu/repository/handle/JRC130291.

Symon, E. 2024. "Apple Fires over 600 Workers from Silicon Valley Office in First Post-COVID Layoff by Company." *California Globe,* April 5, 2024. https://californiaglobe.com/fr/apple-fires-over-600-workers-from-silicon-valley-office-in-first-post-covid-layoff-by-company/.

Thormundsson, B. 2025. "Number of New Computer Science Graduates in the United States and in Canada from 2010 to 2022, by Study Level." *Statista,* June 24, 2025. https://www.statista.com/statistics/1472952/new-computer-science-graduates-us-canada/.

US Bureau of Labor Statistics. 2024. "Job Openings and Hires Decline in 2023 as the Labor Market Cools." *Monthly Labor Review,* September 2024. https://www.bls.gov/opub/mlr/2024/article/job -openings-and-hires-decline-in-2023.htm.

World Bank. 2025. "Skills and Workforce Development." Last updated April 25, 2025. https://www .worldbank.org/en/topic/skillsdevelopment.

World Bank. Forthcoming. *Digital Skills for Africa Report.* Washington, DC: World Bank.

Zojceska, A. 2019. "How to Create Newspaper Job Ads?" *TalentLyft,* February 22, 2019. https://www .talentlyft.com/blog/how-to-create-newspaper-job-ads.

Conclusion | 6

Urgency for policy action

As artificial intelligence (AI) becomes part of the fabric of everyday lives across the world, millions cannot be left on the sidelines to watch as innovation transforms society. Some argue that AI has limited relevance for lower-income countries (LICs) and middle-income countries (MICs), raising doubts about whether these nations should prioritize AI. Governments in LICs and MICs, facing more urgent needs such as health care and infrastructure, may question the wisdom of investing in a technology with current dubious benefits.

However, such views may be short-sighted. People tend to overestimate the short-term impacts of new technologies and underestimate the long-term impacts. AI's current limitations should not overshadow its potential and the inevitability of its continued improvement. Thus, proactive, strategic actions from governments are required to prepare for potential disruptions.

As AI adoption accelerates in advanced countries, delayed action in LICs and MICs could leave them further behind. Advanced countries lead AI innovation and are poised to adopt AI faster and more broadly, reaping more productivity gains. The gaps in productivity and living standards between frontier economies and LICs may grow further. The long-term consequence could be a stark bifurcation of the global economy, with AI-empowered advanced economies pulling further ahead and developing countries struggling to maintain economic and social progress.

Unlike within-country redistribution, where national governments have mechanisms to mitigate inequality, no well-established global institutions exist for large-scale redistribution across countries. Therefore, the potential for AI to exacerbate global inequality is much greater, and the policy challenges are far more complex (Korinek 2024).

Delayed AI adoption may also mean dwindling export-led growth opportunities and shrinking space to create good jobs. AI will reshape countries' comparative advantages and global production specialization. For developing countries, the race is not only with advanced economies but also with each other. The speed, scale, and depth of their AI adoption can affect how much they benefit. Export-led growth, which has been pivotal to many developing countries, is under threat. Just as automation precipitated premature deindustrialization, generative AI (GenAI) may lead to premature deprofessionalization, capping the share of good white-collar jobs at lower levels before countries reach higher income levels (Liu 2024).

With AI-powered machines further threatening manufacturing jobs and GenAI disrupting digitally deliverable services, export opportunities for developing countries could shrink. In such cases, most jobs left in developing countries will be in either farming or low-skilled services, which is insufficient to sustain broad-based economic development.

Although AI is diffusing rapidly in developing countries compared with earlier technologies, its intensity of usage and overall effectiveness remain significantly lower than in advanced economies. The relative ease of AI adoption stems from its ability to piggyback on existing digital devices and services; the availability of low-cost, open-source tools; and the flexibility to easily switch between providers. Unlike earlier general-purpose technologies, AI and digital services benefit from network effects that enable rapid scaling across populations. Yet, the lack of high-quality energy and digital infrastructure, along with the unaffordability of digital devices and services, continues to hinder widespread internet access in some developing regions. Consequently, although consumers and firms in these countries may be using AI, they represent only a small fraction of the overall population or businesses.

Furthermore, the frequency and depth of AI usage in developing countries remain limited compared with advanced countries, because effective AI use often depends on sufficient digital skills and localized adaptations—resources that are still scarce in many developing economies. This limited intensity and effectiveness of AI adoption restricts developing countries from deriving the full benefits of the technology.

More important, developing countries that are more digitally mature cannot afford to be only passive consumers of AI; they need to strive to customize AI models to adapt to local demand and even become AI producers and innovators if they are to capture more benefits. In digital and AI technologies, increasing returns to scale and scope, network effects, and "winner-takes-most" dynamics mean that those who produce and own the technology capture most of the gains. The least-AI-ready countries may start by adopting off-the-shelf AI solutions such as ChatGPT for individual and small firm usage. Developing countries with some AI capabilities can realize greater value from AI by customizing and adapting these technologies to their local contexts. More sophisticated countries can foster their own AI start-ups and build a foundation for AI innovation in key niches and applications to tap into the full potential of AI. This work will create opportunities not just to consume but also to contribute to and shape the global AI development landscape.

Eventually, governments must balance the risk of inaction or delayed action against the risk of premature, misallocated investment. Regardless of whether AI fully lives up to the hype, its value in specific applications is substantial, and its economic significance will continue to grow as innovation continues and adoption accelerates. This creates a strategic imperative for early action: Innovators and early adopters stand to gain significant advantages from knowledge spillovers, economies of scale and scope, and first-mover advantages, whereas late movers risk falling behind. However, premature or misdirected investments could yield suboptimal returns and divert resources from other critical areas.

Investing in the 4Cs

Investing in the 4Cs—connectivity, compute, context (training data, models, and applications), and competency (digital skills)—represents a strategic, largely no-regret approach for LICs and MICs although specific priorities must be tailored to each nation's unique circumstances (refer to table 6.1). A key factor contributing to AI's limited impact thus far is significant implementation lag, a challenge that is acute in developing economies. Even if AI's transformative potential proves less dramatic than some anticipate, strengthening the 4Cs is essential for the broader digital transformation efforts already under way. These foundational elements—robust computing

TABLE 6.1 Prioritize AI investments on the basis of AI readiness

AI capability and 4Cs	Country AI readiness level		
	Low	Medium	High
AI capability	Adopt	Adopt and adapt	Adopt, adapt, and innovate
Connectivity	• Provide universal access to electricity • Improve broadband coverage, quality, and affordability • Support device ownership and access	• Upgrade broadband infrastructure • Provide internet exchange points • Promote digital goods and services exports	• Upgrade broadband infrastructure • Support and develop the local digital sector and digital ecosystem
Compute	• Rely mostly on cloud computing and foreign data centers	• Invest in domestic data centers • Provide data embassy and regional data centers for small countries • Partner strategically with foreign cloud and AI chip providers	• Develop and purchase cutting-edge AI chips • Build high-performance computing systems • Build AI data centers
Context	• Rely largely on translation and existing AI models • Collaborate and partner with global companies and initiatives to collect local data • Improve government statistical and data collection capacity	• Combine translation of and investments in local data sets in select domains; develop synthetic data • Customize open-source AI models • Develop local AI applications in niche markets	• Invest in local training data across major domains • Customize open-source AI models; create cutting-edge domestic models • Enhance data governance
Competency	• Improve digital literacy, as well as basic and intermediate digital skills	• Focus on intermediate and advanced digital skills • Attract and retain talent	• Develop advanced digital and AI skills • Develop and support top-notch AI researchers • Attract and retain talent

Source: Original table for this publication.
Note: AI = artificial intelligence.

infrastructure, high-quality training data, and a digitally skilled workforce—are prerequisites for participating in the modern digital economy, regardless of the precise trajectory of AI development. Building a strong foundation in the 4Cs will not only position LICs and MICs to capitalize on the opportunities presented by AI but also will enhance their ability to leverage other digital technologies for economic growth and social progress.

In the digital and AI age, a country's size—particularly in the form of a vast, integrated domestic market—confers a significant advantage. Digital technologies, including AI, exhibit powerful economies of scale and scope. Once built, platforms and models can be deployed at near-zero marginal cost while value grows rapidly along with user numbers because of network effects. This creates winner-takes-most dynamics, where the largest markets breed the most-competitive firms, which in turn attract more users, data, talent, and investment. A large domestic user base enables firms to scale rapidly, iterate products faster, and gather the vast and diverse data sets essential for training AI models. Unlike in fragmented or smaller markets, companies in large, unified economies can test and refine AI applications across millions of users and sectors without facing regulatory or linguistic barriers.

Moreover, scale enables more concentrated and sustained investments in research and development and compute infrastructure—both of which are prohibitively expensive and central to AI leadership. Countries with large markets can justify long-term public and private investment in frontier innovation, from AI chips and data centers to foundational models. They also benefit from talent agglomeration, because researchers, engineers, and start-ups cluster around rich ecosystems of demand, finance, and digital infrastructure. These dynamics are, importantly, self-reinforcing: Early advantages in scale can rapidly snowball into global dominance, as seen in China and the United States. In contrast, smaller and more fragmented economies risk being perpetually dependent on foreign platforms, models, and norms—consumers of AI, not creators or shapers.

Although scale matters for AI innovation, intensity of AI capacity—measured on a per capita basis—is critical for effective AI adoption and diffusion. High per capita availability of compute, training data, and digital skills ensures that AI tools are not just developed but meaningfully used across sectors, firms, and individuals. In countries with low AI intensity, even if aggregate investments are rising, adoption may remain limited to a few cities or elite institutions, leaving most of the economy untouched. Conversely, countries with high AI intensity can embed AI in public services, small businesses, and everyday workflows, enabling more inclusive and widespread productivity gains. Per capita capacity also determines resilience: When AI compute, context, and capacity are widely distributed and locally accessible, more firms, governments, and individuals can experiment, adapt models to local needs, and generate greater value. In essence, AI intensity reflects how deeply the technology penetrates society.

Scale and intensity together determine a country's position in the global AI value chain and its overall readiness to benefit from AI. Countries with great scale are well positioned to attract global investment; lead foundational AI innovation; and develop local compute capacity, training data, homegrown models, and top-notch AI researchers. Their scale creates strong incentives for AI firms to enter, compete, and grow. Smaller countries, although less likely to drive frontier innovation, can still excel by focusing on AI adoption and customization in high-value niches or specific sectors in which local context matters.

Tortoise Media's Global AI Index measures both scale and intensity of a country's AI readiness (refer to figure 6.1). China and the United States dominate in scale because of their vast, digitally mature domestic markets and concentration of compute infrastructure, massive training data sets, and abundant AI firms and talents. In contrast, smaller countries such as Israel, Singapore, and Switzerland rank high on intensity thanks to focused investments and efficient ecosystems. Countries such as France, Germany, and the United Kingdom perform well on both dimensions, combining critical mass with deep penetration. Large middle-income economies such as Brazil and small high-income nations such as Estonia and Iceland fall into the mid-range of AI readiness. Meanwhile, LICs such as Ethiopia and Kenya underperform on both scale and intensity, highlighting the need to invest in foundational enablers such as affordable and high-quality broadband, digital literacy, and workforce skills. For these countries, building readiness means prioritizing the basics that unlock broader AI adoption.

FIGURE 6.1 Country AI readiness level, 2024

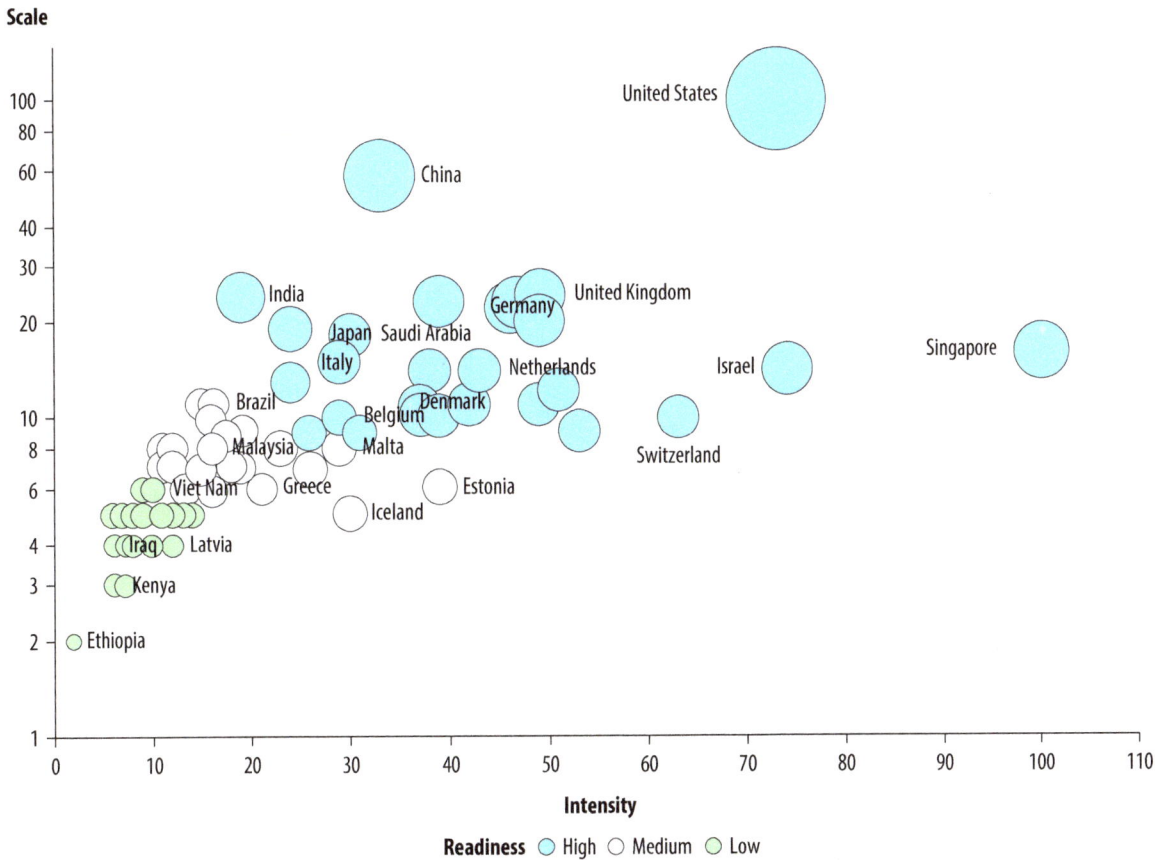

Scale

Source: Original figure for this publication using calculations from the Tortoise Media's Global AI Index (https://www.tortoisemedia.com /data/global-ai).
Note: AI = artificial intelligence.

In addition to strengthening the foundations, the AI era requires a fundamental rethinking of fiscal, labor, education, and social protection policies and global AI policy coordination and collaboration. Although AI holds great potential, it also risks exacerbating inequality, eroding worker bargaining power, and amplifying global divides. The rising concentration of wealth and job displacement and polarization are top concerns. In addition, AI misalignment (that is, "rogue" AI systems that would not pursue their initial purpose and would instead diverge from human intents) and AI misuse are major risks, particularly for the development or acquisition of chemical, biological, radiological, and nuclear (CBRN) weapons, the exploitation of cybersecurity vulnerabilities, and the production of misinformation and disinformation at scale. Addressing these risks will require coordinated domestic policies and international cooperation.

Some economists argue for steering AI innovation away from replacing humans toward augmenting human capabilities. This includes rethinking how performance benchmarks are designed—focusing less on AI outperforming humans at isolated tasks and more on how AI can complement human judgment, especially in areas such as prediction and decision-making. However, this is difficult to implement. First, complementarity does not guarantee job preservation—if productivity outpaces demand, jobs may still disappear, as seen when tractors reduced the number of farmers despite enhancing productivity. Second, most AI tools today complement rather than fully replace workers, automating tasks rather than entire occupations. Third, defining benchmarks for augmentation is far more complex than measuring how AI mimics human performance. Moreover, aging populations, labor shortages, and cost pressures give firms strong incentives to develop labor-saving AI systems.

Fiscal policy: Reducing inequality and providing a safety net amid potential disruptions

Fiscal policies must play a larger role in reducing inequality and addressing the winner-takes-most dynamics. Taxation policies could be more progressive and shift from labor income toward taxing other factors and rents. Tax policies that favor capital over labor distort the direction of progress toward saving labor (Acemoglu, Manera, and Restrepo 2020).

Some of the monopoly rents of digital giants can be taxed without introducing major distortions into the economy (Korinek and Stiglitz 2018, 2021). Higher taxes on capital gains, corporate profits, and wealth could fund social programs and worker retraining. However, capital's high mobility in the digital age means individual countries face constraints in raising capital taxes without triggering capital flight. Digital advertising taxes and data usage fees represent novel approaches to capture value from AI-driven business models. Although potentially significant revenue sources, such taxes face implementation challenges, including defining the tax base, preventing pass-through to consumers, and addressing cross-border transactions. In addition, unilateral implementation risks triggering digital trade disputes.

More aggressive redistribution policies, such as universal basic income or expanded social protection, could help ensure AI's benefits reach broader populations. However, financing such programs requires substantial fiscal space—a luxury many developing countries lack, given high debt levels and limited tax bases. The coronavirus disease 2019 pandemic has further strained public finances, constraining countries' ability to implement new social programs just as AI-driven disruption accelerates.

The international dimension presents additional challenges, because AI's benefits tend to concentrate in advanced economies with strong digital infrastructure and skilled workforces. Traditional development assistance may prove insufficient to prevent growing cross-country inequality. New international mechanisms may be needed to redistribute AI gains globally, such as digital development funds or technology transfer programs. However, designing and implementing such mechanisms face significant political and practical hurdles.

Developing countries face additional constraints in implementing redistributive policies. Weak tax administration, large informal sectors, and limited social protection infrastructure make it difficult to identify and reach vulnerable populations. Coordinated global action will be essential to avoid a race to the bottom in taxation and a widening AI divide. However, achieving such coordination will require overcoming significant collective action problems and reconciling divergent national interests.

Labor and education policy: Future-proofing workers

It is important to update labor and education policies to future-proof and protect workers because AI may accelerate the shift toward short-term, precarious employment and create huge uncertainty in skills demand. Predicting the specific skills and training needed for emerging employment opportunities beyond the short term is difficult. AI likely will reinforce the need for an effective lifelong learning system for the workforce (National Academies of Sciences, Engineering, and Medicine 2025). Intellectual curiosity, critical thinking, general adaptability, social and communications skills, and capacity for continued learning are likely to remain valued worker attributes. Developing these capacities throughout all levels of formal and adult education and training opportunities will be crucial.

Gaps in existing labor regulations have already spurred legislative reforms in multiple countries. For example, the European Union (EU) platform work directive (European Union 2024), approved in April 2024 and adopted shortly afterward, represents a key policy milestone. The directive aims to improve working conditions for platform workers and provide clarity on their employment status (Mirzadeh et al. 2024). Under the directive, a platform worker cannot be fired because of a decision made by an algorithm or an automated decision-making system. The directive also obliges EU countries to establish a rebuttable legal presumption of employment at the national level. Countries such as Costa Rica and Kenya have introduced sector-specific labor regulations, especially in transport.

Several principles can help point policy makers in the right direction when considering how to improve platform work. First, providing clarity on the employment status of platform workers and ensuring minimum rights for all platform workers are key. Second, nongovernmental forms of protection can be used to complement labor regulations. Recently, "platform cooperatives"[1] have been spotted in some sectors, such as transport or home services (Frey and Osborne 2023).

Third, effectiveness also depends on enforcement, which is more challenging for developing countries because of limited administrative capacity to enforce laws and high levels of informal economic activity (Acemoglu 2025). As countries expand legal coverage for platform workers, it is essential to ensure that efforts for enforcement and compliance are adequate. Fourth, data and evaluation can help design more effective regulations. Finally, government regulations and policies should be updated to balance flexibility and protection in the AI era. This often requires tailor-made policies that are based on quality data and a thorough examination of the impacts policy and regulatory changes will bring to workers' lives.

Managing AI risks through trustworthy and responsible AI systems

AI research and adoption are advancing rapidly, but many governments, particularly in developing countries, lack the resources and capacity to effectively manage the new risks that AI brings. A key concern is AI misalignment, in which AI systems optimize for objectives or outputs that diverge from human intentions or from their initial purpose. Misaligned AI behaviors may not be immediately visible and could cause harmful outcomes, especially when AI is applied in critical sectors such as health care or finance. Addressing AI misalignment is not solely a technical challenge: It requires stakeholders to establish processes that ensure AI systems are reliable, predictable, and aligned with public interest objectives before and after deployment (for example, cybersecurity exercises as well as incident detection and response mechanisms).

AI systems are also subject to cybersecurity and privacy risks. First, AI expands the digital attack surface by increasing data flows and system integrations, creating more entry points for adversaries. AI models can also be manipulated with malicious inputs, for example, through prompt injection or data poisoning—causing the system to produce incorrect or unsafe outcomes. Such techniques can enable malicious actors to "jailbreak" AI systems and entirely bypass security filters, undermine public-facing services, and even alter decision-making processes in sensitive domains. These concerns are not speculative; AI incidents are already happening in practice.[2]

Privacy risks are also heightened, because large AI models often process vast data sets containing personal or sensitive information. If effective safeguards are not in place, AI systems may inadvertently expose personal data through their outputs. This is critical in developing countries, where data protection frameworks may still be limited or enforcement capabilities may remain weak.

For policy makers, the priority is not necessarily to create new AI safety regulations from scratch but rather to strengthen the country's practical risk management capacity. Governments can foster compliance with international standards and emerging good practices (for example, the OECD AI principles; International Standard for Organization/International Electrotechnical Commission 42001; and the National Institute of Standards and Technology AI Risk Management Framework) and participate in global initiatives such as the Group of 7 Hiroshima AI Process and the OECD AI Incidents and Risk Repository, which provide platforms for shared learning and collective risk monitoring. Key policy actions include enhancing cybersecurity readiness to address AI-specific vulnerabilities, establishing protocols for incident reporting and response, and ensuring that AI deployments—especially in critical sectors—are subject to clear accountability requirements for safety and data protection.

Government leadership will be essential to coordinating these efforts and prioritizing a risk-based approach to AI safety. This involves setting baseline expectations for AI system reliability and security, working with private sector and international partners to build institutional capacities, and ensuring that AI's benefits can be realized without exposing societies to unmanaged risks.

More broadly, governments in developing countries must continue monitoring the risks associated with AI, such as misalignment, cybersecurity, privacy, CBRN weapons, fairness, algorithmic bias, misinformation, and copyright infringement. AI—and especially GenAI—can turbocharge misinformation, undermine decision-making processes, and distort economic activities (Hajli et al. 2022; Strasser 2023; Suciu 2023). AI platforms rely heavily on extensive data, often sourced from the internet without explicit permission, to train their models (Edelman et al. 2023). Such practices can lead to copyright infringement, posing potential liabilities for both AI platforms and their users. The World Bank (2024b) explores the emerging landscape of AI governance and highlights key considerations, challenges, and diverse approaches to regulating and governing AI.

Government strategies must navigate the ever-evolving and cross-cutting nature of AI, carefully balancing a spectrum of policy objectives, such as economic growth, job creation, transparency, privacy, national security, safety, and inclusion (World Bank 2024a). The intensification of AI's role in defense and critical sectors necessitates stringent cybersecurity measures and ethical considerations to counteract potential misuse, with overregulation posing risks to domestic AI advancements and international competitiveness. Increasing regulatory obligations may impede innovation, particularly for small-scale entities, with the potential for industry leaders to manipulate regulatory landscapes to curtail competition and innovation.

Notes

1. *Platform cooperatives* refers to a project or business that primarily uses a website, mobile app, or protocol to sell goods (for example, data) or services, and relies on democratic decision-making and shared community ownership of the platform by workers and users. As a people-centric model, platform cooperatives prioritize the voices and needs of workers, giving them greater control over its apps, platforms, and protocols (for more details, refer to Scholz 2023).

2. Refer to OECD's AI Incidents and Hazards Monitor, https://oecd.ai/en/incidents.

References

Acemoglu, D. 2025. "The Simple Macroeconomics of AI." *Economic Policy* 40 (121): 13–58.

Acemoglu, D., A. Manera, and P. Restrepo. 2020. "Does the US Tax Code Favor Automation? No." w27052. National Bureau of Economic Research, Cambridge, MA.

Edelman, S. L., P. Kumar, S. G. Rothaus, H. Weingrad, and A. Richman. 2023. "The Risks and Rewards of Generative AI." *Davis+Gilbert Alert, Emerging Issues,* March 31, 2023. https://www.dglaw.com/the -risks-and-rewards-of-generative-ai/.

European Union. 2024. "Directive (EU) 2024/2831 on Improving Working Conditions in Platform Work." *Official Journal of the European Union.* http://data.europa.eu/eli/dir/2024/2831/oj.

Frey, C. B., and M. Osborne. 2023. "Generative AI and the Future of Work: A Reappraisal." *Brown Journal of World Affairs* 30 (1): 161.

Hajli, N., U. Saeed, M. Tajvidi, and F. Shirazi. 2022. "Social Bots and the Spread of Disinformation in Social Media: The Challenges of Artificial Intelligence." *British Journal of Management* 33 (3): 1238–53.

Korinek, A. 2024. "Economic Policy Challenges for the Age of AI," Working Paper 32980. National Bureau of Economic Research, Cambridge, MA.

Korinek, A., and J. E. Stiglitz. 2018. "Artificial Intelligence and Its Implications for Income Distribution and Unemployment." In *The Economics of Artificial Intelligence: An Agenda,* edited by A. Agrawal, J. Gans, and A. Goldfarb, 349–90. Chicago: University of Chicago Press.

Korinek, A., and J. E. Stiglitz. 2021. *"Artificial Intelligence, Globalization, and Strategies for Economic Development,"* w28453. National Bureau of Economic Research, Cambridge, MA.

Liu, Y. 2024. *Generative AI: Catalyst for Growth or Harbinger of Premature De-Professionalization?* Washington, DC: World Bank.

Mirzadeh, I., K. Alizadeh, H. Shahrokhi, O. Tuzel, S. Bengio, and M. Farajtabar. 2024. "GSM-Symbolic: Understanding the Limitations of Mathematical Reasoning in Large Language Models." Preprint, last revised August 27, 2025. arxiv.org/abs/2410.05229.

National Academies of Sciences, Engineering, and Medicine. 2025. *Artificial Intelligence and the Future of Work.* Washington, DC: National Academies Press. https://doi.org/10.17226/27644.

Scholz, R. T. 2023. *Own This!: How Platform Cooperatives Help Workers Build a Democratic Internet.* Verso Books.

Strasser, A. 2023. "On Pitfalls (and Advantages) of Sophisticated Large Language Models." arXiv. Preprint arXiv:2303.17511.

Suciu, P. 2023. "The Next Threat from Generative AI: Disinformation Campaigns." *Forbes,* June 9, 2023. https://www.forbes.com/sites/petersuciu/2023/06/09/the-next-threat-from-generative-ai -disinformation-campaigns/.

World Bank. 2024a. *Digital Progress and Trends Report 2023.* Washington, DC: World Bank.

World Bank. 2024b. *Global Trends in AI Governance: Evolving Country Approaches.* Washington, DC: World Bank. https://hdl.handle.net/10986/42500.

Appendix A
Thematic Case Study Summaries

Introduction

Appendix A of this report features the summaries of three thematic case studies showcasing how artificial intelligence (AI) is used in different sectors to help address critical development challenges. The complete case studies are available in the World Bank Open Knowledge Repository at https://hdl .handle.net/10986/43822.

Each case study focuses on a distinct development pillar: prosperity, people, or planet:

- *Prosperity* highlights efforts to foster economic growth and job creation, supporting countries in building more resilient and self-reliant economies.
- *People* centers on improving quality of life by expanding access to basic services, strengthening participatory governance, and promoting human capital and well-being.
- *Planet* emphasizes the need to safeguard the environment by tackling climate-related risks and advancing sustainable natural resource management.

The case studies explore existing AI use cases, perceptions of key stakeholders, early impacts, and barriers to AI adoption in these areas, specifically examining AI applications in digitally delivered services (DDS; prosperity), education (people), and agriculture and energy (planet) (refer to figure A.1).

Three main messages are highlighted in the case studies:

- AI can accelerate development in key sectors, but without inclusive design and targeted support, its benefits will be concentrated among those who are already advantaged.
- Developing countries are not passive consumers of AI; they are adapting and innovating under constraints but need infrastructure, governance, and investment to scale.
- AI adoption is already reshaping work, learning, and production; governments must act now to manage disruption, close readiness gaps, and steer AI toward shared prosperity.

FIGURE A.1 Thematic case studies: AI and the three pillars

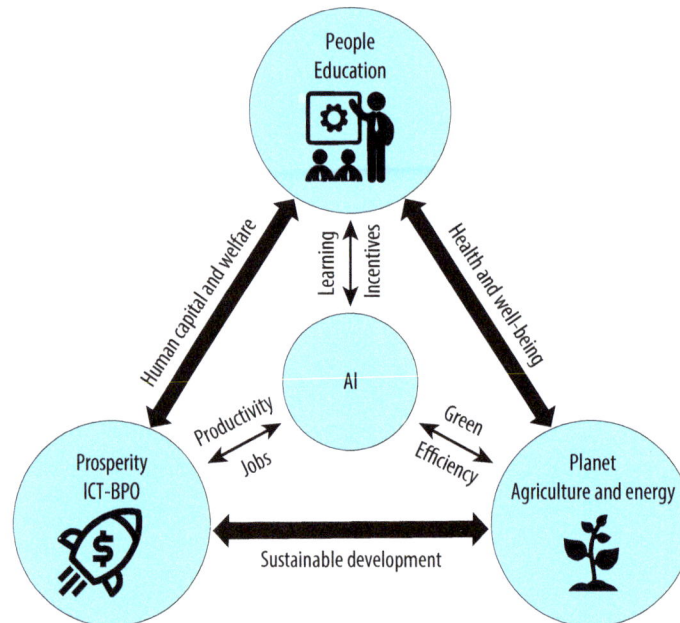

Source: Original figure for this publication.

Note: AI = artificial intelligence; ICT-BPO = information and communication technology and business process outsourcing.

Case Study 1—People
Exploring AI's Disruptive Promise for Education Systems in Low- and Middle-Income Countries

Sharada Srinivasan and Alex Twinomugisha

- AI is being adopted across education systems in low-income countries (LICs) and middle-income countries (MICs) to improve learning outcomes through personalized learning, support teachers in lesson planning and content development, and streamline administrative tasks, but AI use is still uneven, and initiatives are fragmented.

- Linguistic diversity in LICs and MICs results in a smaller corpus of training data that is often costlier to train with, and infrastructure constraints to both develop and deploy AI tools in education persist.

- Without tailored guidance regarding the use of AI in education and effective capacity building at all levels of the education system, AI tools may exacerbate inequalities and weaken critical thinking. Policy makers must act swiftly to ensure safe, equitable, and effective integration.

AI has emerged as a potentially transformative force in education systems across LICs and MICs, offering new tools to address persistent challenges, such as poorer learning outcomes, teacher shortages, and limited infrastructure. This case study, drawing on interviews and focus groups with nearly 150 stakeholders across India and Nigeria, explores how AI—particularly generative AI (GenAI)—is being implemented in educational settings and what barriers, opportunities, and tensions are shaping its use. It focuses on three key actors in the education ecosystem: students, teachers, and administrators.

Across both countries, AI tools are being deployed to personalize learning, expand access to educational resources, and enhance operational efficiency. Student-focused tools are especially prominent at the secondary and tertiary levels, where platforms such as ConveGenius, India's Doubtnut, and The Apprentice Project deliver regional language content, test preparation, and adaptive learning via WhatsApp. These platforms reach millions of users, especially in urban and peri-urban settings. In Nigeria, applications such as uLesson and Simbibot provide similar services, targeting students preparing for exams and seeking supplemental instruction. At the tertiary level, students increasingly use general-purpose AI platforms such as ChatGPT for coursework, research, and skill building, although this adoption tends to occur informally and without institutional guidance.

Teachers, meanwhile, are using AI to streamline lesson planning, automate grading, and experiment with professional development tools. Platforms such as the EkStep Foundation's content generators in India or Schoola's Curri AI in Nigeria support educators by producing multilingual instructional materials aligned with local curricula. Tools such as Smart Paper have made it possible to digitize and grade millions of handwritten tests quickly and cost-effectively—freeing teachers' time and expanding assessment reach. Although many teachers rely on free-tier services because of cost constraints, they report significant time savings and improved efficiency. Some initiatives, particularly in India, are beginning to explore how AI can be used for pedagogical coaching and feedback for teachers.

Administrators are also adopting AI tools to support system-level functions. In India, command-and-control centers such as Gujarat's Vidya Samiksha Kendra use real-time data from AI-enabled platforms to track attendance, monitor school meal programs, and inform decision-making. In Nigeria, higher education institutions are using AI-powered learning management systems to support course matching and distance learning, enabling universities to significantly expand their student base. These tools are beginning to shift how educational systems operate, even as implementation remains uneven and often dependent on partnerships with the private sector.

AI tools in both countries reflect innovation under constraint. Developers are creating lightweight models that can run on phones with simpler features and function offline, an essential adaptation given the widespread challenges of unreliable electricity, limited internet access, and low-end devices. Linguistic diversity presents a further barrier, because digital data for many local languages are insufficient to train accurate and efficient AI models. Initiatives such as India's Bhashini and Nigeria's LangEasy are attempting to fill this gap through crowdsourced data collection and small language models tailored to local dialects. Yet performance remains highly uneven, particularly for non-Latin scripts, and the technical demands of tokenizing complex text in non-Latin scripts often increase operational costs and reduce tool effectiveness.

Despite these innovations, significant barriers remain. Infrastructure gaps persist in both countries, particularly in rural areas, where many schools lack basic connectivity and hardware. The high cost of computing infrastructure and limited access to graphics processing units restrict the development of local AI tools. Data privacy frameworks are underdeveloped, and few safeguards exist to protect student data, especially that of minors. The lack of national policy frameworks means that

AI integration is occurring in a fragmented manner. Schools and subnational governments struggle to assess the quality of competing tools, manage data responsibly, and provide teachers and students with clear guidance on appropriate AI use.

Stakeholders across the education ecosystem bring different, and sometimes conflicting, perspectives on the role of AI in learning environments. Teachers, particularly those in urban or better-resourced settings, often highlight the practical benefits of AI tools in reducing lesson preparation time, generating teaching materials, and automating grading. These functionalities are especially useful for overburdened educators and are seen as boosting instructional efficiency. However, many teachers also express concern that students may become overly dependent on AI-generated outputs, potentially undermining the development of independent thinking, problem-solving, and creativity. Some worry that when students rely on AI to complete assignments or generate answers, the classroom risks shifting from being a space of inquiry to one of passive consumption.

Students—especially at the tertiary level—are among the most-enthusiastic adopters of AI tools, frequently using platforms like ChatGPT to support a range of academic tasks, from writing essays to coding assignments and preparing for exams. Many view these tools as essential for managing their workload, especially when faced with limited access to traditional learning resources or academic support. However, interviews revealed a growing self-awareness among students about the limitations of this reliance. Some acknowledged that they would struggle to complete assignments without AI assistance and that this dependency might hinder their development of core academic skills. This duality raises important questions about how educational systems can foster digital fluency while still promoting cognitive rigor and original thinking.

Policy makers, however, tend to frame AI adoption within the broader narrative of economic competitiveness and workforce development. They see AI integration in schools and universities as a strategic tool to align education with future labor market demands, particularly in sectors requiring digital and analytical skills. Yet, they also recognize a fundamental disconnect between this vision and current educational realities: rigid curricula, outdated assessment systems, and limited teacher capacity to adapt to AI-enhanced pedagogy. This misalignment fuels a deeper tension. Although AI promises to increase educational productivity and help bridge resource gaps, its uncritical adoption risks diluting learning quality and reinforcing existing inequalities. The challenge, then, is not whether to adopt AI but how to integrate it in a way that enhances both learning outcomes and long-term student agency.

To ensure that AI serves as a tool for equity rather than exclusion, the case study calls for more coherent policy responses. Key priorities include establishing national benchmarks for evaluating AI tools, clarifying data governance and privacy rules for education settings, reforming assessment methods to reflect AI-enabled learning environments, and integrating AI literacy into curricula. Equally as important is investing in tools designed for low-resource environments and fostering partnerships that ensure public ownership of educational data while leveraging private sector innovation. India and Nigeria provide important lessons for other developing countries. They demonstrate AI's potential to reshape educational systems and also the risks of unregulated expansion and uneven access. With the right policies, infrastructure, and institutional capacity, AI can support more inclusive, efficient, and resilient education systems. Without them, it risks reinforcing existing inequalities and undermining learning.

Case Study 2—Planet
Harnessing AI for Efficiency: Transforming Agriculture and Energy Sectors

Antonio Martins Neto

- AI can significantly improve efficiency and sustainability across agriculture and energy systems, but adoption remains limited in developing countries because of systemic barriers.

- Localized, inclusive AI models and tools are critical to ensure AI works for smallholder farmers and underserved communities.

- Realizing AI's potential will require a comprehensive policy approach that combines short-term subsidies and training with long-term investments in infrastructure, regulation, and skills.

This case study explores AI's potential in the agriculture and energy sectors, emphasizing how AI can enhance productivity, sustainability, and operational efficiency. As global challenges such as climate change, environmental degradation, and resource scarcity intensify, AI technologies are increasingly being applied to optimize processes and decision-making. These technologies promise to support economic development by addressing inefficiencies in sectors that are both economically and environmentally pivotal.

In agriculture, AI is being applied across the entire value chain—from seed production to processing and retail—to address long-standing challenges related to productivity, resource efficiency, and environmental impact. One of the most-pressing issues in many LICs and MICs is the limited access to agricultural extension services, which leaves farmers with insufficient information to adopt sustainable practices. GenAI chatbots such as Farmer.Chat are emerging as scalable solutions that offer real-time, localized guidance on crop management and pest control, among others. These tools dramatically reduce the cost of delivering expert advice, expanding access even in remote areas. However, their effectiveness hinges on the availability of localized data and language support. Without robust data sets reflecting local agroecological conditions and linguistic nuances, these tools risk offering generic or inaccurate recommendations, particularly for smallholder farmers.

Beyond advisory services, AI is transforming how farmers manage pests, water, and livestock. Many companies have developed AI-powered platforms using aerial imagery and predictive analytics to detect pest outbreaks early, minimizing pesticide use while protecting yields. In Brazil, an initiative has demonstrated that AI-based pest control can reduce pesticide use by up to 30 percent while improving forecast accuracy and market logistics. AI has also advanced precision irrigation systems that monitor soil moisture and weather patterns to optimize water use. Platforms such as CropX and Kilimo have achieved significant water savings and yield improvements, with the latter reporting water savings exceeding 200 million liters in São Paulo alone.

AI is also playing a growing role in reducing food loss and livestock-related emissions, two major contributors to global greenhouse gases. In retail and food service settings, machine learning tools are being used to optimize inventory management and pricing strategies, helping businesses minimize spoilage and waste while boosting profitability. For example, AI-powered platforms can track purchasing patterns, shelf life, and consumption rates to automatically adjust stock levels or recommend dynamic pricing, preventing overstock and reducing losses. In commercial kitchens, computer vision systems are deployed to monitor discarded food in real time, allowing restaurants to refine procurement decisions and cut waste by more than 50 percent. At the same time, AI is transforming livestock management through precision feeding systems and wearable devices that monitor animal health, behavior, and nutritional intake. These tools not only improve animal welfare and productivity but also significantly reduce methane emissions by tailoring diets to their needs and identifying early signs of illness. Beyond operational tools, AI is accelerating research into biological methane inhibitors, with early-stage studies indicating that AI-assisted compound discovery could reduce livestock methane emissions by up to 30 percent.

AI adoption in agriculture across developing countries faces a set of persistent and interconnected barriers that go beyond mere technological readiness. At the most-basic level, limited digital infrastructure, particularly poor internet connectivity and unreliable electricity in rural areas, prevents smallholder farmers from accessing AI-powered advisory services or precision agriculture tools. Even when connectivity is available, the high cost of AI solutions and required devices places them out of reach for many. Small-scale farmers often operate with tight margins, making them less likely to invest in unfamiliar digital technologies without strong incentives or demonstrable short-term gains. Compounding these constraints is a lack of high-quality data, which limits the effectiveness of AI-driven recommendations. For example, recommendations may be too generalized to be useful at the plot level or inaccessible because of language barriers. Finally, many farmers lack the digital literacy needed to interact meaningfully with AI tools, particularly those using interfaces that require reading, typing, or smartphone navigation.

To address these barriers, a multipronged policy response is required. In the short term, governments should expand mobile-based connectivity solutions, subsidize internet access and AI-enabled devices for smallholder farmers, and establish community internet hubs to bridge the rural-urban digital divide. Public support is also needed to scale localized AI models, establish data quality protocols within agricultural programs, and partner with local agricultural experts to ensure that AI tools reflect regional conditions and practices. Medium-term strategies should focus on building enabling infrastructure and institutional support. This includes investing in broadband infrastructure across first-, middle-, and last-mile networks, promoting competition to reduce access costs, and strengthening regional data sets for AI training. Over the long term, closing the digital divide will require improving power grid reliability in rural areas to guarantee stable connectivity. Governments should reduce trade barriers for digital goods, encourage market competition in the agricultural technology sector, and establish national agricultural data repositories to centralize, govern, and standardize data access.

In the energy sector, AI is playing a critical role in driving efficiency and supporting the transition to cleaner, more resilient energy systems. Renewable energy, although crucial for decarbonization, presents operational challenges because of its intermittent nature. AI offers robust forecasting solutions that improve the accuracy of wind and solar generation predictions. Systems such as DeepMind's wind forecasting model and IBM's Watt-Sun have achieved notable improvements in prediction accuracy. In addition, AI is revolutionizing predictive maintenance by detecting faults in critical infrastructure before they result in costly failures. From hydropower turbines at Itaipu Dam to wind turbines monitored by drone-assisted AI systems, maintenance has become more proactive, reducing downtime and operational costs.

Grid optimization and energy theft are other areas in which AI is providing important gains. By analyzing real-time energy flows, AI helps balance supply and demand, integrate decentralized energy sources, and reduce losses from outages or inefficiencies. Companies such as Sensewaves are using AI to support real-time energy forecasting and system stability. Furthermore, AI has been deployed to combat energy theft—an issue that can account for more than 50 percent of electricity losses in some regions—by identifying consumption anomalies and fraudulent patterns with high precision.

AI is also enhancing energy efficiency in buildings through smart heating, ventilation, and air conditioning management. Solutions developed by firms such as BrainBox AI and Verdigris have demonstrated energy savings of up to 25 percent while reducing emissions. At the same time, AI is being leveraged to expand energy access in underserved regions. Projects by Atlas AI and Omdena have used geospatial analytics and predictive modeling to identify optimal locations for mini-grid deployment, reducing electrification costs and increasing renewable energy uptake in remote areas. AI-driven fintech tools, such as those developed by Nithio, are also improving investment decisions and credit risk assessments for clean energy projects, making financing more accessible in low-income regions.

Despite these promising developments, the energy sector also faces significant barriers to AI adoption. Legacy infrastructure, cybersecurity risks, regulatory complexity, and a shortage of skilled professionals continue to impede progress. One significant challenge is the prevalence of outdated analog infrastructure that is ill-equipped to support real-time data processing or AI-driven optimization. Many developing countries still rely on fragmented or centralized grids that were not built with digital integration in mind. Upgrading these systems to accommodate smart meters, distributed energy management, and predictive analytics often requires large-scale capital investment—resources that are often scarce or subject to political and institutional bottlenecks. In addition, the digital backbone needed to enable AI—stable internet, cloud computing access, and Internet of Things sensors—is frequently absent or unreliable in remote or underresourced regions. These constraints prevent utilities from leveraging AI to reduce losses, manage demand, or optimize renewable energy flows.

Cybersecurity and data interoperability add further layers of complexity. As energy systems become more digitized, the risk of cyberthreats increases, yet many utilities in developing countries lack the expertise or protocols to adequately secure their networks. A shortage of skilled professionals in both energy engineering and AI-specific domains further slows deployment, particularly when public utilities face hiring and retention constraints. Regulatory uncertainty is an additional challenge; outdated energy laws and rigid approval processes leave little room for experimentation or public-private collaboration on AI solutions.

Addressing these barriers requires a combination of short-, medium-, and long-term policy actions. In the short run, governments should offer targeted tax incentives, grants, or concessional financing for utilities and private providers to invest in AI-ready infrastructure and pilot applications, such as predictive maintenance or smart billing. Public-private partnerships can play a critical role in scaling innovation while sharing risk. Medium-term policies should focus on building institutional capacity by training regulators and utility staff, promoting cybersecurity protocols, and establishing common data standards for interoperability. Over the longer term, regulatory frameworks need to evolve to support decentralized, data-driven energy systems. This includes building space for sandboxes or innovation zones where AI can be tested safely. With such coordinated efforts, AI can play a central role in modernizing the energy sector, improving grid reliability, expanding access, and accelerating the shift toward renewable and resilient systems.

Case Study 3—Prosperity
Co-worker, Coach, or Competitor? How AI Is Transforming the Future of Digitally Deliverable Services

Johan Bjurman Bergman and He Wang

- AI is reshaping digital services by enhancing productivity and enabling higher-value work, but its benefits remain uneven across firms, sectors, and workers.
- Firms report modest signs of AI-driven job displacement in digital services jobs focused on simple tasks, especially in mature service-exporting economies.
- Without proactive policy action, AI adoption could deepen divides between large and small firms, high- and low-skilled workers, and advanced and emerging economies.

DDS—including software development, information technology (IT), customer support, creative services, and specialized back-office tasks—have become critical drivers of economic transformation in developing countries. Global exports of DDS surpassed US$4.25 trillion in 2023, with developing countries increasingly relying on this sector to generate good jobs, drive economic growth, and attract foreign exchange and investment. The rapid emergence of AI—especially GenAI—is reshaping the sector's structure, workflows, and competitive dynamics. This case study examines how AI is being adopted by digital services firms in the Philippines and Uzbekistan, the ways in which it is transforming firm operations and worker experiences, and the broader risks and opportunities it presents for inclusive development and global competitiveness.

Early impacts are already visible, with AI enhancing productivity in areas such as customer support, software development, and health care services. Firms report that AI assistants reduce task times, enhance customer satisfaction, and improve training outcomes. For example, call summarization tools reduce handle times in contact centers by up to 10 percent, and AI-powered medical coding tools are automating parts of the process of translating medical records into bills. In the software industry, GitHub Copilot and similar tools have led to time savings of more than 50 percent for developers, particularly benefiting those with lower baseline skills.

Across the case study countries, AI tools are primarily viewed as co-workers and coaches rather than as direct competitors with humans. Workers and firms widely recognize AI's potential to improve efficiency, quality, and learning outcomes—especially by automating repetitive tasks, aiding second-language communication, supporting code generation, or enhancing customer service workflows. However, only a fraction of AI's capabilities are currently being used by the interviewed firms. Smaller firms and lower-skilled workers tend to adopt off-the-shelf tools in limited ways, whereas larger and more technologically mature firms leverage AI to customize workflows and develop client-facing solutions.

AI is also shifting how value is created and captured in the digital services space. Technology-driven firms—for example, in software development—are adapting and moving up the value chain, offering custom solutions, automating internal operations, and even selling AI services and products. Meanwhile, labor-intensive firms—for example, those in business process outsourcing (BPO)—are becoming more vulnerable to automation. Foreign-owned firms, especially those integrated into global value chains with access to proprietary AI tools, are better positioned to benefit. This issue is driving a growing gap between high-skilled and low-skilled firms, workers, and countries.

Nevertheless, the case study also documents signs of displacement—especially for entry-level and routine-based roles. Although layoffs are still modest, some Philippine firms expect AI to take over up to half of simple customer service tasks within three years. Labor market data already show steep declines in job postings for IT and BPO roles since the launch of ChatGPT in late 2022, with few signs of recovery. These impacts are most acute in mature, labor-intensive sectors that face price pressures from global clients.

The case study outlines a four-archetype framework to help countries navigate the AI transition in DDS. Each archetype—digital export leaders, high-skilled high potentials, mature low-skilled exporters, and emerging builders—reflects a different position in the global services landscape and faces distinct challenges and opportunities as AI reshapes work. Digital export leaders such as Malaysia are already well integrated into global value chains, with strong digital infrastructure and growing in-house AI capabilities. Their focus now is on ensuring inclusive benefits, avoiding excessive concentration of value among top-tier firms, and investing in broader workforce upskilling. High-skilled high potentials, such as Viet Nam, have a strong human capital base and growing digital sectors but limited penetration in global services exports. AI offers these countries a chance to leapfrog into more sophisticated services—such as cloud engineering or data analytics—without passing through low-end outsourcing. However, proactive investments in frontier digital skills, innovation ecosystems, and a supportive regulatory environment are required.

Mature low-skilled exporters such as the Philippines face a more urgent threat. Their economies have long depended on large-scale customer support and back-office processing—precisely the types of jobs most vulnerable to AI-driven automation. Although firms in these countries are adopting AI for internal efficiency gains, their ability to move up the value chain is limited by gaps in skills, innovation, and intellectual property ownership. Emerging builders such as Uzbekistan are still developing their digital services industries, with limited current exposure to AI disruption. Yet this issue also presents an opportunity: These countries can support the development of AI-driven digital services sectors from the get-go, without the burden of legacy systems. By investing in foundational digital infrastructure, digital literacy, and local innovation, they can position themselves for future growth in AI-enabled services.

The case of the Philippines illustrates both the promise and the perils of this transformation. The country is a global leader in contact center services, employing 1.6 million workers. Firms are adopting AI tools to train agents faster, analyze customer sentiment, and automate basic queries. However, the shift to software-based services risks transferring value creation outside the country because few IT departments are based in the Philippines. Health care outsourcing faces a similar challenge: Although AI is improving efficiency in medical coding and patient coordination, jobs may be reduced and value redistributed to regions in which AI systems are built and managed.

In contrast, Uzbekistan—a less-mature player in the DDS space—is still in the early stages of AI adoption. Firms in IT, logistics, and business process services are experimenting with AI for recruitment, human resources, and content creation, often using off-the-shelf tools such as ChatGPT. Despite enthusiasm, adoption remains limited by gaps in digital infrastructure, human capital, and policy clarity. However, as an emerging builder, Uzbekistan may be able to leapfrog legacy systems and build AI capabilities natively, particularly in government services, e-commerce, and financial technology (fintech), where the use of digital platforms is rapidly expanding.

Across the case study countries, firms cite similar barriers to deeper AI integration: limited digital and data infrastructure, uncertainty over data privacy and AI governance, insufficient skills to develop or deploy advanced models, and the high cost of custom AI development. Many firms report having to learn by doing, experimenting internally without much government support or regulation.

Policy makers face a core challenge: how to promote the use of AI as a tool that complements and augments human workers rather than replacing them. Thus, creating the conditions for widespread, responsible AI use—especially among small and medium enterprises and lower-skilled workers is needed.

Without proactive responses, however, countries risk deepened inequality and further lost ground in the global digital economy. To address these risks, the case study's key recommendations include reducing policy uncertainty by establishing clear, stable regulations to guide responsible AI use and relaxing overly restrictive cross-border data laws that currently hinder access to international cloud services and high-performance computing. Addressing infrastructure gaps, particularly in regions outside major cities, is also critical to unlocking local talent and ensuring broader participation in the digital economy. In parallel, governments must adopt a cohesive approach to developing AI-specialized talent through education and university partnerships while also scaling up proactive AI reskilling and upskilling programs for workers—especially in lower-skilled sectors increasingly affected by automation. Without such coordinated actions, firms in many developing countries will struggle to compete globally, with the benefits of AI remaining concentrated among a narrow set of actors in high-income economies.

Common insights and policy considerations

AI is increasingly integrated into education, digital services, agriculture, and energy. The case studies from India, Nigeria, the Philippines, and Uzbekistan and the overview of cases in the agriculture and energy sectors show that AI is already generating tangible benefits. These include improvements in efficiency, learning outcomes, service quality, and productivity. However, the scale, equity, and sustainability of these benefits depend on the readiness of local ecosystems, the capacity of institutions, and the governance frameworks guiding AI development and use.

Across all sectors, AI is largely being integrated as a tool to support and enhance human work rather than replace it. In classrooms, teachers are using GenAI to help plan lessons and produce teaching materials. In health care services, AI supports nurses and care coordinators with patient tracking and communication. In contact centers, agents are using AI for on-the-job coaching and performance evaluation. Farmers are turning to AI-enabled chatbots for localized agronomic advice. In each case, AI functions more as a co-worker or a coach—amplifying human capacity and streamlining tasks—than as a direct substitute. When these tools are well designed, adapted to local contexts, and embedded into existing workflows, they tend to augment human effort rather than displace it.

Yet, despite the enthusiasm and early signs of value creation, AI's full potential is not being realized. A common pattern across the studies is the underutilization of AI capabilities, particularly among smaller firms, workers with lower digital skills, or institutions operating in resource-constrained environments. Many users rely only on the most-basic features of GenAI tools, and more advanced use cases, such as personalized instruction, predictive analytics, or workflow optimization, remain out of reach. These advanced applications typically require access to significant computing capacity, and in-house expertise, all of which are often limited or prohibitively costly in developing country settings.

Language and localization challenges are a major constraint to AI's inclusive use. In education, the effectiveness of AI-powered tutoring tools is undermined by the lack of training data in many nondominant languages, especially those using non-Latin scripts. Agricultural platforms require region-specific content, local dialect support, and data calibrated to local farming conditions—elements that global AI systems are not typically designed to accommodate. In digital services, many frontline workers operate in environments with low digital fluency and struggle to adopt AI tools built for high-resource users. Without dedicated investments in local language models and culturally relevant interfaces, AI risks replicating and even reinforcing existing inequities in access to information and services.

Underlying all of these challenges is a foundational weakness in data quality and governance. AI systems across sectors depend on structured, reliable data, but in many LMIC contexts, the inputs—whether student records, farm-level environmental data, or client service logs—are often incomplete, inconsistent, or fragmented. These technical issues are compounded by the absence of clear data privacy and accountability frameworks. Particularly in education and health, where minors or sensitive personal data are involved, the lack of safeguards erodes trust and increases the risks of misuse. Without stronger policies and oversight, the expansion of AI in public service delivery may inadvertently expose users to harm or exclusion.

A final shared concern across the case studies is that AI may exacerbate inequality if left to market forces alone. In digital services, lower-skilled workers are already experiencing early signs of job displacement as AI automates routine tasks. In education, students with better internet access or greater English proficiency tend to benefit more from AI tools, and others fall behind. In agriculture, large commercial farms are often better positioned to adopt precision tools and predictive systems than smallholders operating with limited connectivity and capital. The risk, in all three domains, is a widening gap—between large and small firms, between skilled and unskilled workers, between urban and rural communities, and between countries that produce AI technologies and those that merely consume them.

To address these shared challenges, a coordinated policy response is needed. A foundational priority is strengthening digital and data infrastructure. Reliable electricity, internet access, and access to cloud services are prerequisites for using and scaling AI effectively.

Equally as important is establishing robust governance frameworks. Sector-specific rules for data protection, informed consent, and algorithmic transparency are needed particularly in education and health, where vulnerable populations are at risk. Governments can support innovation while ensuring safety by piloting regulatory sandboxes, developing standards for AI tool procurement, and mandating explainability for high-stakes decisions.

People must also be prepared to work with AI. Therefore, investing in large-scale upskilling and AI literacy efforts is needed. Teachers, health workers, civil servants, and farmers all require tailored training to use AI effectively. This training can be done through integration into existing curricula, vocational programs, and sector-specific training modules.

To democratize access to AI, public policies should also address cost and capacity gaps. Financial incentives, such as grants, subsidies, or tax credits, can help smaller firms and public institutions adopt AI tools. Support for open-source solutions and shared digital infrastructure can lower barriers for actors operating at the margins.

Finally, governments must anticipate labor transitions and manage them with foresight.

Taken together, these policy directions can help ensure that AI becomes a driver of inclusive development rather than a source of deepening divides.

www.ingramcontent.com/pod-product-compliance
Lightning Source LLC
Chambersburg PA
CBHW050908210326
41597CB00002B/63